ATROPOS PRESS
new york • dresden

© 2012 by Andrew Spano
Second Edition
Think Media EGS Series is supported by the European Graduate School

ATROPOS PRESS
New York • Dresden

151 First Avenue # 14, New York, N.Y. 10003

cover design: Peggy Bloomer

all rights reserved

ISBN 978-0-9857146-1-1

Abduction Topology: The Psycholinguistics of Discourse

By Andrew Spano

Table of Contents

Part 1: Preliminaries

Part 2: The Apparatus of Language

Part 3: The Discourse of Space and Time

Part 4: The Psychology of Discourse

Part 5: Morphology of Abduction (Abdication)

Abduction Topology:
The Psycholinguistics
of Discourse

ATROPOS PRESS
new york • dresden

PART 1: **PRELIMINARIES**

In the proposition a state of affairs is, as it were, put together for the sake of experiment.

— *Wittgenstein*[1]

1. The Categorical Exclusion

1.1 Coming into Being (*le devenir*)

For us to understand how a thing comes into being, it is necessary to follow its etiology to the start. A thing comes into being when it crosses a certain linguistic threshold where it may be said about this thing that it is. But where does this threshold lie, and what is its push-pull mechanism? Why does a thing tend to come into being and then out of it? What is the mechanism, and is there meaning in the human sense? To begin this discussion we will consider a proposition, that the difference between zero and one is greater than the difference between one and any other number. To express this idea, we use the following notation: $(0 / 1) > (1 / n)$.[2] Between the first enclosed part of the proposition and the last lies the threshold where a thing comes into being in the linguistic sense. The reason why coming-into-being (*le devenir*) is discussed here only in the linguistic sense is that being has no attribute, therefore we cannot speak of it as we can speak of the thing itself. However, as a linguistic

---

[1] Wittgenstein, Ludwig. *Tractatus Logico-Philosophicus*. C. K. Ogden, trans. New York: Barnes & Noble, 2003, p. 45.

[2] Mathematical notation (unless otherwise obvious or improvised) follows the table on pages xii-xvii of *Discrete Mathematics for New Technology* by Rowan Garnier and John Taylor, Bristol: Institute of Physics Publishing, 1999. There are at least two or three other systems of expressing mathematical philosophy, the most prominent being that of North and Whitehead. Where other systems are used, notation is made as footnote.

phenomenon, we may discuss it in several ways: as a thing, as a word and sound (parole), as an idea, and as a part of a syntactic concatenation with other like ideas which create an expression called a discourse. It is this discourse that is the being of thought.

When an absolute threshold has been crossed, such as coming-into-being, then we have observed a *categorical exclusion*. In this case, we are concerned with four values: 0, representing a negation of 1; 1 itself, representing the negation of 0; 1 in relation to 0 as infinitely greater; and finally n in relation to 1, which is any number created by adding 1 to n. For there to be a definite number after 1 (n + 1), it must be expressed as a definite number and cannot simply be termed "infinity," which in the categorical exclusion is not a value but a concept. And while 1 may be infinitely greater than 0, zero nevertheless is a definite number. We say then that 0 is *excluded* from all other numbers, as a number. Sometimes this property of 0 is expressed as $\aleph 0$ or aleph null, the smallest infinite cardinal number.

To look at the categorical exclusion another way, we may take Peano's three primitive propositions, summarizing their significance to the discussion of coming-into-being using an axiom of Russell's. Peano argues that "1) 0 is a number, 2) The successor of any number is a number, and 3) No two numbers have the same successor."[3] More to the relevancy of the discussion of being, Russell restates Peano's propositions thus: "The successor of the number of terms in the class *a* is the number of terms in the class consisting of *a* together with *x*, where *x* is any term not belonging to the class."[4] By successor is here meant the number following another number. The immediate predecessor is, of course, the number immediately before another number. In the categorical exclusion, the relationship between 1 and n is always excluded from the class of the relation of 0 and 1 because they are both categorical negations of each other as expressions. Referring to Russell above, x = 1 and a = 0. The value a is excluded from the class (n + 1), though the value x is shared by both classes as the threshold itself, the > serving as an expressive operator and nothing more.

What comes into being, then, is the singularity of 1, which is an Event which cannot be reversed. The difference between the coming-into-being and the iteration of being, theoretically infinite though it may seem, is

---

[3] Russell, Bertrand. *Introduction to Mathematical Philosophy*. London: George Allen and Unwin, Ltd., 1956, p. 5.
[4] Ibid., p. 23.

what is categorical despite the shared value of 1 as indication of threshold. Which brings us to one more possibility in the formation of the existential ontology of a thing as language: recursion.

1.2 Iteration and recursion

The possibility of a number recurring seems to violate Peano's primitive proposition that "no two numbers have the same successor." This, however, is not necessarily the case. For example, I may form any number with the formula n + 1, but what if I am using clock arithmetic? In other words, what if a number repeats itself ad infinitum as it does on a clock face (e.g. every 12 or 24 hours the number 1 recurs)? For example, if I apply n + 1 to 1 the outcome is 2, etc. If I apply n + 0 to 1 of course the outcome is 1. But if I do away with the arbitrary idea of ordinality (immediate predecessor [a] < successor [b], or a < b), then I may see the term n + 1 as a infinite iteration of a recursion. Apparent ordinality, which will be called the progressive fallacy, presumes that value increases with each successor. As we shall see, this simple idea, which is a prima facie view of the concatenation of numbers or the counting of beans, is the source of much mayhem in thought and language.

Before we get to the linguistic, ethical, social, and cultural implications of these ideas, there is still more to show regarding iteration and recursion.

For instance, presume we play a game. The goal of this game is to reach a 0 value by effecting a progression which includes possession. The idea of reaching a 0 value by progression contradicts the standard idea of progress itself as an endless series of increase based on the successor being greater than the immediate predecessor.

Game 1: a and x are in love without possession, but x is married to y. Nevertheless, a and x enter into a relationship. The asymmetry is that a plays a zero-sum game in that if a loses x, then a is back to 0 in the progression of the attempt at possession of x. On the other hand, if x loses possession of a, x still has possession of y, and therefore remains at the value of 1 possession which, we will assume here, is equal to n + 1 possessions and represents a non-zero-sum game. A nuance of this game is the asymmetry of x possessing n + 1 lovers, creating the non-zero-sum for x.

Game 2: a is in love with x, and is married to b, as x is married to y. Now the game is symmetrical. The symmetry of the game is that now lovers a and x possess a lover and are both in a non-zero-sum game individually, even with losing one lover (assuming there is only one play here and you may only lose or gain one lover per play — and there are only three plays). The problem is now one not of augmentation but of negation. The sets $(a + b) = (x + y)$ each show a non-zero-sum game where the subtraction of one value from each set does not leave a the 0 empty set. Looked at as subsets of a larger set, the sum is now zero for both subsets, as we shall see in Game 3: $[(a + b) = (x + y)]$. Both subsets and a and x have an equal chance of losing b or y and therefore crossing the threshold between non-zero and zero-sum. Taken as one proposition then, it is a zero-sum in Game 3 because no more partners can be gained, only lost. *Ontologically then, in Game 2, despite the symmetry of their non-zero-sum status of the subsets, the inevitability of Game 3 means the sum is already zero in the larger set.*

Game 3: In the third and last game, either a or x loses either b or y. The problem here is one of negation and not progression. The progression of a to the non-zero-sum position creates the possibility of either a or x losing a partner in the last play. Our conclusion is this: *the progression from games 1 to 3 resulted in the sum of zero. Zero is a reset or recursive modularity of the progression.*

Another example can be drawn from Wittgenstein.[5] We may call this the PQR game after the names of the three columns in the table. The goal of the game is to reduce all three True and False columns to all False in as few moves as possible, starting with all three columns (p, q, r) containing the value True on the first line of the table. If we substitute the number 1 for True and 0 for False, then we have a goal of reducing all three 1 columns to three 0 columns. As with the Lovers' Game above, progression is revealed to be a fallacy if we define progression as the increase or decrease of rational numbers using Peano's mechanism of $n + 1$. Here there is no ratio, only a relationship and a total transformation of values (True $\rightarrow$ False, 1 $\rightarrow$ 0). while the matrix table is more revealing, for our purposes here it will suffice to describe the transformation of TTT to FFF, or 111 to 000.

For this to be a game, there must be two players. The player who goes first is chosen by calling a coin flip. The goal, again, is to reduce 111 to 000. The first move is set: call 111. Now there are seven possibilities for the second call, but the rule is that each player may only negate the value

[5] Wittgenstein, Ludwig. *Tractatus Logico-Philosophicus.* C. k. Ogden, trans. New York: Barnes & Noble, 2003, p. 65.

of one digit. There are six possible steps between 111 and 000: 011, 101, 110, 001, 010, and 100. Player 2 wins because his turn is after Player 1 announces the only possibility left: 100, leaving 000. This is a zero-sum game because the sum of 0 has been reached and one player must lose for the other to win. It shows the progressive fallacy because in the entire sequence of reduction there has only been one nontrivial transformation: 1 → 0. Also, the game could easily be reversed with the goal of reaching 111 (0 → 1), and since both 0 and 1 are negations of each other as real numbers, either version of the game results not in the attainment of a score but in the flip-flop negation of "different" values that have no ratio, but only the relationship of being infinitely different. Seen against clock arithmetic and binary math, progression is an illusion created by rational integers and is, therefore, a fallacy.

1.3 Modularity and quantization of values

What we enter into here is the world of modular arithmetic, or the arithmetic of recursion and not progression in the sense that Peano means in the idea that no number is the successor of itself. This concept is critical to the understanding of the components of the exclusion. Before we discuss modularity, a few words about these components are essential.

The exclusion consists of the following parts which work together like a machine:

a) The difference between 0 and 1
b) The difference between 1 and n
c) The difference between a and b
d) The threshold between a and b (1)
e) The reset from successor to immediate predecessor (always n - 1)
f) the categorical exclusion (0 /1) > (1 / n)

We have discussed the immediate significance of the differences, and somewhat of the threshold. What truly concerns us here are e and d. The reset and the exclusion are exclusive of each other. There are two types of exclusions here: the coming-into-being of 0 / 1, and the point at which there is no possibility of reset (return to a previous state). For example, once the threshold 0 / 1 has been crossed, it is possible to reset to 0 as we saw in the

Lovers' Game above. Once a and x enter into a relationship, the threshold has been crossed and the game begins with a at a disadvantage in a zero-sum game. When a possesses b, however, then the game resets to 0 where both a and x are equal in terms of the game's language rules.

The attempt to prove Fermat's Last Theorem ($a^n + b^n = c^n$, where n is any multiple greater than 2 and a, b, c have no nonzero integers), provides us with the most recent example of the usefulness and curious iconoclastic properties of modular arithmetic. Andrew Wiles' breakthrough using modularity to at last prove the theorem thrust so-called clock arithmetic into the philosophical foreground. Put simply, clock arithmetic is recursive not linear. The linearity of a proposition presumes that n + 1 will bring us to any number, just as a transcontinental train will bring us to either side of a continent — though in this case ad infinitum in both the positive and negative directions.

In clock arithmetic 2 + 2 may not equal 4. For example, if my clock has three hours on it, with 3 being the top hour, then 2 + 2 will equal 1, which is in the fourth position from 3. How is this useful in mathematics? Singh explains what significance modular arithmetic had for Wiles in his proof: "By simply changing the values of a, b, and c, in the general elliptic equations mathematicians can generate an infinite variety of equations, each one with its own characteristics, but all of them just within the realm of solubility."[6] The problems Wiles and others faced and perhaps that Fermat decided to pass on to posterity as a joke, is that starting with the multiple 3, every case for every cardinal number after would have to be proved to prove once and for all that the theorem was true. This method is an impossibility.

Here the progressive fallacy expressed indirectly in Peano's primitives, that one number must succeed another, and that no number may be the successor of itself, falls to the ontological argument that being is encapsulated in quanta or modules, and that within the module "an infinite variety of equations, each with its own characteristics" may be generated, iterated, or recur.

As we shall see, these simple ideas have brought us to a new threshold of discourse, which is the no-man's-land between Cartesian-Newtonian and quantum physics. The prevailing thesis here, told in various ways, is that mankind has entered into a new paradigm tacit in the creations and revelations of what Wolfgang Schirmacher calls Homo Generator:

This other modernity beyond postmodernity reveals itself as

---

[6] Singh, Simon. *Fermat's Enigma.* New York: Walker and Company, 1997, p. 165.

"artificial life," and leaves behind a once-raging debate about who will determine and control this artificial life. In information technology and media as well as in biotechnology and the biological sciences, one can observe how long-since obsolete paradigms abuse their power to define when faced with new phenomena. Whether ethics and public acceptance attain a key position in this regard and mobilize criticism or whether a linear optimism of progress prevails, remains of secondary importance, for both positions bear the stamp of anthropocentrism and are deeply undialectical.[7]

Here Schirmacher aligns technology and media to the revolutions in science — little reported and less understood — that have occurred in chemistry, nuclear physics, neuroscience, and materials science since 1993 when Wiles first reported the proof of Fermat's Last Theorem. Furthermore, Schirmacher points to the misalignment of the Cartesian-Newtonian paradigm with the applications of these discoveries and the ethics and politics of the contextual cultures in which these discoveries were bred. As mentioned earlier, much of the mayhem of modern life is the symptom of the Progressive Fallacy, that the mere succession or concatenation of iterations is in itself our temporal and ontological context. The potentialities of modular arithmetic, discovered by the ancient Greeks and studied by Diophantus[8], is just an example of what modern mathematicians such as Carl Fried Gauss in his *Disquisitiones Arithmeticae* bring to our understanding of how we may operate functionally as Homo Generator. The primary obstructions to evolution of thought and behavior are the Progressive Fallacy and the traditional Cartesian view of man as the manipulator of a mechanized nature and mathematics as an immutable language containing the discourse of a metaphysical Creator.

It may perhaps seem that the games played by logicians, mathematicians, and even social scientists using computer modeling do not effectively extend into the *materia* of the space-time vectors we casually call being, or life. Observing the process of coming-into-being at the threshold then, we may find some curious deconstructions of our tacit assumptions about our place in the existential context.

---

[7] Schirmacher, Wolfgang. "After the Last Judgment: Hegel as Philosopher of Artificial Life." European Graduate School. Articles. Retrieved on 29 May 2011.

[8] Singh, Simon. *Fermat's Enigma*. New York: Walker and Company, 1997, p. 165.

1.3.1 When there is nothing left to prove

Before we step further, we must meditate on what it means to prove something. To begin with, we now become acquainted with the Discourse. The Discourse (hereafter with a lower-case initial letter) is the shared understanding of the story of our place in the spatial and temporal continuum as the greater set, and in the subsets of what is for the most part the fate of our births. To understand the dynamic between these sets (e.g. whether or not a subset includes a monotheistic god) is to understand human life on a cultural scale. However, in the dimensions of space and time, we come to an understanding of man as a thing, a physical fact that can be or not as that thing.

Proof can only occur within the context of this discourse. Therefore, the implicit definition of "proof" is often "conforms to the discourse." Deviations are termed errors, and therefore are not proof conclusive. Here is the basis of epistemology from the view of the mind that is itself a node in the network of the discursive system or constellation. Epistemological investigation begins with testing. Ronell indicates that discovery, proof, or the truth of a proposition is a negative enterprise based in the "overthrow" of the discourse.

"The [...] scientific stance, then, involves the strength to try to overthrow rather than to establish the solution at which thought arrives. The point is to let go in good faith of the massive defense mechanisms that attend thought, to allow if not to provoke the dissolution of the solution, to affirmatively invite failure by losing the attachment to a solution made in service to dogmatic principles."[9]

The "dogmatic principles" here are not the casually metaphoric dicta of the professions, or the prohibitions of the church, but rather the metaphysical assumptions we make about the physical world and which are near impossible to see through without a serious analysis of the apparatus of discourse. A serious analysis of discourse is, indeed, the mission of this study.

Kant, in his Introduction to the Critique (IV), shows how the majority of our thinking is synthetic, or based on unprovable propositions, and that the few provable propositions are too few in number to build a world. The implication is that therefore the world as we perceive it is largely a creation of our imagination. The exception here is in when we are in "the extreme limit of pain," says Holderlin, where "nothing remains but the condition of time and space,"[10] the two a priori of Kant's Dasein.

[9] Ronell, Avital. *The Test Drive*. Chicago: U. Illinois Press, 2005, p. 35.
[10] Agamben, Giorgio. *Homo Sacer: Sovereign Power and Bare Life*. Standford: Stanford U.P., 1998, p. 185.

In "Of the Difference Between Analytic and Synthetical Thinking," Kant divides propositions into two groups: explicative and argumentative. The first group corresponds to analytic propositions "because the former [propositions] add in the predicate nothing to the conception of the subject, but only analyze it into constituent conceptions, which were thought already in the subject [...], the latter add to our conceptions of the subject a predicate which was not contained in it, and which no analysis could ever have discovered therein."[11] Herein we begin to see the first quanta of the discourse of propaganda: the predicate and its relationship with the subject of a sentence. This is the building block of the edifice of thought.

The key is "experience" as Kant refers to it; the processing of space-time as an entity "being" in the existential context, flavored with the irregularities of cultural implantation. "By the addition of such a predicate [...] it becomes a synthetical judgment. Judgments of experience, as such, are always synthetical" and therefore must be argued or are, epistemologically, negotiable. Argumentative propositions are the woof of the fabric of the discourse, whereas explicit are the warp. The determining threshold is found in the predicate of the sentence. Examples given by Kant suffice: it is analytic to say that things have the property of extension, but it is synthetic to say that the shortest distance between two points is a straight line, or even that a body set in motion tends to stay in motion. In the first synthetic example the phrase "the shortest distance" is a relative, judgmental proposition. In the second, Newton betrays even himself with the word "tends," and we can thank him for having the decency to do so. To assert otherwise is to enter into the discourse of dogma.

Kant cites Newton's argument that for every action there is an equal and opposite reaction as an example of a synthetic proposition. "For in the conception of matter, I do not cogitate its permanency, but merely its presence in space, which it fills."[12]

What is most significant in Kant's analysis is the priority of the a priori. Things extend in space a priori, so that we might say of them, "This is a thing" because it extends (note the close etymological similarity to the word existence). Whereas nothing is a priori straight, long, short, or tends. Kant plunges further into his analysis by condemning mathematical absolutism as synthetic: "Mathematical judgments are always synthetical."[13] Which brings us back to the proposition of 2 + 2 equaling 4. In this statement "2

[11] Kant, Immanuel. *Critique of Pure Reason*. New York: Barnes & Noble, 2005.
[12] Ibid., p. l.
[13] Ibid., p. xlviii.

+ 2" is the subject, in other words "If I add these two numbers together what happens?" the predicate, which defines the proposition, says "the sum is the number 4." But we have seen that in our modular arithmetic this is not so in a three-numbered recursion. The answer then is 1. This example is given only because the discourse uses the example of "2 + 2 = 4" as a popular, vernacular way to define the a priori, what exists immutably before all synthetic propositions.

1.4 Artificial worlds

As Zizek has stated, what is significant in the modern age is not virtual reality, but the reality of the virtual. Ayer takes up this proposition, calling the the idea of a virtual reality where "unicorns exist" as superstition. "In general, the postulation of real non-existent entities results from the superstition [...] that, to every word or phrase that can be the grammatical subject of a sentence, there must somewhere be a real entity corresponding," giving an example as the statement "Unicorns are fictitious."[14] Prima facie this statement may seem to hold as much truth as the statement "all dogs are faithful," but a look at the predicates — *fictitious* versus *faithful* — reveals the respective priority of the statements. A priori, unicorns are fictitious. A posteriori a dog may or may not be faithful. To house the synthetic propositions, the discourse creates a world where such utterances are commonplace. "For there is no place in the empirical world for many of these 'entities,' a special non-empirical world is invoked [...]."[15]

This special world becomes the business of the discourse. As such, the discourse is in need of propaganda to support its world the way a parent supports his or her children by having a job. Advertising, books, periodicals, speeches, architecture, products, music, education, money, lifestyle — there is no end to the encapsulation that must be accomplished to maintain the ever-crumbling edifice of the discourse that describes a world that is not Dasein, but that Dasein encloses the way an aquarium encloses fish in an ersatz sea.

---

[14] Ayer, A.J. *Language, Truth and Logic*. New York: Dover Publications, Inc., ND, p. 43.
[15] Ibid., p. 43.

1.4.1 Beyond the special world of the artifice

So we may see this special world as a kind of veil hanging between the explicit and argumentative worlds. In the latter, rhetorical structure reigns as the organizing principle of argument. We will analyze examples of rhetoric later and in some depth. However, here let it suffice to say that a traditional advertising copy pattern consists of three sentence types in concatenation: interrogative — declarative — imperative. Often the imperative has exclamation as its adjunct. For example:

Interrogative: Do you want to be rich?
Declarative: There are three reasons why people are poor.
Imperative: Give us money and will will teach you the secret of getting rich.

Of course, the punch line here is that the secret disclosed after payment is that selling the secret of getting rich is what makes you rich, revealing the entire expression to be tautological, simplified thus: getting money makes you rich. A similar proposition is found in a dialogue between characters in an Esquire magazine article written by Ernest Hemingway in 1926 titled "The Rich Boy" where Scott Fitzgerald observes, "The rich are different from you and me." "Yes, they have more money." We learn from Ayer, however, that we can always rely on tautologies to be true because, as Kant describes, a thing that extends exists, which is as much as invoking Aristotle's first Law of Thought: A is A. However, discovering a true tautology from a false one also lies on the borderline between the explicit and the argumentative, making the obviousness of tautology easy bait for the invocation of the reality of the virtual. A dragon in a three-dimensional movie presentation may be frightening though the viewer knows such a creature does not exist, just as the audience at the Lumiere Brothers' presentation of a clip of a train coming into the station frightened the audience out of its wits regarding a machine that does exist in the theater. "A man can always sustain his convictions in the face of apparently hostile evidence if he is prepared to make the necessary ad hoc assumptions."[16] Ayer presents part of the famous syllogism beginning "All men are mortal" as an example of an evidently tautological statement. His analysis, however, reveals that for the statement to be both true and tautological, we can only verify the following, that "everything which has the other defining properties of a man also has the property of being mortal [...]."[17]

---

[16] Ibid., p. 95
[17] Ibid., p. 96

Which brings us back to Kant's statement that mathematical statements are always synthetical. If Kant declares that experience is the a posteriori negating the explicit nature of an analytical proposition, wherein lies the experience in abstract mathematics or number theory? We could say that empirical methods of calculation such as counting beans or fingers show us that both methods of adding and subtracting are almost invariably reliable, but even schemes for using notation to complete multiplication, division, and logarithms are so fraught with error and misunderstanding that we tend to rely on memorization, machines, and tables to complete the functions.

So then do we place mathematics on the explicit or argumentative side? We could say that with the dawn of the Homo Generator paradigm of Schirmacher, the mathematician, indeed the poet and the scientist, enter the post-Cartesian territory — a terra incognita by definition — where at last the birth of the recognition of the synthetic a posteriori nature of the discourse becomes more clear as "the hope and the angst of the post-Hegelian philosophers, a Dasein beyond metaphysics, a human being which [sic] needs no Being, no certainty, no truth. Modern technology is the birthplace of homo generator [...]"[18]

We may consider Andrew Wiles as a suitable example of homo generator at least in the sense that in the almost 400 years after Fermat's death no one came close to proving the theorem, yet he did prove it. Why? It could be that at least in certain strains of theoretical endeavor, such as mathematics and science, maintaining "convictions in the face of apparently hostile evidence" was no longer possible. This may be optimistic. Revolutions in quantum physics, number theory, and cognitive science alone show a clear, demonstrable, and categorical break with the past which was often littered with cherished synthetic propositions about everything from diet to astronomy. The rise and fall of psychology during this period may also be considered, especially its yield to psychophamacology marking the transition from metaphysician to physician. (In some ways, however, dogma supported by propaganda in these domains was only reinforced, making homo generator beat a retreat.)

---

[18] Schirmacher, Wolfgang. "Homo Generator: Media and Postmodern Technology." (1994.) European Graduate School Articles. Accessed 29 May 2011.

1.4.2 Lifting the linear equation

Let us return to the original proposition of this discussion: (0 / 1) > (1 / n) and search for the transcendental (Kant) lifting of the prevailing paradigm. The categorical exclusion makes way for the modular lifting we can find with the progress of any form of sequential development and event. After the threshold, we may have n + 1 or 1 + n. In the first case, we simply inch along the endless time line one integer at a time without ordinal relationship. In the second, we commence an ordinal relationship supplying any number for n, such as 10 or 100 but extending on for infinity. In both cases we have infinity, but in the first case no ratio (making infinity an irrational number), and in the second a ratio (making infinity a rational number). In the first I can express a number by adding 1, but I do not have the ratio of 1 and n. In the second, I have the ratio of 1 and n, where n can be any other number.

We can add a third kind of infinity if we consider the number lying in the a priori position of the threshold: 0. Peano states that 0 is a number, it has value, and we can say that 0 is a negation of 1 and that 1 is a negation of 0, making both 1 and 0 rational. However, we may also have $\aleph 0$(aleph null), the smallest infinite cardinal number. So there is 0 as a whole number, and 0 infinity. Finally, we have Wiles' proposition presented to an audience, appropriately at the Newton Institute in Cambridge, England on June 23, 1993 where he first announced the tentative proof of Fermat's theorem:

If p is a prime number, u, v, and w are rational numbers, and $up+ vp+ wp= 0$.

According to Rubin and Silverberg, Wiles' presentation was part of three talks with the overall title of "Modular forms, elliptic curves, and Galios representations."[19] Once again, modularity brings the proposition back to 0 rather than concatenate toward a linear infinity, creating the illusion of progression. Coming-into-being, then, is cyclical rather than progressive. The crossing of the threshold from 0 to 1 is an infinite divide and as such is never quite effected except as appearance. The appearance of things in the world, with their singular property of extension, does not give them being for, as Kant states it, being itself is not an attribute, thus invoking Zeno's paradox.[20]

[19] Rubin, K. and A. Silverberg. "A Report on Wiles' Cambridge Lectures." (1994.) American Mathematical Society.

[20] Ayer, A.J. *Language, Truth and Logic.* New York: Dover Publications, Inc., ND, p. 43.

The problem of an infinite divide between 0 and 1 is overcome by what Kant refers to as the Transcendental Aesthetic, in the "pure" sense. "I call all representations pure, in the transcendental meaning of the word, wherein nothing is met with that belongs to sensation."[21] At the moment 1 is achieved, sensation begins and knowledge becomes sense based on a posteriori. The a priori, according to Kant's aesthetic, includes space and time, as it does not take our perception of sensory stimuli to live in extension in those two vectors. Space is "not a conception which has been derived from outward experiences."[22] Furthermore, "time is a condition a priori of all phenomena whatsoever — the *immediate* condition of all internal, and thereby *mediate* condition of all external circumstances."[23]

It is worth exploring the difference between the terms "immediate" and "mediate" here. By time as a pure transcendental Kant means it is not the result of empirical experience, and that it is an a priori. Therefore, time is immediate and not the past or future, both of which originate from experience, one as a record of it and the other as a projection of it. Furthermore, it is the medium in which we exist, or the region of Dasein. This medium exists a priori and has no attribute though all attributes arise in its region or context. But there is also a modern interpretation of this idea of a "medium."

The vessel of the propagation of ideas is the mass media, which of course take many forms that do not need to be listed here. The media are foremost concerned with time: air time, prime time, standard time, time zones, run time, and so on. The audience's interaction with the media product is always immediate, even if one is reading an old newspaper from decades ago. Screenplays are written in the present tense. But tense is irrelevant because the media product arrives before the audience in the only time there is: Kant's pure time of transcendental aesthetic (TA). Many media products (of course including books) are concerned with depiction of the ancient past, or the distant future. In fact, there is almost no other form of such representation (and this includes historical religious scriptures predicting a future end time). "Time travel" is the prerogative of the media.

However, there is one aspect of time that Kant considers to be a posteriori and outside of the TA: the time line of rational numbers. "[B]ecause this internal intuition presents to us no shape or form, we endeavor

---

[21] Kant, Immanuel. *Critique of Pure Reason*. New York: Barnes & Noble, 2005, p. 2.
[22] Ibid., p. 3.
[23] Ibid., p. 9.

to supply this want by analogies, and represent the course of time by a line progressing to infinity, the content of which constitutes a series which is only of one dimension [...]."[24] Which brings us back to Wiles' dilemma when approaching the theorem, with proofs extending on the line of rational integers forever as all multiples above 2. Fermat's joke was that you would have to provide proof for every multiple over 2, with a, b, c having no nonzero integers. Only fools would dare undertake the proof. But through modular arithmetic, in particular two forms of it: the Tanayama-Shimura Conjecture applied to ellipsis, and the Galois Lifting, providing a simultaneous and parallel solution via two paths for one problem, he was able to limit the proofs while accounting for all instances of the theorem. (We will discuss simultaneous parallel ontologies and ontic threads in Part 2 of this discussion.)

2.1 The set of all sets and its significance to the sovereign

Russell describes the set of all sets as that which contains itself if and only if it does not contain itself. This apparent paradox is actually a rational reading of what "set of all sets" means, despite Wittgenstein's complaint to the contrary (3.333). Primary to the discourse is the sovereign, and the sovereign power. The sovereign power uses the discourse through propaganda vessels to accomplish its aims. In this way, the prevailing discourse is propagated and inculcated as the official language of the sovereign and its adjacent interests. However, mere words and images are not enough (as Joseph Goebbels proved by relying too much on them). There must be a juridical solution, longitudinally prosecuted and exercised, where The Word of the law crawls out from its primordial slime of ontological obscurity as analytical proposition, and into the light of empirical authority. As Ayer pointed out earlier, the mind is ever ready to accept the substitution — or *abduction* — of individual ontological sovereignty and a priori intuition of space and time for the beautiful lie of appearances and empirical a posteriori experience. As Agamben describes it, "The paradox of sovereignty consists in the fact the sovereign is, at the same time, outside and inside the juridical order [....] 'I, the sovereign, who am outside the law, declare that there is nothing outside

---

[24] Ibid., p. 9

the law [...].' "[25] Here is the first mention of topology. "The topology implicit in the paradox is worth reflecting upon, since the degree to which sovereignty marks the limit [...] of the juridical order will become clear once the structure of the paradox is grasped."[26]

What is the topology of this paradox? The nesting "set of all sets" that is not a set of itself can be described as, $[a(n) \rightarrow n(\sim a)]$ where $\rightarrow$ operates as "if, then," a is the set of all sets, and n is any number of sets within the set of all sets, including the set "not a." The expression reads if a is the set of all sets then a must not be one of the sets.

If the law is all powerful, then the sovereign power must be outside of the law because it is the law. This is a land of great uncertainty, another terra incognita where what is "known" epistemologically is only what is synthetical. While the analytic may be intuited within this system, it never appears, as its appearance is to the topology what a magician's tricks are to the illusion he creates. Since the juridical powers may not conduct all-out war on the population with success, they must employ other means. The state therefore turns to the apparatus of propaganda, just as a manufacturer cannot force you to buy its products but must convince you through argument of the merits of surrendering tokens of sovereignty in the form of money.

Through this glass darkly, we see Kant and his pure Transcendental Aesthetic from a great distance. We see the formulations for overcoming the discourse of infinity in time and space as if these were the illusions themselves, and that the synthetic, argumentative reality substituted in the abduction of individual sovereignty is in fact the analytic, explicit reality. "There is no rule that is applicable to chaos," says Agamben.[27] "The sovereign's monopoly over the final decision is the essence of State Sovereignty and must be properly defined not as the monopoly to rule but as the monopoly to decide [...]."

Critical to the sovereign power is the "state of exception," where the power may be exercised outside of the law as it is written and propagated. Exception is a form of negation, in this case negative of the positive law of enforcement. Returning to the categorical exclusion, we may say that the state of exception is a form of reset back to the state of chaos where rules

---

[25]Agamben, Giorgio. *Homo Sacer: Sovereign Power and Bare Life*. Standford: Stanford U.P., 1998, p. 15.
[26]Ibid., p. 15.
[27]Agamben, Giorgio. *Homo Sacer: Sovereign Power and Bare Life*. Standford: Stanford U.P., 1998, p. 16.

do not apply, the irony being that such a decision was made by another set of rules allowing return to no rules or chaos. "The exception is a kind of exclusion," says Agamben, and as such is a negation of 1 to 0, a reset. "The rule applies to the exception in no longer applying, in withdrawing from it. The state of exception is thus not the chaos that precedes order but rather the situation that results from its suspension."[28]

The situation here is that there is a return to the natal state — at least for the sovereign. But also there is opportunity for the citizens, who are cued by the fiats of the leader. There is a rise of the rule of the camp, which includes martial law, but at the same time there is looting — a forcible redistribution of income. "The situation created in the exception has the peculiar character that it cannot be defined either as a situation of fact or as a situation of right, but instead institutes a paradoxical threshold of indistinction between the two."[29] In the categorical exclusion, the threshold lies at the position 1, which is part of both sides of the transformational equation as both infinitely greater than 0, and in ratio to infinity with n. When sovereign power steps outside the law, invoking the law of the camp, it simultaneously restores personal sovereignty to the citizen by revoking the rule of law which was the very apparatus of abduction of the citizen's sovereign persona. The rule of the camp always possesses the following characteristics, it: 1) Suspends rule of law, 2) Is temporary, 3) Restores sovereignty to the citizen ("Law of the Jungle"), 4) Uses or threatens direct violence, 5) Requires the sovereign to step outside of the rule of law.

The "freedom" that ensues can be the barbarism of torture and murder, or a liberation from disaster, oppression, or genocide. Agamben cites Arendt as describing the totalitarianism of the camps as a state where "everything is possible [....] because the camps constitute a space of exception [...] in which not only is law completely suspended but fact and law are completely confused — everything in the camps is truly possible."[30] The problem the bourgeoisie has in appreciating this freedom is because state torture and murder on the one hand and looting and rape on the other are not sanctioned deontological behaviors. When they are sanctioned by the parasite classes of government, church, schools, banking, and media, they must be performed teleologically by proctors (soldiers) or performed on an "other" class of excluded individuals who

---

[28] Ibid., p. 18-19.
[29] Ibid., p. 18.
[30] Agamben, Giorgio. *Homo Sacer: Sovereign Power and Bare Life*. Standford: Stanford U.P., 1998, p. 170.

are both within and outside of the state of exception via the ban, which places them in the same position as the sovereign, but rather as homo sacer.

Not enough has been said so far regarding the anti-bourgeoise presence of the ultimate *auslander*: the willful criminal, who, like the sovereign, is always already in a state of exception by his own a priori personal fiat. Agamben describes his state as "in many ways similar" to homo sacer, the sacred man who may be killed without juridical penalty. "He has been excluded from the religious community and from all political life" and is therefore free of the nomos. His status as a kind of holy man helps illuminate the vernacular sainthood gangsters and criminals receive from their "audiences" who are often also their victims.

The issue in transformational law is what Agamben calls "inclusion." The categorical exclusion (CE), by its nature, has an inverse relationship to inclusion. It is a negation of it, and vice versa. What is excluded from the category is determined by the sovereign power. By remaining as the arbiter of juridical power within the law, the power excludes the citizen from exercising the same (e.g. "taking matters into his own hands"). Under this regime we may say that the citizen's sovereignty has been "abducted," creating a topology or territory with inclusion at one end and exclusion at the other. This state of affairs is perfectly described by the CE, thus: The transformation from 0 to 1 crosses the threshold from personal sovereignty in a lawless terrain to the rule of law and the abduction of sovereignty. The transformation from 1 to n is iterative, for example swapping one form of political economics for another as capitalism, communism, theocracy, dictatorship, and the like. What matters is not what form the abduction has taken — a bag over the head and shoved in a car, hijacked in a plane and made to land in hostile territory, armed seizure of a facility — but that the abduction has taken place.

Below, Agamben describes the push-pull mechanism of the abduction along the infinite positive and negative value track of the CE:

> The exception does not subtract itself from the rule; rather, the rule, suspending itself, gives rise to the exception and, maintaining itself in relation to the exception, first constitutes itself as a rule. The particular "force" of law consists in this capacity of law to maintain itself in relation to an exteriority. We shall give the name *relation of exception* to the extreme form of relation by which something is included solely through its exclusion.[31]

---

[31] Ibid., p. 18

The push-pull negation here can be likened to the trucks of an electric train with self-powered cars and no engine. In such an arrangement, each car has two trucks with sets of electric powered wheels. The rear truck (based on the direction the train travels) pushes the car, while the front truck, engaging the same mechanism, pulls the car. The "exception" is the front truck, and the "rule" is the rear. Both propel the force of law toward its exteriority, and as such are in a state of *the relation of exception* in that they negate each other and yet propel the juridical "force" in the maintaining of a set of all sets where "something is included solely through its exclusion." If p is the pull mechanism (exception) and q is the push mechanism (rule) and n is the arrow pointing to exteriority, then $[\sim (p \vee q) \rightarrow (p \wedge q) n]$. In other words, if not pull or push, then pull and push is exteriority. While this may seem absolute, we must consider that *there is no exception to the state of exception. It is — absolute.*

The state of exception serves as the threshold between what is inside and outside.[32] It also serves as the transformational position for the normal situation and chaos. The relation of exception, then becomes the topology of abduction/abdication through which both the sovereign and the citizen navigate in their *pas de deux* of hegemony.

2.2 Personal sovereignty and exclusions

When we talk about language, we talk about psychology. Language has been described as a concatenation of binary values. Something is good or bad, right or wrong, hot or cold, up or down. In the coming-into-being, the thing is at last judged in language and by language. For example, one is either the sovereign or not, one is either male or female (at least at first), one is either rich or poor. In the Kantian sense, none of these values is explicit or analytical. However, there remains one value which is the same for all: all are born with personal sovereignty. Immediately this proposition seems suspect because there is the fact of the sovereign. It could be asserted that there cannot be personal sovereignty unless the sovereign suspends the rule of law. Even where there is no direct sovereign power, such as in an isolationist religious sect, the state retains the ultimate power to persecute, disband, prosecute, and otherwise determine the form of life for the separationists.

---

[32] Ibid., p. 19

A further argument against a priori personal sovereignty is that in many countries a child is born as state property, straight from the womb. Until a certain age, for instance sixteen, the child must attend state schools or their equivalent, must be a registered citizen through a birth certificate, must be counted for in the census, and can be taken away from the parents and made a "ward of the state" at the slightest provocation and with almost no legal recourse to the contrary.

Nevertheless, suicide defies the hot brand of ownership. Suicide offers us the ultimate reset of the categorical exclusion. By killing oneself, one "excludes" oneself from the discourse, and from the realm of the sovereign while exercising the ultimate sovereignty. However, it is not to be taken as an exception to the state of exception. Negations here are slavery versus suicide, the former being the least state of personal sovereignty and the latter the most. The slave who kills himself "cheats" the sovereign out of his possession, his investment, and the potential labor that could be expected from that slave. There is a good reason why jail and prison authorities take away prisoners' shoelaces.

Schopenhauer uses the very origin of the state sovereign and the discourse — theocracy and scripture — to wonder at the prohibition both make against taking one's life. "Thus we read that suicide is the most cowardly of acts, that only a madman would commit it, and similar insipidities; or the senseless assertion that suicide is 'wrong', though it is obvious there is nothing in the world a man has a more incontestable *right* to than his own life and person."[33]

It is worth repeating the phrase here "there is nothing in the world a man has a more incontestable right to than his own life and person." This is the quintessential statement of personal sovereignty, and *in extremis*, where one's life is being taken by one's own hand. Were personal sovereignty not an a priori, then it would be something we would have to argue into existence. All the arguments of the church men of all ages have not slowed the urge to die willingly. Once it was performed at the points of enemy swords. Today in most places it is a solitary act of direct or indirect intention.

We may take the statement that the suicide prohibition is supported by the liturgy and scripture as indicating an obtuse relationship to the act. Schopenhauer shows that the clergy has little juridical ground upon which to make suicide illegal as the majority of scriptures offer no such

---

[33] Schopenhauer, Arthur. *Essays and Aphorisms*. New York: Penguin Books, 1970, p. 77.

prohibition — perhaps because death came so readily when they were written suicide was not needed. Though we do have the example of Judas doing so after betraying Jesus, but this scene is cast as justice for the act of betrayal.

"In my opinion it ought [...] to be demanded of the clergy that they tell us by what authority they go to their pulpits or their desks and brand as a crime an action which many people we honor and love have performed and deny an honourable [sic] burial to those who have departed this world voluntarily — since they cannot point to a single biblical authority, nor produce a single sound philosophical argument; it being made clear that what one wants are reasons and not empty phrases or abuse."[34]

The passage above is rich in exception and exclusion. To begin, he asks "by what authority" the ban (as we shall call it) is justified? Lacking in explicit text, he must fall back on the criminal laws. But criminal laws provide no rationale as religious teaching do. Laws are not teachings. Therefore, Schopenhauer asks for a reason, a teaching, not "empty phrases or abuse." Moreover, reason leads us to question such a ban when we weigh the merits of a life well lived and of peace and generosity against the judgment of guilty which always befalls the suicide. There is no trial or defense lawyer; the suicide is a priori guilty without having the right to be a priori sovereign!

There is perhaps no better metaphorical image of "exclusion" than being "excommunicated" from the church upon killing oneself. In the case of the suicide, though, the exclusion takes on the lurid image of being denied burial in "sacred" ground. The suicide must be interred in profane space, alien territory, indeed in the region of the topology of the categorical exclusion where one is a priori unabducted. Again, by invoking the state of exception for the suicide, the sovereign succeeds in restoring the suicide's personal sovereignty just as in declaring martial law there is what Agamben calls the ensuing "situation" of relative freedom.

The situation, though, is not as simple as all this. The idea that the sovereign "wants" to enslave or even rule is to assume to much. Moreover, the citizen, precisely at the point the sovereign state seems to seize the most power, is thrown back on personal sovereignty — a situation the citizen is not accustomed to. For abduction to be complete, there must be acquiescence on the part of the abductee. Seldom does that acquiescence come "up front." But often does it come on the back end of the kidnapping tale. For instance, in many Russian folk tales the abductee is a child, taken from the world of prohibitions ("Do not go near that forest!") to a land

---

[34] Ibid., pp 77-78

where he does not have to work, and gets to play with golden apples — a matter we shall return to later.[35] So the citizen, and indeed the child subject, must be presented with an a posteriori argument to motivate the abdication of personal sovereignty (which then may be taken back through suicide or martial law). This is called hegemony or the species where there is push-pull mechanism. In other words, the sovereign power pulls and the citizen pushes. Built into this situation is the potential for the citizen to revoke his voluntary abduction, which may be possible without suicide, but abdication is by definition final unless the crown is seized by force.

In this passage, Achilles, the greatest hero of Troy, and a protosovereign in and of himself, has second thoughts about freedom when it entails death:

O shining Odysseus, never try to console me for dying.
I would rather follow the plow as thrall to another
man, one with no land allotted to him and not much to live on,
than be a king over all the perished dead.
— Achilles' soul to Odysseus, Homer, *Odyssey*, 11.488-491

There are many twists and turns of the matter of sovereignty here. His first proposition is, in effect, "I would rather be a slave," in other words, he states, explicitly, that he would prefer to be in a state of overthrow or abdication of personal sovereignty than his current position. If x is death and p is slavery and q is sovereign power, then Achilles' statement or preference follows this form (where →means "if, then"): q(x) →p, in other words, if sovereignty comes with death, then I would rather abdicate my sovereignty and be entirely abducted as a slave.

However, what is fascinating here it the proposition without x: q →p. Could we possibly imagine Achilles, the greatest hero Troy has ever known, voluntarily abdicating his personal sovereignty and state sovereignty to "follow the plow as thrall to another"? Furthermore, we have excluded one form of sovereignty from the formula so far: the lack of land ownership by the slave owner Achillies would slave for. We can abstract lack of ownership of land to the idea of lack of possession. A slave may possess or not. Either way, a slave *is* possessed, as a nonslave, presumably, is not. Land ownership was and in some ways is requisite for full participation in parliamentary proceedings and even voting for representatives. Achilles' formula, then, if we indicate possession as y, becomes: q(~y [x]) →p, the addition being slavery without possessions.

[35] Propp, Vladimir. *Morphology of the Folktale*. Austin: U. or Texas press, 1988, p. 98.

Schopenhauer addresses this resistance to freedom of suicide: "But there is something positive in it as well: the destruction of the body. This is a deterrent, because the body is the phenomenal form of the will to live."[36]

3.1 The language of the sovereign

For there to be language, there must be apparatus. Apparatus is the grammatical and rhetorical forms the language operates in — its social architecture. As such, language is the apparatus. Sovereign of the sovereign. The reason? Communication. For the sovereign to communicate, he must use language. It can be the mute language of masques and dance, or the articulated languages of newspapers, the internet, and books. *It hardly matters what medium conveys the message. What matters is the message itself.*

Agamben has said that language was the first liturgical apparatus. the moment words were strung together into syntactical relationship, the apparatus was born.[37] Herein lies the crux of propaganda's mechanism. The sovereign power in the end is only a figurehead for the true ruler: language itself. There are many definitions of language. For the sake of this discourse, let us say that language is a concatenation of speech parts that, together, form a whole idea. We may suggest that this concatenation produces thought, which previously was an *a morphous* mass of impressions.

"Language is the sovereign who, in a permanent state of exception, declares that there is nothing outside language and that language is always beyond itself. The particular structure of law has its foundation in this presuppositional structure of human language. It expresses the bond of inclusive exclusion to which a thing is subject because of the fact of being in language, of being named. To speak [*dire*] is, in this sense, always to 'speak the law,' *ius dicere*."[38]

3.1.1 The socket of language

To what does language speak, and from where does it utter? How is the apparatus constructed and what are its parts? Let us begin by saying that to live without a sovereign power is the same as living without language. The Critical Period in speech and listening development has been described as

---

[36] Schopenhauer, Arthur. *Essays and Aphorisms*. New York: Penguin Books, 1970, p. 79.
[37] Agamben, Giorgio. Personal conversation. Saas-Fee, Switzerland, 2009.
[38] Agamben, Giorgio. *Homo Sacer: Sovereign Power and Bare Life*. Standford: Stanford U.P., 1998, p. 21.

from age 0 to 12. It has been noted that lack of development in the form of speech interaction causes permanent loss of speech capability despite training.[39] Perhaps the same could be said for living without a sovereign power. Nevertheless, what we seek here is the social socket, the place where language as a non-native phenomenon acquired through social interaction, takes hold in the early development of the child. What we also seek is the position where personal sovereignty is abducted by the social and political discourse. These are psychological positions in child development.

To Agamben, language abducts the principal position of the one who wields hegemony: "language is the sovereign who, in a permanent state of exception, declares that there is nothing outside language and that language is always beyond itself."[40] He goes on to say that the morphology of law is human language itself, expressing the "bond of inclusive exclusion." The critical propositions here are that the sovereign always already is in a state of exception (and not by self fiat) and that the exclusion is "inclusive." *Therefore, the state of exception is an a priori.* In the second, we discover another paradox expressing Russell's, in this case that the state of exception, as exclusion, is part of itself if and only if it is *not* part of itself. The mechanism here is "being named," which ropes the individual into the nomos in both the ancient and modern senses of being in the spirit of the law and being the worldview (Weltanschauung) of invididuals.

This set of all sets (exception/exclusion) includes the example, which is the nomos, the case law, defining the juridical state the citizen is subject to. "From this perspective, the exception is situated in a symmetrical position with respect to the example, with which it forms a system."[41] The system is a kind of solar system, with the exclusion orbiting the inclusion, the exception orbiting the rule of law, and the outside orbiting the inside of the set — *while always already contained within the set as coming-into-being.* But of course there must be an exception to the exception for the sovereign to be always already in such a state with or without fiat. Therefore, the paradigm of the exception is always excluded from the set, "shown beside," as the class of juridical nomos "can contain everything except its own paradigm."[42]

---

[39] Lust, Barbara. *Child Language*. Cambridge: Cambridge UP, 2006, pp, 79, 93.

[40] Agamben, Giorgio. *Homo Sacer: Sovereign Power and Bare Life.* Standford: Stanford U.P., 1998, p. 21.

[41] Ibid., p. 21.

[42] Ibid., p. 22.

The language socket here is in the usurpation of the sovereign's autonomy by language itself. The sovereign's hegemony is on loan from language. Its a priori state is the result not from some special or holy quality about the sovereign bestowed by god or the gods, or even by apparent wealth. Rather, it is a priori because language exists before the sovereign as the state in which the sovereign is included and others are excluded from in a state of exception. The arbiter or the nomos, then, may assign whatever value is expedient for the situation to the word associated with it. This is a common practice of power and is indeed the root of divisive propaganda, which should not be confused with the mere propagation of ideas and its psycholinguistics.

3.2 Psycholinguistics of the "Ideal I"

The concern here for language is not so much in the cognitive science and neuroscience of its acquisition and development, as much as it is in the subject-object relationship between communicators. Already contained in the terms "subject" and "object" are the seeds of the citizen-sovereign positions which are, according to Agamben, symmetrical. The developmental psychology of this relationship is described by Lacan as "the mirror stage" in which the individual passes though two critical stages: the Ideal or Specular and the Social or Real.[43] To these distinctions we will add two more states for the sake of providing a kind of bracket for them: the 0I (i.e. zero sense of "I"), and the Ix (i.e. the sense of "I" abducted by discourse through voluntary hegemony). This way Lacan's two states of personal development will have entry and exits states as brackets for the two principal phases.

What Lacan is concerned with is the development of the sense of "I." Following the rule of negation we have used throughout this discussion, the arising of the I must be coupled with the arising of the you, they, them, thou — the other. Without an I to speak, there is no human speech. There may be other forms of speech, such as natural language processing and production, but there is no I needed for synthesized language (despite the irritating use of the personal pronoun by such machines). Moreover, we must also invoke the rule of exchange, that components in the topology of negation are interchangeable. Each I is a you, each subject an object, each 0 a negation

---

[43] Lacan, Jaques. "The mirror stage as formative of the function of the I as revealed in psychoanalytic experience." *Ecrits: A Selection.* New York: Norton, 1977, p. 2.

of 1 for, as Peano expresses in the first of his propositions on integers, "0 is a number," not the absence of a number, just as the object is not the absence of a subject or I.

Before we enter into the teeth of the discussion, though, it is useful to link it with the idea of the camp, in particular Agamben's idea of "bare life." As we are in part analyzing negation here, we may define by negation. What happens when 0 is merely the absence of a number? What happens when subjectivity is removed from the parallel ontological threads of subject-object? Bare life is only possible when the subject is objectified in such as way that subjectivity is excluded, in fact excluded a priori for at no point in Nazi theory did Jews lose their subjectivity. They never possessed it. *"The state of exception thus ceases to be referred to as an external and provisional state of factual danger and comes to be confused with juridical rule itself."*[44] In other words, the state of exception from the law becomes the law when the object is desubjectified. This process is called in the topology of propaganda psychology "abduction/abdication." The subject is both abducted (pull mechanism) and abdicates (push mechanism). In so doing the subject enters what was once the objectification of the state of exception, which finds its coming-into-being through the act not of fiat but of capture (kidnapping).

Agamben describes the dual mechanism of the hegemony of abduction/abdication in Nazi jurisprudence. "National Socialist jurists were so aware of the particularity of the situation that they defined it by the paradoxical expression 'state of willed exception [...].' "[45] A caveat here is that "a state of willed exception" and "abdication" should not be construed as Jews in Poland, for instance, or American Japanese during World War II "wanting" to be interned. Rather, each had the ultimate sovereign act at their disposal: suicide, or even the mercy killing of loved ones such as children. The abduction of their sovereignty therefore contained an element of negative volition because the ultimate sovereign act (in Schopenhauer's sense) remained. Also, "willed," a term dear to Hitler (e.g. *Triumph de Willens*), is a nonspecific referent here and may be assigned to the volition of both the abductor and the abductee.

At what position in early development does the sense of I begin, and what is its relative position to a sense of others? While Lacan does

---

[44] Agamben, Giorgio. *Homo Sacer: Sovereign Power and Bare Life.* Standford: Stanford U.P., 1998, p. 168.
[45] Ibid., p. 168.

not specify age, he makes it clear there are certain periods in which such changes occur. Identification of these periods relies on what relationship a child has to her own image as seen (or not) in a mirror. Moreover, he (and other psychologists such as Kohler), tie the perception of self as both subject and object through mimesis as a critical stage in the development of intelligence, which we may assume here to be the "general intelligence," or the "g," of psychometricians. "This recognition is indicated in the illuminative mimicry of the *Aha-Erlebnis* [sudden realization], which Kohler sees as the expression of situational apperception, an essential stage in the act of intelligence."[46]

Again, we have a "situation" in the sense Agamben describes as what occurs when the juridical power is removed from the state — not chaos, but a kind of "freedom" to interact with others as others, either in a state of acknowledging their personal sovereignty or violating it through objectification. As such we may return to the categorical exclusion (CE) and apply it here. The crossing of the threshold from 0I to 1I (the Ideal stage) requires a recognition that "I am," the cogito. For a person not a thing, this is coming-into-being. For a thing, it entails recognition and naming by the persona. Until then the thing is not a thing at all but as Heidegger calls it, is the "furniture of the world." These two designations of coming-into-being as the persona and the thing complete what Heidegger called the "Monolith of Being" or what Agamben refers to as "form of life." Palmer describes the dynamic between persona and thing as a interplay of exclusion and inclusion:

"In effect Heidegger is saying that the two kinds of Being he identifies are equiprimordial rather than choosing one as a fundamental basis. Thus he designates what might be called the Monolith of Being as a combination of these two kinds of Being and posits that we are continually moving back and forth between the two modalities, sometimes keeping hold of them in tandem."[47]

Again we have the push-pull mechanism in the equiprimordality of coming-into-being, as the Monolith indicates the a priori nature of both the I of the persona and the bestowing of thingness on the object. For the child the sense of "I" always already exists as a latent inevitability at conception

---

[46] Lacan, Jaques. "The mirror stage as formative of the function of the I as revealed in psychoanalytic experience." *Ecrits: A Selection*. New York: Norton, 1977, p. 1.

[47] Palmer, Kent D. "Beyond Dynamic Ontologies to N-ontologies and the foundations of Emergence in Fundamental Ontology" (*The Applications of General Schemas Theory*). White paper. Accessed 3 June 2011.

(much debated but little understood by both sides in the abortion debate). For the thing, the fact of its existence precedes its naming. Note that a persona which never develops a sense of I is not considered to be "alive" in the interpersonal sense (though it may be in the juridical and medical sense), and that a thing which is never named either does not exist in the personal ontology of the persona, or does but simply contains no cognitive value since it is not a part of thought. As the set of all sets, the sovereign power contains both the persona and the thing, proclaiming dominion over both, and is therefore a "meta-operator" in determining what is the furniture of the world and exactly how it will be transformed. For example a forest few are aware of remains yet part of the world's furniture. It becomes a "resource" when the meta-operator decrees that it shall be stripped of trees for wood, laid bare for grazing, torn open for minerals, and gutted for coal.

The reverse is true too as negation. Coming-into-being is negated by non-being only in the sense of unawareness of the presence of a thing, or in the case of the developing child mind, the existence of the other. Objects which are not "ready-to-hand" do not come into being, just as in the pathological development of the sense of I the result is narcissism (and/ or sociopathy) in the absence of a sense of others as sovereign subjects. Successful dictators often possess this asset in their domination of others. "[W]hen something ready-to-hand is found missing, though its everyday presence [*Zugengenzein*] has been so obvious that we have never taken any notice of it, this makes a break in those referential contexts which circumspection discovers."[48] In the absence of referential context, the thing (or the person) is excluded.

3.3 Psycholinguistics of the "Social I"

All is not necessarily well in the development of the sense of I. The child, a priori because of the "bare life" fact of existence, and the latent inevitability of its I, already possesses a sense of sovereignty. As Palmer describes, it is equiprimordial in the process of coming-into-being as a push-pull mechanism between inclusion and exclusion as modalities. *As a result, the sense of "self" with a small "s," and the sense of Self with a capital initial immediately come into conflict.* This conflict is exploitable.

---

[48] Heidegger, Martin. *Being and Time.* New York: Harperperennial Modernthought, 2008, p. 105.

(We shall arrive at that discussion soon.) "[T]he important point is that this form situates the agency of the ego, before its social determination, in a fictional direction, which will always remain irreducible for the individual alone, or rather, which will rejoin the coming-into-being (*le devenir*) of the subject asymptomatically, whatever success of the dialectical syntheses by which he must resolve as *I* his discourse with his own reality."[49]

The "discourse with his own reality" of course becomes his discourse, or the story of his life as it unfolds in coming-into-being of all things. There will always be a sense of otherness or alterity about this "I." The lack of complete identification makes it possible for the sovereign to offer the lure of abdication and its freedom from the responsibility of the form of life, which will become a life of form. It makes it possible for the state to abduct the personal sense of being a Jew and replace it with the antagonistic state idea of being a Jew, symbolized by the yellow star. This becomes the I's new *I-dentity*, repetition, inculcation, and context making it "so" in the ontic sense. At this point the abducted persona branches into two ontic threads that are always at odds but which bear the same name: an a priori personal Jew, and an a posteriori state Jew. In fact, the second life must be lived with more vigor than the first in simultaneous parallel ontology, because it has now been identified by the primordial self as a threat to the Monolith of Being which was previously only associated with the first sense of being a Jew. The second ontic thread now becomes the Self.

From this irritation the Social I arises like a pearl in an oyster. The relationship of the ideal I to the primordial I provides the paradigm for the more significant relationship between the ideal and the social, sometimes called the "Real" stage, with the Ideal stage sometimes called the "specular" stage. Our dichotomy will be between the Ideal and Social, as these words best convey the nature of the stages, for to the narcissist society is less than ideal, and to society the narcissist is hardly welcome except as packaged commodity (more on this later).

The mirror stage effectively ends once the child realizes that there are others like itself with this same sense of mimetic I. The territory is then left behind for the pathological, those like Narcissus in the myth who pines for himself as he gazes into his reflection in the pond while his lover Echo, unable to do anything except repeat his empty phrases, pines for him nearby. This too is the point at which neuroses and the pathologies of the social

---

[49] Lacan, Jaques. *"The mirror stage as formative of the function of the I as revealed in psychoanalytic experience." Ecrits: A Selection.* New York: Norton, p. 2.

I begin to spread roots, fertilized by the rich soil of discord between the primordial and ideal I. "It establishes in the defenses of the ego a genetic order [...] and situates [...] sessional inversion and its isolating processes, and the latter in turn as preliminary to paranoic alienation, which dates from the deflection of the specular *I* into the social *I.*"[50]

The end of the mirror stage also brings on social conflict as the fledgling entity establishes its role in the psychodrama of other its needs, wants, love, hates. "This moment in which the mirror stage comes to an end inaugurates, by the identification with the imago of the counterpart and the drama of primordial jealousy [...] the dialectic that will henceforth link the I to socially elaborated situations."[51]

We can inventory some of the characteristics of the persona at this stage: coming-into-being is in deep time, having emerged from the equiprimordial into the ideal, then through the struggle between the two ontic orientations emerged into the rudiments of the social, where a new struggle begins between competing individuals. The political creature emerges in this struggle, as does the desire for the sovereign. Without the sovereign, the disparate selves remain in an inefficient state of conflict with themselves and with the others as analogues of self in a jealous situation characterized by strife. They then look to a sovereign for relief. In their "turning to," they abdicate, while during their turning to the sovereign abducts. We have abduction/abdication. The interesting particles in these two words are "duct" and "dict," the first meaning to convey and the latter meaning to speak. If we combine their meanings, we have the term "conveying speech," which is known to us as propaganda in the larger sense.

What inevitably happens, though, is the sovereign becomes a reflection of the society that was abducted and that did abdicate. The mirror stage has now realized itself again but on a colossal scale not as a stage in development but as a "state" in the meaning of a condition or mode that is permanent. The sovereign makes this situation possible by the a priori state of exception. And herein we discover the permanent state of exception in which the sovereign lives *if and only if he does not live in this state!* It should be noted, as it had not been earlier, that often the child's first "other" is the mother (whose name so neatly rhymes with "other"). At least the immediate others in the child's life begin usually with parents, associating

---

[50] Ibid., p. 5.
[51] Ibid., p. 5

for all time a sense of alterity with the parent diad.

How a child relates to others will largely be determined by this first relationship. By the time the state (with its five-part apparatus of *government, church, schools, banks, and mass media*) is the foremost presence in the persona's life, often adulthood has been reached. In the reiteration, its proportion cubed, of the mirror stage, and in its transformation into the permanent state of exception, the state becomes equated with the parents. The natal pleasure of that first encounter with parents — those who provide protection, awe, education, food and shelter, and who support the whole operation by their endeavors — is transferred through the usual channel of libidinal conduct to the accoutrements of the state power. A grudging affinity arises, where the state continually chides the citizens for not living up to the ideal, and citizens begrudge the do's and don'ts of the juridical "discontents," as Freud would put it. For instance, sexual intercourse with one's step sister is considered "incest" by many states and is illegal with varying penalties. As much as Mr. X may want to have sex with his step sister, he is stopped by what seems to him a senseless law. He is too shy to complain about it, lacks the means to fight against it, and therefore abides by it or does it in deep secret because he is still grateful for the parent state even with its arbitrary laws and therefore is either in awe of it or is merely obedient.

Before we dive deeper into the psychological mechanism of propaganda and abduction, we must look at the schematic of the transitions described above. We will use the already-stated notation: 0I, I1, I2, Ix, meaning the primordial I (0I), the mirror-stage ideal I (I1), the real or social I (I2), and the abducted I (Ix, where x = abduction). Furthermore, we must look at this concatenation using the categorical exclusion (here a move will be indicated using an arrow, and each position will be parted by a comma): 0I→I1, I1→I2, I2→Ix. The concatenation ends when the category is excluded. For instance, there is only the permanent state of exception as the set of all sets, therefore there is nothing beyond Ix. There is nothing before 0I because it is the equiprimordial state perched between inclusion and exclusion.

However, we have not taken into view the "reset" function of the CE. If we do, the series changes significantly: 0I↔I1, I1↔I2, I2↔Ix. *It is possible to set a state backward.* Sometimes this is called "revolution," which is an unpromising term because of its all-too-obvious shortcoming of indicating a 360-degree return to the starting point. Rather, we may borrow a term from structural linguistics and call these steps from state to state "transformational."

When we move from 0I to I1, the step is categorical, meaning it is a negation of the previous step, just as 0 and 1 are negations of each other. It cannot be reversed except by an act of suicide (voluntary nonbeing). I1 and I2 are negations, and I2 and Ix are negations, but they are not categorical. As negations, they can be reversed. We will call the return of one state to its predecessor a "reset," and the advancing to the next step a "transformation" (*not* a progression!). The rule is that no state can be either reset or transformed without moving in sequence, so to reset to 0I from Ix, one must move through first I2 and then I1 successfully: Ix→I2→I1→0I. There are also combinations and oscillations. There are five possible combinations of reset (if we include suicide), but any number of oscillations. For instance, an entity may oscillate between I1 and I2 indefinitely, inserting itself into the hegemonic order, and then removing itself or being removed. This being removed is called "exile" or a "ban." "He who has been banned is not, in fact, simply set outside the law and made indifferent to it but rather abandoned by it, that is, exposed and threatened on the threshold in which life and law, outside and inside, become indistinguishable."[52]

This movement between I2 and I1 needs mention because it is an apt demonstration of the reality of the reset and its relationship to the threshold. We commonly refer to the brink of any transition "a threshold." However, in a categorical sense, a threshold is a point of no return. That is, once it has been crossed there is no effective return. As one can be exiled from the social order by the hegemon, it is possible to make a move from I2 to I1. It is also possible to be reinstated from I1 to I2 (as Dante was). It is also possible to move back and forth between states, as professional spies do (I1↔I2), and it is possible to either escape or be rescued from abduction (Ix→I2). However, it is not possible to reset from I1 to 0I because it is at once a categorical exclusion, a negation, and a transformation, whereas I1, I2, Ix are transformations and negations of each other which is why the "I" precedes the order number. Furthermore, no transformation may be made if the position has no predecessor. As 0I is the equivalent of ℵ0, the smallest infinite cardinal number, it has no predecessor.

There is one exception, and that is in the state of exception. In a state of exception "bare life" becomes possible. Bare life is a total reset to 0I, and from any position, because it is a kind of murder/suicide. But this is not

---

[52] Agamben, Giorgio. *Homo Sacer: Sovereign Power and Bare Life*. Stanford: Stanford U.P., 1998, p. 28.

a viable form of reset in the sense that there is no preservation of persona, no preservation of thingness. Agamben describes this form of bare life as a place where "life [...] has been entirely separated from the form of life that bore the name," and as such it becomes trivial. The other transformations without categorical exclusion are nontrivial.[53]

Finally, reset is not possible if the current position is permanent, creating a categorical threshold. The permanency of a position is a coming-into-being of the CE, whereas the threshold between OI and I1 as it is a permanent categorical threshold having the above-mentioned properties. For there to be a coming-into-being of the CE at any transformation between states, there must be an Event — a warp on the psycholinguistic topology of thought. The event must create a permanent position or state, including but not exclusively the state of exception (as there can be the inclusion of exception and exception of inclusion). For example, in the Ix position one may find oneself in prison — for life. Therefore, no matter what, there will never be a reset to the previous two positions because the prisoner has literally been abducted. The prisoner will never be free, though he may be living in a permanent state of exception which sets him free from many of the obligations of the non-incarcerated population. Another example is that of the excommunicated priest. He will never be reinstated (reset) into the set of "the church." He has now entered a new set, that of the excommunicated. There is a reason why Dante chose "rings" of Hell in the Inferno. They are sets with categories of sinners, nested within each other so that "Hell" becomes the set of all sets — which, it turns out in the Purgatorio and Paradiso, is and is not a set of itself otherwise there would be no Beatrice and no redemption.

3.3.1 The topology of language as thought

Thought is language as landscape. L.S. Vygotsky has made a strong argument for thought being composed primarily of language (though he knew well that it was also impressions and images).[54] Certainly, when it is spoken or written it is the best approximation of thought, though we would never say that synthesized language is thought, even if interactive or

---

[53] Ibid., p. 168.
[54] Vygotsky, Lev. S. Alex Kozulin, ed. *Thought and Language*. Cambridge: MIT Press, 1986.

says "am thinking." At best it is a kind of recording, highly responsive, but ultimately mimicking thought rather than generating it. This is the difference between what Schirmacher calls Homo Generator and artificial life without generation.

"Truth is a gift of being, which is our place and activity in the world's process. As artificial beings by nature, our body as well as our mind is 'a happening of truth at work' every lived-through moment. Even in the most inhumane enterprises, truth is still at work in humanity as a silent cry toward its absence. According to Heidegger, truth is not about being right or wrong but accepting 'aletheia,' the powerful interplay of revealing and concealing, which shapes humanity's destiny. Today's media, taken as one of our body's splendid incarnations, is involved in the interplay of instrumental technology and life technology, torn between the murder of the body and its elevation (Hegel's) to an unknown status."[55]

Schirmacher does not condemn artificial life, but dismisses the confusion over human thought and so called articifical intelligence or intelligent agents. He looks toward a day when the categorical divide between what is not even bare life and something resembling it is created through the hybrid of biology and computers. "But realized by biotechnology and communication technology alike, artificial life could overcome its genesis in technocratic ideology and mend the flaws of its anthropocentric intentions. 'Artificial life' is a prospect which should enable humanity to attain its own fulfillment instead of triggering our resistance."[56]

The obstacle may not be with the technology itself. After all, is it not an indulgence of the progressive fallacy, that the mere passage of time will somehow overcome the technological limitations as it seems to have in the past (an illogical projection of the record of the nonexistent past into the hallucination of a never-existent future). Rather, the obstacle is within humans themselves. Thought itself fails Kant's test of whether a proposition is synthetic or analytic, whether it is explicit or must be argued. When synthetic propositions are presented as analytic ones, the analytic statements are not analytic but synthetic. If there is no argument over the proposition then, the argumentative has been presented as explicit thought.

---

[55] Schirmacher, Wolfgang. "Homo Generator: Media and Postmodern Technology." (1994.) European Graduate School Articles. Accessed 29 May 2011.
[56] Ibid.

None of this is necessarily a problem in itself. However, if we take de Saussure's description of thought as the case, there may be a problem in organizing thought in such a way that it can begin to approach the epistemological questions raised in this study and by the psycholinguistic mechanism of propaganda and the topology of abduction/abdication. "In itself, thought is like a swirling cloud, where no shape is intrinsically determinate. No ideas are established in advance, and nothing is distinct, before the introduction of linguistic structure."[57] The structure is itself the apparatus, the discourse of the sovereign, not its content — but the linguistic structure. For example, in a simple statement it is possible to gauge the ontological status of thought: Tom runs. What we learn from this paring of a subject and verb is Kant's two a priori absolutes; in Tom's world there is space and time for he needs both to run. Furthermore, we see that this is an analytical statement provided it is meant literally. If we say Tom runs quickly, the statement then turns synthetic because "quickly" is not part of space and time in any categorical way but belongs to thought is its power of judgment and its subjective assessment of phenomena. Finally, if we add a complete predicate we have, Tom runs quickly to the store, showing us that there is more than one thing in Tom's world: a store. The predicate "quickly" to the word "store" becomes a discourse built upon an analytic statement. Therefore, in six simple words we create a discourse of thought highly nuanced. Concatenate thousands of sentences and parse them for sense and we see that predicates tend toward the synthetic, which is the introduction of our subjectivity into the world of objective phenomena.

The topology of language as landscape begins with the conversion of language into thought and ends with the reconversion of thought into language. This reciprocal process — each a negation of the other — provides the push-pull mechanism in which the Weltanschauung is manufactured as discourse. The input is propaganda, the output discourse (though professional communicators learn to reverse this process). What is most significant here, though, it the thought process as a topological surface upon which events occur. Each event creates a warp in its fabric, just as gravitational fields create a warp in the woof of space-time. This landscape can be navigated, mined, lived in, drawn (abstract art), attacked.

---

[57] de Saussure, Ferdinand. *Course in General Linguistics*. Chicago: Open Court 2008, p. 110.

"So we can envisage the linguistics phenomenon in its entirety — the language, that is — as a series of adjoining subdivisions simultaneously imprinted both on the plane of vague, amorphous thought, and on the equally featureless plane of sound."[58] Here de Saussure makes his famous distinction between *langue* and *parole*. Sound itself can be viewed as a wave in various forms, creating the undulating hills and valleys of language topology.

But of course de Saussure takes sound (phoneme) not just as a physical property but as a sign that is auditory rather than visual. The sound itself (with rare exception) is utterly detached from the semantics of the word or particle. "Every linguistics sign is a part or member, an articulus, where an idea is fixed in a sound, and a sound becomes the sign of an idea."[59] The articulus is described by Chomsky as a Markov chain, where the present word determines (generates) the rest of what he indicates as Sentence. For example if the word is turtle, then the *extensa* of the subject could be there is much to learn about the turtle and and the varieties of habitat in which it is found. Both predecessor and successor of the noun are generated simultaneously from any part of the Sentence. Even the article "the" generates "about the," implicating a noun-subject, and the, indicating the noun-object. "We can now extend the phrase structure derivations [...] so that we have a unified process for generating phoneme sequence from the initial string Sentence."[60] Besides the generative position of the word in the Markov articulus, there is also the stochastic — or predictably unpredictable — nature of generative grammar. Often the predicate can go either way into opposing propositions. The Subject "the invention of sliced bread is" can terminate in the Chomskian sense with either: "the best idea ever" or "the worst idea ever." How it will cleave semantically is a mystery to the listener until the Markov chain has moved to the predicate link, yet both propositions are generated by the same noun phrase.

It is axiomatic in natural language processing that the way people speak and hear is based on concatenation and not discrete units (words or phrases). The print before you, however, looks that way. But if it were read aloud, then parsed using a signal sampling device, it would be one

---

[58] de Saussure, Ferdinand. *Course in General Linguistics*. Chicago: Open Court 2008, p. 110.

[59] Ibid., p. 111.

[60] Chomsky, Noam. *Syntactic Structures*. The Hague: Mouton Publishers, 1975, p. 33.

continuous wave of sounds with hardly a break. The thought process with its ancillary cognitive functions then parses the wave into quanta which become the furniture of the topology of the world of thought.

"The characteristic role of language in relation to thought is not to supply the material phonetic means by which ideas may be expressed. It is to act as intermediary between thought and sounds, in such a way that the combination of both necessarily produces a mutually complementary delimitation of units. Thought, chaotic by nature, is made precise by this process of segmentation."[61]

But what is this world, this topology? That it has furniture in the form of quantized phonemic input, that it has hills and valleys in the form of sound waves processed, that it has images and sensory impressions, that it has industries of word generation and the shaping of propaganda for the discourse makes it seem substantial. But in fact what we are looking at here is form, not substance. "Linguistics, then, operates along this margin, where sound and thought meet. *The contact between them gives rise to a form not a substance.*"[62]

Lacan's social I is closely tied to the acquisition of language in that it is social agreement on meaning that transforms the arbitrary phonemes attached to semantic values into mutually agreed upon signs (de Saussure) with the least amount of ambiguity. The stochastic properties of the Markov chain extend to the unpredictability of semantic phoneme assignment. The reverse would be words that always somehow "sounded" like their object, as in onomatopoeic words. But they are a small set (in English words such as plop, screech, slither, pop). But as most words are abstract or general (e.g. "mankind"), such correlation is not possible.

In fact, says de Saussure, phonemes arise on a simple principle of negation and difference. As long as one phoneme sounds different from another, it is useful, which is perhaps why homophones are the class of sounds with the greatest number of grammar errors in usage. "Speech sounds are first and foremost entities which are contrasting, relative and negative [....] In the language itself, there are only differences."[63] Although the grapheme for rice porridge is the same in both Mandarin and Cantonese

[61] de Saussure, Ferdinand. *Course in General Linguistics*. Chicago: Open Court 2008, p. 110.
[62] Ibid., p. 111
[63] de Saussure, Ferdinand. *Course in General Linguistics*. Chicago: Open Court 2008, p. 118.

dialects of Chinese, the phonemes are entirely unrelated, even as opposites. In Mandarin the single-syllable word is pronounced with a level tone as *zhou*, but in Cantonese the word has two syllables: *congee* and more than one tone. Here the phonemic assignment to the grapheme and the semantic object itself is utterly arbitrary, requiring social confirmation within the two language spheres. "The arbitrary nature of the sign enables us to understand more easily why it needs social activity to create a linguistic system. A community is necessary in order to establish values. Values have no other rationale than usage and general agreement. An individual, acting alone, is incapable of establishing a value."[64]

Perhaps narcissistic individuals are glorified in modern cultures because they are trapped in the mirror stage while at the same time possessing some commodity in demand, such as a baseball player or a musician or a politician possess. The adulation and remuneration they receive for being in a state that cannot be abducted serves as a preventative against their transformational shift to the real or social stage where, in the case of particularly charismatic or talented individuals, damage could be done to the discourse. They are as de Saussure describes, "incapable of establishing a value." *As such, they are not a threat to the masses as homo generator, who creates words, language, ideas, and thoughts and is therefore the most dangerous man.* Furthermore, their inculcation into the permanent state of the mirror stage with no reset often begins at the close of the Critical Period (CP) 0-12 years of age, when language and thought are friable properties, as state educational institutions and product advertisers well know. (It should be noted here that there is no reset for children who do not learn listening and speaking during the CP. They seem to be incapable of it after the end of the CP.[65])

It is impossible to generalize about the mass media from the rare pathologically narcissistic individuals who attain stardom. It is the exception. The rule is that abduction/abdication must occur during the socialization stage after the mirror stage. This is the "place" where, as de Saussure puts it, "sound and thought meet," giving rise to the form of life. *"[T]he language itself is a form, not a substance.* The importance of this truth cannot be overemphasized."[66] The form of life, then, is the topology of thought which shapes the exterior world and is in turn shaped by what it has, in concert with other members of society, created as homo generators.

---

[64] Ibid., pp. 111-112.
[65] Lust, Barbara. *Child Language*. Cambridge: Cambridge UP, 2006, pp, 79, 93.
66 Ibid., p. 120.

4.1 Prison as the set of the state of exception

There will not be an attempt to summarize here. Throughout the sections above summary has been given. However, we will pause to consider where we are in the larger scheme of this investigation into the topology of abduction through the psycholinguistic use of propaganda. Part 1 analyzes the logic behind the mechanism of abduction, in particular the categorical exclusion and the concatenation of the stages of the development of sovereignty. The purpose has been to show correlations between these states, the state of exception, language, juridical functions, and propositions relevant to all of these. Part 2 explores the simultaneity of states as parallel ontic threads and ontologies and what affect they have on language.

That language itself is sovereign, which produces thought as a continuous discourse, should make us suspicious (another form of thought) of the very tale you are reading now. Have you found something interesting? Is there the ring of truth about it all? Has it affected how you see things? Is there anything here — even the quotations themselves — that has changed the way you view the world? These are questions to ask considering that *this study is itself a discourse, no different from any other*. There are no good or bad discourses. It is the fact of the discourse itself that is the mechanism, and it is the mechanism that orders Dasein in such a way that we are even able to identify its parts and our place in it. But what of the social order?

Lacan makes an appeal for the exploration of the morphology of how we know anything. It is a plea for an epistemology of development and language, and language's place in the formation of thought. If "the camp" is the contemporary form of life, then there must be an antecedent to it that ushered the state of exception in. To Lacan, the camp creates an age of anxiety where the measure of all value, including linguistic value, is based on the utilitarian niche it occupies. In other words, *government, schools, church, banks, and mass media use the utilitarian yardstick to determine the promotion or ban of a value in any domain*.

Moreover, says Lacan, the consequences of abduction/abdication into the world of the camp through the psycholinguistics of propaganda, and the concomitant relinquishing of personal sovereignty creates a kind of freedom within the state of exception that is the word-bond of servitude of all: "freedom that is never more authentic than when it is within the walls of a prison [...]; a voyeuristic-sadistic idealization of the sexual relation; a personality that realizes itself only in suicide; a consciousness of the other [that] can be satisfied only by Hegelian murder."[67]

---

[67] Lacan, Jaques. *Ecrits: A Selection.* New York: Norton, p. 6.

PART 2: **THE APPARATUS OF LANGUAGE**

We are ourselves the entities to be analyzed.

— Heidegger[68]

1. Simultaneous Parallel Ontologies

1.1 Ontic threads: ethics and morality

In the great tragic moment in Plato's *Apology*, Socrates explains to his followers that he prefers death to what he sees as ignominy. Perhaps in this passage we see the universe of ethics and morality, the contradictions and parallels. The oppositions and convergences. But certainly we feel the passion behind the *res cogitans* that argues not for a definition of right and wrong, but for an auspicious death. Socrates invokes the rule and the exception when he cites the law and war. In both, he says, "ought any man to use every way of escaping death."[69]

"The difficulty my friends, is not in avoiding death, but in avoiding unrighteousness; for that runs faster than death. I am old and move slowly, and the slower runner has overtaken me, and my accusers are keen and quick, and the faster runner, who is unrighteousness, has overtaken them."[70]

We may recall Achilles' statements about preferring to be a slave for a poor farmer than be a king of the Underworld. In Achilles' case, he would relinquish his social sovereignty (monarch of Hades) and his personal sovereignty (free man not slave) to avoid death and its consequence, keeping in mind that to the Greeks of Troy, Hades was simply the afterlife and not punishment. In Christianity we would have a more difficult time arguing that

---

[68] Heidegger, Martin. *Being and Time*. New York: Harperperennial Modernthought, 2008, p. 67.

[69] Plato. *Apology*. New York: P.F. Collier & Son Corp., 1937, p. 27.

[70] Ibid., p. 27.

being sovereign of a place such as Hell, designed for unrighteous "sinners" (the killers of Socrates), would be preferable to being a slave in the living world. If we compare Achilles' words to Socrates', we find that they are inversions or negations of each other.

In Socrates' case, death and its consequence (presumably the same Hades) is preferable to unrighteousness in the world of the living. If we define unrighteousness as placing the law and the state of exception above the presence or lack of individual culpability in a specific case, then we have circumvented the juridical mandate of justice, for justice itself is pinioned not to the rule of law but to the exception to the rule of law — the inclusion of the exception. Socrates cites the "justice" of the battlefield where mercy may be wrung from the victors "if a man will throw away his arms, and fall on his knees before his pursuers" and be willing to "say or do anything."[71] In the prostration of the vanquished we find what Agamben calls "chaos," which is not the "Situation" that arises when the state of exception is invoked, though it may be part of it. If a man be willing to "say or do anything," then there is no rule or even exception to a rule but only expediency: he will not be spared if there is no momentary expedience for the victor, making the ethical mode of the entire ritual deontological with no reference to some future teleological state of justice in which both victor and vanquished abide by the same juridical rules.

Nevertheless, the rule of a camp is invoked too. Socrates cites the law and war, meaning the apparatus of the state on the one hand and the state of exception it creates in the military camp. For there is a double meaning of "campus"; it is both the place in which the prisoners are interned, and the place where the soldiers retire, regroup, and plan the next move. Both soldier and prisoner live in camps, often adjacent to each other. If not, then the soldiers live or work in the prisoners' camp, making them, for the time they are there, prisoners too, but not of the fences and barbed wire and armed guard towers (for they may come and go freely), but rather of what Socrates calls "unrighteousness." When Berlin fell on 2 May 1945, "the fast runner, who is unrighteousness," had overtaken the German army in the form of Hitler's passion for the destruction of the fatherland. This is not divine providence, fate, or even punishment. To Socrates it is simply the result of injustice. Therefore, he sees no need to flee his death sentence, or to reproach himself for having made the intellectual and philosophical argument he made. "I thought that I ought not to do anything common

---

[71] Plato. *Apology*. New York: P.F. Collier & Son Corp., 1937, p. 27.

or mean in the hour of danger; not do I now repent of the manner of my defense, and I would rather die having spoken after my manner, than speak in your manner and live."[72]

So we may use Socrates as the benchmark of moral and ethical behavior in that he is willing to die for what he considers to be righteousness. It is difficult to say that a person is immoral or unethical if he is willing to die either for what he may be guilty of by his own admission, or may not be guilty of by some other standard. Taking both Socrates and Achilles into consideration in our discussion, we can parse some of the implications of their words and deeds.

First, we will discover the schemata in their statements. In Socrates' statement if death is y and unrighteousness is x, then we have an either/or situation expressed $x \leftrightarrow y$. He has a choice. But since y runs faster than x, we must express the relationship thus: $y < x$. The slower runner, presumably age (but perhaps also his accusers) has overtaken him in the race of life, and is represented by a. His accusers, who are "keen and quick," and have at least overtaken him as the slower runner has, and are represented by b, expressed $b > a$. However, unrighteousness is the fastest runner of all and has overtaken his accusers but not, by implication, Socrates (n), because of his suicide, represented by n(y) — the ultimate sovereign act. We will represent this relationship thus: $n(y) > [(x > y), (b > a)]$. Socrates chooses death not because he wants to martyr himself (always a suspision in such situations), but because death was simply the greater of all propositions or arguments. Rather than join the ranks of the unrighteous and plead for his life as the vanquished soldier does, and rather than flee as the coward does (Socrates was known for his austerity and implacability in battle), he chose the sovereign act of suicide to recapture his abducted sovereignty and is the ultimate victor in the battle with unrighteousness. It is the victory of voluntary death, not the ideas of right and wrong here, that is the ethical and moral standard.

1.1 The extrinsic and intrinsic arguments

We will reiterate Achilles' case from Part 1 and make a comparison. First he believes that, "I would rather be a slave." His preference is for being in a state of overthrow or abdication of personal sovereignty. If x is death and p is slavery and q is sovereign power, then Achilles' statement or preference follows this form (where →means "if, then"): $q(x) \rightarrow p$, in other words, if

---

[72] Plato. *Apology*. New York: P.F. Collier & Son Corp., 1937, p. 27.

sovereignty comes with death, then I would rather abdicate my sovereignty and be entirely abducted as a slave.

What is interesting is the proposition without x: $q \rightarrow p$. Achilles abdicates his personal sovereignty to plow fields with a poor farmer as a kind of indentured servant. A slave *is a* possession. Achilles' formula, if we indicate possession as y, becomes: $[q(\sim y \ [x]) \rightarrow p]$, the addition being slavery without possessions.

Contrasting the argument of Socrates with that of Achilles (z) we have:

1) $n(y) > [(y > x), (b > a)]$

2) $[q(\sim y \ [x]) \rightarrow p] > z(y)$

These arguments may be considered inverses of each other and are therefore negations. Argument 1 is for recapturing sovereignty through volitional death (suicide), whereas argument 2 is for abdicating sovereignty for life rather than death. From the point of view of personal sovereignty then, we may conclude that if personal sovereignty (s) is the greater value, then Socrates is the winner of the Death Game. On the other hand, if life (l) is of greater value than death, then Achilles is the winner. We may express these conflicting values as: $s > l$ and $l > s$. Which one is "better" is not the aim of this analysis. Rather, the aim is to place both on equal footing. After all, Achilles is to the state what Socrates is to the stateless, having been "banned." Therefore, the choice of priority of one over the other is in truth a choice of the state or the non-state. This choice is trivial because the "non-state" cannot exist without the state. Furthermore, Socrates honors the state's prerogative to sentence him to death for his crimes, which is the chief impediment to fleeing. "[...] I went, and sought to persuade every man among you that he must look to himself, and seek virtue and wisdom before he looks to his private interests, and look to the State before he looks to the interests of the State; and that this should be the order which he observes in all his actions."[73]

The priority here is for the intrinsic values of "virtue and wisdom" and "the State" over the extrinsic values of "personal interests" and the "interests of the State." We may assume that both the intrinsic and extrinsic values are, in their groups, of equal value and meaning. In other words,

---

[73] Plato. *Apology*. New York: P.F. Collier & Son Corp., 1937, p. 25.

virtue, wisdom, and the State are in the same group, a matter more clear in the extrinsic case where both share a common word: interests. It is this word that is most interesting here. It would seem that one's "personal interests" would be, *prima facie*, intrinsic, that is, inwardly the most important to a sovereign individual. But when we contrast it to the other value in the group: "interests of the State," we see that these two values cannot be material equivalents if the first is to mean what is most inward to the self or intrinsic, for the interests of the State are by definition *extrinsic* to the individual and may even be at odds with the individual's intrinsic interests — as they are in Socrates' case.

If "personal interests" are in the same group as State interests, then what are these interests and how are they somehow extrinsic if they are personal? The answer may be that State interests and personal interests are one and the same in the entity in its abducted position, having passed the mirror position (I1) into the social position (I2) and on into the abducted position (Ix). Without listing the details of care of self in the abducted "personal" position, it is fair to say that the interest of the persona here is foremost to follow the law, whether or not there is a state of exception. Secondary are the usual concerns such as preservation of life. But to Socrates this is not an intrinsic value, since the state itself obviously has the power of life and death. When a state has this power, then the only recourse to win back personal sovereignty is suicide — if the choices are to 1) beg for mercy, 2) pay for clemency, 3) flee from the law, and 4) commit voluntary death. Socrates chooses 4 because 1, 2, and 3 are unacceptable being within the abducted position and therefore *extensa* of the state apparatus and extrinsic not to his personal interests, but to his sense of justice which transcends the personal.

In the case of Achilles, there is only personal interest. His care of self does not go beyond his desire to be alive again, a desire of self interest and not even of the State, which entirely goes against Socrates' position on the matter of death as expressed (in a consoling way) to his followers, Plato among them, and even to the judges who voted against him. "Wherefore, O judges, be of good cheer about death, and know this of a truth — that no evil can happen to a good man, either in life or after death."[74] We might assume, through Achilles' soul's extreme unhappiness, that he was somehow being punished as a sinner. But as a Greek Trojan, he at least possessed an *apre*

---

[74] Plato. *Apology.* New York: P.F. Collier & Son Corp., 1937, p. 29.

mort in kind with the philosopher. So why the disparate reactions to the inevitable? First, Achilles has already expressed his desire to abdicate, whereas Socrates has expressed his desire to recapture his sovereignty through suicide. Second, Socrates warns that one should always "look to himself" (a = intrinsic ontology) before looking to extrinsic cares of the *pro forma* (b), and third, he even goes so far as to say that if his children put *b*before *a,* "punish them; and I would have you trouble them, as I have troubled you [...]"[75]

Finally we must discuss the difference between looking to the State and looking to the interests of the State. Herein lies the essential political argument, and the essence of the significance of the state of exception. Achilles shows disdain for statecraft in Hades by eschewing both the possibility of being sovereign there, and the possibility of being a sovereign in the world of the living (by abdicating to slavery). Although his concern for his care of self is self interested but not intrinsic, he is an extrinsic. But his lack of care for the interests of the state does not make him, in this sphere, an intrinsic. It seems as if his disdain may be in kind with Socrates', but in fact it is extrinsic to the State which requires the "look" or "gaze" of the citizen to exist and serve its purpose! The unenvisaged state soon fades (as did so many unenvisaged empires of history). The gaze of the citizen makes the state arise. All citizens participate in statehood and statecraft by their labor, no matter what system. When they cease to participate, even as lumpen proletariat, then they are slaves, captives in prison, or stateless. Achilles chooses to participate only as a slave, removing his gaze from both the state of the living and the dead. By complying with the death sentence handed to him by the state, Socrates shows that his gaze is fixed on the state, but that the state's interest — suppressing the voice of those who would criticize it — is extrinsic to Socrates' care of self. To those who voted against him in a close judiciary vote, he says, "For if you think that by killing men you can avoid the accuser censuring your lives, you are mistaken; that is not a way of escape which is either possible or honorable [...]."[76] By killing men the state at once exercises the rule of law and the state of exception by obliterating sovereignty through state killing as in a mode of war, creating the camp.

[75] Plato. *Apology.* New York: P.F. Collier & Son Corp., 1937, p. 25.
[76] Ibid., p 28.

1.2 Extrinsic and intrinsic as parallel ontologies

We may map the extrinsic and intrinsic strategies to the topographical geometry of the eccentric and centric. Visualizing a circle with a dot in the center, we can see that the topology consists of certain regions: outside the circle, inside the circle, outside the dot, and the dot. We could also say that for the dot there is outside the dot *and* outside the dot and circle, or two outer regions (there is no "inside the dot"). As these are categorical distinctions, there are no degrees of being inside or outside. Therefore, everything is either at or outside the dot, which is of course the center. What is "at the dot" is *centric*, and what is not is *eccentric*.

Transposing Plato's distinctions of care of self as "virture and wisdom" and care of Self as the demands made on one by the social apparatus, and envisaging the State versus supporting or succumbing to State interest, we arrive at a correlation between intrinsic as centric and extrinsic as eccentric. The values can be expressed thus: $a = x$, $b = y$. Topographically, if the center is p and the surroundings are q, we have $ax(p) + by(q)$ as the total topographical area.

Heidegger's distinction between public and private space falls within $ax(p) + by(q)$ territory. Also, ontologically it expresses the whole topography of the territory. What is ready-to-hand expresses what Plato describes as "personal interest," things that are in our possession and reflect our extrinsic concerns. (What is present-at-hand is there but is not possessed.) Both what we have and what is there are possessed by the alterity of the extrinsic/eccentric: other, society, state (government, church, schools, banking, media). Heidegger describes the territory between the centric position and the plane of the eccentric: "We have shown earlier how the environment which lies closest to us, the public 'environment' already is ready-to-hand and is also a matter of concern [mitbesorgt]."[77] It is a matter of concern because it surrounds the intrinsic/centric position with the constant threat of what Heidegger calls "they," the abduction into the Ix position from the I2 socialized position. "In utilizing public means of transport and in making use of information services such as the newspaper, every Other is like the next. This Being-with-one-another dissolves one's own Dasein completely into the kind

---

[77] Heidegger, Martin. *Being and Time*. New York: Harperperennial Modernthought, 2008, p. 164.

of Being of 'the Others', in such a way, indeed, that the Others, as distinguishable and explicit, vanish more and more."[78]

The "they" form the Other. This Other territory is within and without the borders of the camp, which is the surface area of the circle (finite), and the area outside the circle (infinite). The number for the surface area outside of the circle is always n, meaning any number beyond the number of the surface area inside of the circle. William James once observed that since one cannot see the entire ocean from its shore, one takes what one sees and multiplies it beyond the horizon of conception. "We think the ocean as a whole, by multiplying mentally the impression we get at any moment when at sea."[79] So too do we think of Others, the circumference of the circle being our collective identity (e.g. Jews, Christians, Muslims, Americans, students on a certain campus, fans in a baseball stadium at a home game).

Just as we give names to places, nations, and teams, so too do we give names to the psychological topography of extrinsic/eccentric, intrinsic/centric, abduction/abdication, inclusion/exclusion, rule/exception. The Euclidean paradigm projects into mental space just as physical space projects into the Euclidean paradigm of spatiality and location. According to Tuan, "sensorymotor and tactile experiences would seem to lie at the root of Euclid's theorems concerning shape congruence and the parallelisms of distant lines; visual perception is the basis for projective geometry."[80] Therefore, the concatenation of the stages of the development of the sense of I follow a clear geography, as expressed previously: 0I, I1, I2, Ix. We have moved a bit beyond the Categorical Exclusion (0 / 1, 0I → I1) to focus on the dramatic topography of abduction/abdication after the social I stage (I2 → Ix), with → representing position transformation here (and not the conditional "if then"). Nevertheless, the transformations in the grammatical sense are negations of each other and may be described in Euclidean terms as topological.

1.3 Equality of all binary positions

We have explored the topology of the state of exception where the sovereign officially steps outside of the law (which has always been the case by the

---

[78] Ibid., p. 164.

[79] Tuan, Yi-Fu. *Space and Place*. Minneapolis: U. of Minnesota Press, 1977, p. 16.

[80] Ibid., p. 17.

nature of sovereignty itself as a permanent state of exception). In the state of exception the sovereign can be outside the law if and only if the sovereign is inside the law, and vice versa. If we use the same mental model (*gedenken* in the sense "to think of") as we have with the eccentric versus centric, we come upon an interesting proposition: namely that the territory outside of the circle may be labeled a, the territory inside b, and the dot capital A, or, with $\rightarrow$ expressing "if, then," $a \rightarrow b \rightarrow A$. *In other words,* if the territory is outside the circle, then the territory is also inside the circle, and is then the position A, which is the centric correlate of the most extreme eccentric position outside of the circle. As in Russell's paradox, then, a is the center of the circle if and only if it is *not* the center of the circle. For you see, if we merely set up a series of oppositional dichotomies such as possession/abduction, included/excluded, intrinsic/extrinsic, centric/eccentric, we would have nothing at all. As each of these positions is the negation of the other, being true to the categorical exclusion's demonstration of the progressive fallacy, we would have to assume that there is some kind of ratio between these values — one better than the other, etc. Otherwise, they are simply $0 \leftrightarrow 1$, interchangeable negations of each other. How then can we say something?

Therefore, we will presume that the dot, and the territories of the circle's area and the region outside of the circle, are all of the same value, though we may speak of them in different ways and assign them to different phenomena. For example, the eccentric position of the "they," in the end, is a collection of centric positions of the I. Moreover, it is as useful to debate the relative merits of here/there, in/out, up/down and even death/life as it is to assign priority of any kind to either position in the topology. Keeping this within our gaze, it is safe to explore the consequences of the strategy as Heidegger describes them. "The 'they' has its own ways in which to be. That tendency of Being-with which we have called 'distantiality' is grounded in the fact that Being-with-one-another concerns itself as such with averageness, which is an existential characteristic of the 'they'."[81] Eccentric territories are not in flux and do not exceed each other. Rather they are in an equilibrium by the *averageness*. In opposition, though, the center stands as extraordinary by comparison — but only by such comparison and not by any intrinsic value apart from the comparison. Nevertheless, the center is under constant stress from the outer territories to abdicate its territory. It always abdicates in the abduction process to relieve

---

[81] Heidegger, Martin. *Being and Time.* New York: Harperperennial Modernthought, 2008, p. 164.

this stress, for, as the Chinese saying goes, the nail that sticks up shall be hammered down!

"The 'they', in its Being, essentially makes an issue of this [....] Every kind of priority gets noiselessly suppressed. Overnight, everything that is primordial gets glossed over as something that has been well known. Everything gained by a struggle becomes something to be manipulated. Every secret loses its force. This care of averageness reveals in turn the essential tendency of Dasein which we call 'levelling down' [*Einebnung*] of all possibilities of Being."[82]

The question remains of by what method, mechanism, or conduct does this usurpation of A occur in its tense relationship with a and b? Heidegger has already hinted as some of the mechanisms when he mentions "public means of transport," and "information services." So consequential are these "ducts" of abduction, that Adorno has written a book on how to con-*duct* oneself *vis-a-vis* these social fixtures in the territory of the apparatus. For instance, in *Minima Moralia* he even discourses upon how one should react to invitations to talk on mass transportation. Conduct in the viaduct.[83]

Which raises the matter of Dasein. For there to be being at A, there must be abduction. Something must equalize the topology of the psycholinguistic territory, just as something must initiate and initialize speech development in a child through social interaction. What brings the child into the next position from the mirror state is precisely the acquisition of language as a social tool. As *the* social tool sine qua non! Dasein does this through insensitivity to "every difference of level and of genuineness and this never gets to the 'heart of the matter' ['auf die Sachen']. By publicness everything gets obscured, and what has thus been covered up gets passed off as something familiar and accessible to everyone."[84]

Ultimately, it is the eccentric position itself that bring about Dasein, not the centric position, just as it is the state of exception which brings about freedom, not the rule of law, and just as it is the sovereign of the state who brings about sovereignty of the individual. How? By negation. One arises from the other, but the other cannot be sustained without the social fabric to support it. "In Dasein's everydayness the agency through

---

[82] Ibid., pp. 164-165.
[83] Norberg, Jakob. "Adorno's Advice: *Minima Moralia* and the Critique of Liberalism." PMLA, March 2011, Vol. 126, No. 2, p. 398.
[84] Heidegger, Martin. *Being and Time*. New York: Harperperennial Modernthought, 2008, p. 165.

which most things come about is one of which we must say that '*it was no one* [italics added].' "[85] The mirror stage is not possible without the primordial 0I stage where there is no identity, just as personal sovereignty is not possible without first relinquishing it to the state and then, perhaps even by suicide, snatching it back as Socrates did.

2.1 What *"no one"* does for everyone

Which brings us to the question of ethics and morality. Are they possible when their author is *"no one,"* as Heidegger describes the law-making body of the Dasein? Is the sovereign no one too? Is the territory A (centric position) also no one? And if they are no one, what kind of rules would no one make. In asking such questions we confront what is in essence a matter of linguistics. And this problem lies in the assignment of meaning to words produced by a machine incapable of meaning.

In natural language programming, phonemes are parsed into code that is mapped to the parts of speech, which are then concatenated into the syntactical units we call sentences. By and large, machines which produce language are not concerned with paragraphs or rhetorical structure. In fact, they are not even concerned with words *per se* since speech, both produced and heard, is rather one long wave of sounds that rise and fall and are articulated in different ways by the body and mind. So when a machine responds with, "I love you," as a chatterbot might to the query, "Do you like me?" there are three fallacies in the simple sentence. First, there is no "I" speaking. Second, the software/hardware cannot feel love (and we do not know what love is anyway), and finally, for there to be a "you" there must be an I, which there is not. Yet, we may even have an emotional reaction to the utterance, just as we may break down in tears at the conclusion of *Les Miserables* by an author long dead but whose words live on breaking hearts and jerking tears. We seem to have, as Heidegger makes clear, a kind of "insensitivity" to the exception and to the etiology of utterance. This, then, is the first problem confronting the synthetic production of language. "Assuming the set of grammatical sentences of English to be given, we now ask what sort of device can produce this set (equivalently, what sort of theory gives an adequate account of the structure of this set of utterances)."[86]

---

[85] Ibid., p. 165.
[86] Chomsky, Noam. *Syntactic Structures*. Mouton: The Hague, 1975, p. 18.

Chomsky shows the relationship between theory and proof-of-concept, as well as the difficulty to ascertain the morphology and mechanism of language production, which he calls "an enormously complex system [...]."[87] He further describes how a simple language-producing machine might work:

"Suppose that we have a machine that can be in any one of a finite number of different internal states, and suppose that this machine switches from one state to another by producing a certain symbol (let us say, an English word). One of these states is an initial state; another is a final state. Suppose that this machine begins in the initial state, runs through a sequence of states (producing a word with each transition), and end in the final state. Then we call the sequence of words that has been produced a 'sentence.' "[88]

In our own example, the machine might work like this:

Library
Subjects: (a) Tom runs (b) Mike walks
Predicates: (p) to the store. (q) to the theater.
Initial state: Declarative statements (excluding interrogatives, imperatives, and exclamations)

Instructions: *Each subject must have a predicate. All predicates must follow the subject. Form all possibilities after tabulating probability and all possible combinations.*

(**Tabulation of probability:** 4; possible combinations: ap, aq, bp, bq)
Output
1) (ap) Tom runs to the store.
2) (aq) Tom runs to the theater.
3) (bp) Mike walks to the store.
4) (bq) Mike walks to the theater.

What makes this "a machine" is that the sentences are complete with predicate only after the machine runs, and that before there existed no form

---

[87] Ibid., p. 18.
[88] Chomsky, Noam. *Syntactic Structures*. Mouton: The Hague, 1975, p. 18-19.

of these sentences uttered by a non-machine. Once the machine runs, we have sensible utterances expressive of the names, gates, and destinations of two individuals. Furthermore, we have some statistical information about the all possible outcomes, and a set of rules to follow that will prevent nonsensical utterances such as "to the store to the theater," though "Tom runs," and "to the store. Tom runs" make *sense*, but not in the optimal way in which the programming brings us.

We can also build a machine called the Kant Engine. This one generates synthetic (argumentative) and analytic (explicit) statements. In its design, function, and output, it resembles how propositions are generated by Dasein in the "averageness" of "everydayness." This machine is designed to create only analytic and synthetic statements and contains a heuristic to prevent their conflation.

Library
Noun phrase subjects: x) The dress y) The coat z) The dog
Analytic predicates: (a) is borrowed. (b) is silk. (c) is male.
Synthetic predicates: (p) is sexy. (q) is nice. (r) is obedient.

Initial state: Declarative statements (excluding interrogatives, imperatives, and exclamations)

Instructions: *Each subject must have a predicate. All predicates must follow the subject. Form all possibilities after tabulating probability and all possible combinations. Heuristic: x and y must not be paired with c and r; z must not be paired with a, b, or p.*

(**Tabulation of probability**: 10; 5 analytic statements: xa, xb, ya, yb, zc; 5 synthetic statements: xp, xq, yp, yq, zr.)
Output:
Analytic
1) (xa) The dress is brown.
2) (xb) The dress is silk.
3) (ya) The coat is borrowed.
4) (yb) The coat is silk.
5) (zc) The dog is male.

Synthetic

1) (xp) The dress is sexy.
2) (xq) The dress is nice.
3) (yp) The coat is sexy.
4) (yq) The coat is nice.
5) (zr) The dog is obedient.

We might predicate that our machines will never make errors. There is no confusion in the instructions, no chaos, no ambiguity, no Dasein! The machine cannot be said to "exist," because it is entirely abstract. It is not even like "the mind," which is contained in a brain which in turn is contained in a neat package called the skull. Here there is nothing/no one. Here Heidegger's words haunt us: "In Dasein's everydayness the agency through which most things come about is one of which we must say that 'it was no one.' " No one is the sovereign, except language. Language is the coming-into-being of the subject and its objects. It is language that makes something hot or cold, good or bad, brown or green, silk or cotton, male or female in the *performative* sense. Language *performs* this function just as our machines perform theirs.

However, there is a problem. Our machines in their simplicity and encodability are more or less infallable. When we consider what Chomsky calls "an enormously complex system" of natural language, the probability (calculated at 4 and 10 above) becomes exponential. Add n number of intentional attempts to shape the discourse through propaganda, and the situation drifts into Dasein with its famous "insensitivity" to heuristic controls. The statements in our second machine are likely to become confused or intentionally manipulated so that the analytic and synthetic subject and predicates will become mixed, violating the heuristics that state that *x and y must not be paired with c and r; z must not be paired with a, z, p, or q.* Statements such as "The dog is sexy," or "The dress is obedient" creep into usage and, as Heidegger states is the mode of Dasein, dissolve into the everydayness of utterances and in doing so, perform the leverage of abduction in psycholinguistic topology for the "They."

2.2 The fallacy of the subject-object dichotomy

In all of the test sentences above, an assumption has been made: that the relation between subject and object, or subject and predicate, is somehow absolute. This assumption starts to unravel when we note the trivial distinction between S-V-O language such as English, and O-V-S language such as Japanese. First, we discover that the prevailing pattern in a language's sentence structure is not somehow a universal necessity. Second we learn that consistent, repetitive, predictable structure is not needed for a language to convey information with more or less accuracy. Furthermore, there are languages which do without particles that seem essential in other languages, such as articles, which are superfluous in Russian and Mandarin Chinese. In the everydayness of any language, the rules of grammar and rhetoric fade into "usage," which varies with region, subculture, fashion, and fad. For instance, in parts of the United States "So don't I" means "So do I" in others, indicating that even negations are not enough to disturb the communicating power of language as long as the listeners concur on the intended meaning in the social position of development. But even this extreme example, which is nontrivial, is more common than we expect. Most statements can be made in the negative or positive with the same intended meaning (in English). For example, in promotional speech ideas about a product are presented in positive form, so that "Our car won't leave you stranded" will be presented as "Our car will get you where you want to go," with the same intended meaning (even if there are nuanced differences between the actual statements).

The concern here is for an *a priori* which goes beyond the limits set by Kant of space and time. The attempt here is to strip down language with Occam's Razor so that we can see at least four possibilities for now: 1) That there is no progression in mathematics or language, which leads to the progressive fallacy, 2 That there is "no one" generating language, but rather it is a universal property called the Language Faculty (Chomsky); 3) That the subject-object (predicate) dichotomy is trivial, and 4) That most propositions cannot be verified and are therefore potentially "false" propositions.

We have already discussed 1 and 2 above. To begin on 3 we must sharpen Occam's Razor with the words of Kant on the limits of the a priori. "Time is a necessary representation, lying at the foundation of all our intuitions. With regard to phenomena in general, we cannot think away time from them, and represent them to ourselves as out of and unconnected with time, but we can quite well represent to ourselves time void of phenomena. *Time is therefore given a priori* [italics added]."[89] If phenomena are *a*, and

---

[89] Kant, Immanual. *Critique of Pure Reason*. New York: Barnes & Noble, 2004, p. 7.

time is b, then Kant's last statement above shows, where $\rightarrow$ stands for "if, then," that $(a + b) \rightarrow \sim (a \sim b)$.[90] The tacit operating mode of Dasein is that time is a priori. (We must make the distinction here between what Spisani[91] designates as T and t in relation to time. "T" is *a priori*time, whereas "t" is the personal, subjective sense of the passing of time which is entirely psychological and is not at all what Kant indicates.) The same can be said of space, as we have already discussed in Part 1. However, a more pointed argument is needed here.

Kant further makes the distinction of the *extensa* as a priori. He uses the example of things that extend into space as a property we can verifiably assert is an attribute of a *thing*. Moreover, space as a territory is a *set of things*, in fact the set of all things, and therefore contains itself if and only if it does not contain itself. Without Russell's paradox, space could not be simultaneously one and many, which is also a paradox. "Space is essentially one, and multiplicity in it, consequently the general notion of space, of this or that space, depends solely on limitations. Hence it follows that an a priori intuition (which is not empirical), lies at the root of our conception of space." (Here too there is S and s, the *a priori* of space as S and psychological space as s [small/large, narrow/wide, etc.]).[92]

The problem is, that human language is based on the empirical assumptions built on the a priori of space and time. Furthermore, the "subject-object" dichotomy in language is again a binary of equal value and not a ratio, meaning the two are mere negations of each other and not distinct entities, just as "here/there" are not in any verifiable way extant; the moment I move from "here" to "there" in space, the polarity is reversed. Therefore the subject-object dichotomy is a synthetic proposition, is empirical, and presents a fallacy when analyzed for verifiability. Ayer seizes upon the relationship, which is really a proposition *about* space and time, to expose its resistance to veracity. "To begin with, we must make it clear that we do not accept the realist analysis of our sensations in terms of subject, act, and object. For neither the existence of the substance which is supposed to perform the so-called act of sensing nor the existence of the act itself, as an entity distinct from the sense-contents on which it is supposed

---

[90] Throughout this text "+" will be used for the operator AND.

[91] Spisani, Franco. *The Meaning and Structure of Time* (*Significato e Struttura del Tempo*). Bologna: Azzoguidi, 1972.

[92] Kant, Immanual. *Critique of Pure Reason*. New York: Barnes & Noble, 2004, p. 4.

to be directed, is in the least capable of being verified."[93]

Again, we are back to a binary: either the entity extends in time and space and is said to "exist," or not: 1 or 0. Thus, the "subject, act, object" (or object, act, subject) progression is the progressive fallacy as language. The extensa are the furniture of Dasein. When we go beyond the furniture in language, we begin to weave the discourse. The discourse is by its nature false, but necessarily so because the world of appearances is an appliance, just as language is. Propaganda, then, is the discourse propagated, which includes purveying the Weltanshauung. The words themselves do not indicate the *world/word* view. Rather it is the structural syntax of the words concatenated that enforces the unverifiable proposition of Being-as-subject in an apparent S-V-O world.

2.3 Being-as-subject and the eccentric position

Being-as-subject is the essential fallacy. From this unverifiable proposition all language flows in its form but not in its entity as expression. Expression is a biological a priori in that it originates from the Language Faculty (LF) and knows only time and space. Without going too deeply into the cognitive science of language acquisition, production, and development, we may at least rely on the T + S superstructure of functional language and presume that since it is based on the two a priorae identified by Kant it is both *primordial and innate*. Chomsky describes the progressive fallacy in language acquisition, throwing the burden of language production on the *a priorae* of Universal Grammar (UG) and the LF, agreeing that it is a *metatheory*:

"The task The task of the child learning a language is to choose from among the grammars provided by the principles of universal grammar [,] that grammar which is compatible with the limited and imperfect data presented to him [by the social *arch*]. That is to say [...] that language acquisition is not a step-by-step process of generalization, association, and abstraction, going from linguistic data to the grammar, and that the subtlety of our understanding transcends by far what is presented in experience."[94]

When we consider the five pillars of the discourse: government,

[93] Ayer, A.J. *Language, Truth and Logic*. New York: Dover Publications, Inc., ND, p. 122.
[94] Chomsky, Noam. *On Language*. New York: New Press, 1998, p. 180.

church, schools, banks and the media, we can see that the idea of a "metagrammar" is subversive. For government it shows that there is an a priori in language that is not issued by fiat (as public education and its frameworks and benchmarks is), that for the church "grammar" even transcends the idea of "God" in that it is innate and not acquired through a salvatory ritual, that for schools language is not really something that can be taught (and even empirical data bears this out, *for children do not learn to listen and speak in school*), that for banking (and its adjunct: commerce) promotional propositions in the forms of advertising and public relations consist of accretions aimed not at the fundamental properties of language but at what is acquired and can therefore be shuffled off, and that for the media — which does not exist in space but in time — only synthetic propositions are possible. "[T]his whole complex of ideas seems linked to potentially quite dangerous political currents: manipulative, and connected with behaviorist concepts of human nature."[95] Here Chomsky refers to what he calls "empiricist learning theories [that are] much too limited to be adequate."[96]

The discourse teeters on a rickety mass of scaffolding swiped from the refuse of the Newtonian-Euclidean-Cartesian universe, which cognitive science and quantum physics are proving to be increasingly inadequate to create social organizations that serve *homo generator.*

3.1 Morality, ethics, and "no one"

Nevertheless, the concern above for "no one" being behind the furniture of Dasein with its languages, cultures, customs, inventions, religions, morality and ethics is underscored by the use of what Chomsky calls "what is presented in experience" which is then translated into artificial systems such as language synthesis. The ready-to-hand nature of grammar rules is ultimately juridical. Rules of grammar are laws, just like the "law of gravity," the incest taboo, and the parking ticket. Morality is an amorphous term used to catch the detritus of a persona's acts and deeds. However, ethics is another matter. Besides being a branch of philosophy, ethics has a morphology. We can even say there are different kinds of ethical strategies, such as deontological and teleological. Furthermore, we have elaborate

---

[95] Ibid., p. 128.
[96] Ibid., p. 127.

and simple systems of ethics constructed by the likes of Kant (Categorical Imperative) and Aritsotle (Nichomachean Ethics).

For Kant, the imperative is, "Act only according to that maxim whereby you can, at the same time, will that it should become a universal law."[97] For Aristotle it is more of a character issue of liberality, magnificence, gentleness, friendship, honesty, charm on a personal level and on the juridical a matter of justice, *distributive and corrective*. But what is the ethical system of the apparatus? In both Kant's and Aristotle's systems, the emphasis falls on the subject; the subject must act this way and that. *In the ethics of the apparatus, the object must act on the subject.* Considering we have already dismissed the subject-object dichotomy for the time being, it may seem specious to then plunge into making such a distinction and adding that the distinction makes all the difference in the effect of the ethical system. However, we must discuss Being-as-subject and its relationship to coming-into-being. The essential difference between the two is that the former is a static state and the latter dynamic. Basing an ethical system on the former is simpler than the latter because it does not bring up the necessity (imperative) of contextual relativism. Since coming-into being is a dynamic state, its ethics must be dynamic too, based on some paradigm or parameter or algorithm which accommodates changes in the ethical topology of decision making.

A third state, however, makes it possible to administer law in a correlated state of exception: Being-as-object. In the state of exception, being-as-object exploits Dasein's "insensitivity" to the particulars of a situation and simply mandates by fiat (dictates) the conditions of the form of life. Moreover, it makes it possible to encode rules of conduct and automate them through testing systems and series of levels and hurdles the persona must navigate to achieve the status of citizen. Ronell describes the place testing holds in the Dasein of Being-as-object:

"The test allows for the maximum freedom of scientific venturing and invites, within its borders, the free play of wholly unjustifiable conjecture. The test promotes incessant field days for the riotous or tentative spin of an unjustifiable conceptual urge. At the same time it serves the function of reality principle to science's pleasure principle, limiting and ordering the possible as it answers the call of the impossible."[98]

---

[97] Kant, Immanuel. James W. Ellington, trans. *Grounding for the Metaphysics of Morals*, 3rd ed.. Indianapolis: Hackett, p. 30.

[98] Ronell, Avital. *The Test Drive*. Chicago: University of Illinois Press, 2005, p. 39

This is as much to say that Being-as-subject is excluded from the state of exception by a kind of ban, putting it outside the pale of verifiability. Herein lies the essential conflict between Kant's *a priori* and the so-called scientific method we derive from Descartes. This is a fine point. While 20th-century science embraced what it considered to be "verifiability" in the sense that Ayer (and Russell and Whitehead and Carnap) means it, in fact what science had its arms around was empiricism using the experimental method of controls and observation advocated by Descartes, and as such spent a century arguing over the greatest discovery in modern times: quantum physics. We owe much of this mayhem to one passage in Descartes' *Discourse on Method*: "I noticed that experimentation becomes more necessary in proportion as we advance in knowledge. In beginning and investigation it is better to restrict ourselves to our usual experiences, which we cannot ignore if we pay any attention to them at all, then to seek rarer and more abstruse experiences."[99]

In short, scientists rely upon *empirical* evidence which, Ayer says, is not verifiable. From the view of the Being-as-subject, empirical evidence is suspect because, in one way or another, everyone knows that perception is just that: what the persona perceives and is not necessarily what is "there." If this were not the case the willing suspension of disbelief in the enjoyment of media spectacles would be impossible. We would stare at the screen thinking: "This is a movie/television production," and not shed a tear when the hero dies or lives happily ever after. Ronell, citing Bacon, says, "For Bacon, the mind has to be purged of anticipations, idols, and prejudices before it can apply itself to an untainted reading of nature."[100] Bacon presumes an "untainted reading" of nature is possible through Being-as-subject. We may hope, though, that clearing the subjective palette will give us at last a "better" view of nature that is less of a projection of our own filtration of Dasein. From the view of Being-as-object, though, verifiability is just a matter of devising an "experiment," which Ronell points out is just another *test*. The test itself is a *homunculus* of the apparatus, doing its bidding to support what Socrates calls the "interests of State."

To separate the empirical and nonempirical forms of verifiability, Popper proposed "falsifiability,"[101] the method by which a proposition must be proven false rather than true. Falsifiability is less a method than a *tocsin*

---

[99] Descartes, Rene. *Discourse on Method*. Lawrence J. Lafleur, trans. Indianapolis: The Bobbs-Merrill Company, Inc., 1975, p. 41.
[100] Ronell, ibid., pp. 38-39.
[101] Popper, Karl. *Logik der Forschung*. Tubingen: Mohr Siebeck, 1934.

rooting out the illogic in the application of verifiability to the scientific method using empirical observation and testing. Popper's spanner in the works thrust the empirical verifiability of a proposal under Being-as-object into the same conundrum or "joke" Fermat left us with as his last theorem. In other words, to falsify a proposition one is in the same position as providing a proof, as in a proof of Fermat's last theorem, but then must show that every instance of the proposition is false, which could prove impossible. For instance, we might want to falsify the idea that man is mortal. To do so convincingly we would have to wait for every human to die, or kill them all to prove our point. In the meantime, new humans would be born, at least one of whom may be immortal. Therefore, Popper's falsifiability is hardly a practical method but is more of a philosophical point regarding the empirical form of verifiability which Popper presents as unjustifiable because it is a test.

3.2 Ethics of the automaton

Homo generator (HG) is at a crossroads between Being-as-object and Being-as-subject. Moreover, HG can look back over his shoulder and see Descartes, Newton, and Euclid lingering behind, still appealing for an audience like a trio of singers from a bygone era. He has three paths to choose, one of which represents *neoteny*, or a return to a previous state. The other two represent, in the case of Being-as-object, the state of exception and the science of the camp based on testing (are you a Jew?); Being-as-subject represents exclusion and the ban under the state of exception while retaining personal sovereignty (exile, house arrest). This is not an easy choice to make, especially when it is made *for* homo generator by the apparatus.

Homo generator appears on the scene of human evolution just at the point where the Cartesian vision is at last a proven concept. Descartes perceives animals, but not humans, as "clockwork," for animals are "not rational, and [...] nature makes them behave as they do according to the disposition of their organs; just as a clock, composed only of wheels and springs, can count the hours and measure the time more accurately than we can with all our intelligence."[102] In the same category as these animals is the *automaton*, or robot. For Descartes, this creature lacks essential human

---

[102] Descartes, Rene. *Discourse on Method.* Lawrence J. Lafleur, trans. Indianapolis: The Bobbs-Merrill Company, Inc., 1975, p. 38.

traits just as the animal. (We will leave the soul out of this discussion for fear of venturing too deeply into theology and metaphysics.)

To begin, there is a kind of Turing test Descartes devises that will determine conclusively whether or not the persona is human or a machine: "The first is that it could never use words or other signs for the purpose of communicating its thoughts to others, as we do [....] The second [...] is that, although such machines could do many things as well as, or perhaps even better than, men, they would infallibly fail in certain others, by which we would discover that they did not act by understanding, but by the disposition of their organs."[103] In other words, even as simulations of humans, the machines would fail the tests.

Today, we strive to create automata that are "more human than human," to cite Nietzsche. Descartes already admits that these machines "could do many things as well as, perhaps even better than," humans. If we could add a measure of ambiguity to their status as either creatures abiding in Being-as-object or Being-as-subject, homo generator would be confronted with the apparatus walking and talking and maybe even cohabitating with its creator. If flesh-and-blood personae can be abducted and perform as extensa of the apparatus, why cannot machines perform as extensa of homo generator? This would be artificial life supreme. But what would its ethics be? And how would it test its human counterparts for their own ethical status?

3.3 The apparatus tests the subject

For the automaton to approach human functioning, it will need more than language. Machines that speak and interact with us are pervasive (if not invasive), and are therefore trivial for our purposes. However, in the state of exception everyone is tested. If the automaton is an extension of the apparatus, its *golem* as it were, how will it test humans to see if they are not machines? How will it enact its instant juridical ethic system upon meeting someone, as humans do with their social codes and elaborate protocols? We will make a little machine here like the language machines, only this one is to determine the statistical probability of whether or not a person belongs, mostly belongs, mostly doesn't belong, or does not belong to the apparatus. It is called the Six-Bucket System,

---

[103] Ibid., p 36.

and it provides s test of whether or not someone should be banned from the state.

The six buckets are in three categories: 1, 2, 3. Each category holds two buckets containing characteristics which are negations of each other, so that 1 contains ab, 2 contains pq, and 3 contains xy. Therefore, ab, pq, xy are negations. For example, ab could be "good/bad, pq could be "rich/ poor," and xy could be "winner/loser." To determine an individual's profile, a series of redundant interrogatives would be presented by the automaton, such as "What is your net worth in dollars?" If it is over \$300,000, then the persona is "rich," and if it is under that the persona is "not rich" (e.g. "poor"). On this point a series of redundant questions in a similar vein could be asked and then a mean determined to increase accuracy, the final decision (rich or poor) based on the mean index.

Running this system, we derive 6 combinations of characteristics in the three columns: apx, apy, aqy, bqy, bqx, bpx. The positive category is to the left of the column, and the negative to the right. The "most positive" score is apx, occupying all three left columns of 1, 2, 3. The most negative is bqy. Therefore, apx is the negation of bqy expressed (apx ~ bqy). The remaining four states are either "more positive" or "more negative." For example, apy is more positive, but aqy is more negative. Bqx is more negative, whereas bpx is more positive, expressed thus: (apy > aqy), and (bpx > bqx). Finally, there are two *logical equivalents*: n (apy ≡ bpx) and m (aqy ≡ bqx). To simplify matters, we can say that there are four possible scores: *apx, n, m and bqy*, with *apx* being the "most positive," *n* being "mostly positive," *m* being "mostly negative," and *bqy* being the most negative.

At last our automaton has tested its subject and has determined if this subject will get the job, the housing, the stipend, the college degree, the license, the mortgage — *in short if it is "banned" from these rewards or not*. If one were to be interviewed by this automaton for any of these desirable commodities, one would be satisfied if the qualifications were based on the result of "mostly positive," though for some especially desired rewards one would of course have to be "the most" positive. Those with the positive scores would be included in the operations of the apparatus in a positive way, whereas *those with negative scores would find themselves excluded or otherwise banned at least from the desirable commodities*.

But as the test itself issues from Being-as-object, there is "no one" who is doing the testing. The test itself is the ontological determinant.

That the subject is judged "most positive" or "most negative" is not a function of the subject's actual state in some analytical way, but is rather a synthetic proposition about the subject, presented, however, as an *objectively verifiable proposition* through "testing." The Six-Bucket System mimics the activity of the empirical experiment's analysis of the data extracted, then presents it as an analytical proposition when in fact it is synthetic! This is how propaganda is used to gain leverage in the abduction/abdication process. The subject abdicates when he takes the test and in particular when he accepts the results of the test. "While the test is a questioning act, and while it may prompt the necessity of counter-examples, it already contains and urges a sense of the correct way to answer its demand [....] [T]he test attacks the epistemological meaning with a kind of ontological fervor."[104]

Epsistemologically, the test creates its own meaning *ex nihilo*. Herein lies the relationship between the apparatus, the discourse, the state of exception, and Being-as-object: as there is "no one" there, meaning must be fabricated through the exploitation of synthetical propositions presented as analytical ones. This exploitation occurs in the I2 position, the successor of the mirror stage, ushering in the abducted position of Ix. Statements such as that attributed to Joseph Goebbels: "Repeat a lie often enough and loud enough and it becomes the truth," historical or not, describe the process well. "To the extent that the test, according to its more constative pretexts, delivers results, corroborating or disconfirming what is thought to be known or even to exist, it can undermine anything that does not respond to its probative structure. The status of the thing tends to topple under the pressure of the test. Somewhat paradoxically, it is not clear even that something is known until there is a test for it."[105]

4.1 Universal grammar (UG), universals, and the a priori

There has been much discussion in the last fifty years regarding whether or not syntax and grammar are "built in" to the mind as an *innate*, a priori installation. The *a posteriori* then is the self and the Self, or the positions at the mirror and social stages of development (with the eccentric Ix position as the terminus). For the sake of this discussion, we will conclude that

---

[104] Ronell, Avital. *The Test Drive*. Chicago: University of Illinois Press, 2005, p. 186.
[105] Ibid., p. 187.

the Language Faculty (LF) is innate, using Kant's vectors of space and time (S + T) as the primordial a priorae, and excluding their psychological equivalent (s + t), for the structure of language is nothing more than an expression of these vectors. The Progressive Fallacy arises when the *a posteriori* development of the LF is mistaken for the *a priori*.

We must at this point make a distinction similar to T + t and S + s: Universal Grammar (UG) and the universals of language. According to Chomsky, "universal grammar *is not a grammar, but rather a theory of grammars*, a kind of *metatheory* or *schematism* for grammar [italics added]" that we are asserting is a priori.[106] On the other hand, "universals" (as described by Osgood) are deep structure concerns in the *a posteriori* language. People confuse "universal grammar" with "deep structure," because by "deep structure" they understand the logical subject-predicate proposition, supposed by philosophers as underlying all language.[107] That error will not be made here. We take the a priori to be no more nor less than Kant states: S + T. Inasmuch as grammar follows this pattern, it is universal. Deep structure [DS], however, is the morphological dimension of learned language, and learned almost exclusively between the ages of 0 and 12 (we are not discussing writing here). So we might make the schematic distinction between UG and DS

Using Osgood's four "fundamental psycholinguistic generalities,"[108] we will begin an analysis of the basal DS language and its comparison to the acquired discourse which informs its progressive development a posteriori. The aim is to differentiate the acquired languages (for even in one tongue there are many languages or dialects) from the basal language, and to parse the modifications made to thought as this basal language develops into a pond fed by the river of the discourse and its *apparatus*. It will be argued that during this process the value of T + S is inverted with its psychological counterpart, so that the equation is (T + S) < (t + s) at the point of abduction.

Osgood's four generalities are:

1) At all levels (phonological, morphological, and syntactic) language systems like other behavior systems will follow a principle of progressive differentiation in their development.

---

[106] Chomsky, Noam. *On Language*. New York: New Press, 1998, p. 183.
[107] Ibid., p. 183.
[108] Osgood, Charles. "Language Universals and Psycholinguistics." *Universals of Language*, 2nd ed. Joseph H. Greenberg, ed. Cambridge: MIT Press, 1966, p. 304-6.

2) At all levels of units in a language, the competing alternatives will be organized hierarchically in terms of frequency of occurrence and a relatively low-entropy distribution approximating the Zipf[109] function.

3) At all levels of language organization, whenever there are competing means of achieving some criterion of communication performances, these competing means will be related inversely as a compensating system.

4) At all levels, the laws of language change (diachronic universals) will be found to reside in the principles and conditions of learning as they operate upon individual speakers and hearers.[110]

The usefulness of these generalizations lies in their position a posteriori from the primordial position of 0I, where all that exists as an organizing principle is S + T. What they show is that the *a posteriori* organizing principles are organic too, but depend upon the social stimulus necessary for the Critical Period (CP) to be successful in the development of the innate LF. While it may seem that "the discourse" and "the apparatus" are somehow "the enemy," particularly using the violent word "abduction" to indicate their mechanism, the fact is they are organic extensions of the a priori and are absolutely necessary for language development, which is their vehicle. Now we will make some brief remarks about the significance of Osgood's generalities.

1) The   *"phonological, morphological, and syntactic"* parameters of language increase in their "differentiation" as the child develops through the 0-12 CP. In quantifiable terms, the number of sounds the child can distinguish (phonologically and as a "sign" in the de Saussurean sense) increases through socialization, as does the understanding of compound words and phrases. The strong threshold of understanding, though, is the final one of syntax, which is the most complex and contains

---

[109] Zipf function: an observation in computational linguistics expressed by George Kingsley Zipf that the most common word will be expressed twice as often as the next most common word, and thrice the next, etc.

[110] Osgood, Ibid., p 304-306.

the most variables (i. e. phonemes contain the least variation because they must be consistent from hearer to hearer within the environmental milieu). As we know, sentence structure can vary dramatically and still produce similar meanings for a particular statement.

2) Using the *Zipf* law of frequency in computational linguistics, the above three parameters are then organized hierarchically to decrease "entropy," that is, the latency which occurs when the three components are retrieved from memory and the language centers of the brain and are then manipulated to produce sense. (Poor Zipf law controls in language development tend to aggravate latency either from physiological causes [e.g. brain damage], to subnormal environmental stimuli).

3) This is a most interesting generality. In the *a posteriori* acquisition of language during the CP, different systems will compete. A typical example would be formal versus informal language, or vernacular versus mainstream, or slang versus proper speech. However, for our purposes we will look at the language of abduction in discourse. After the Ix position is achieved, the previous psychological and linguistic orientation does not "go away." On the contrary, it remains as a *neotenic* refuge for reset to the I2 stage (reset to I1 is extremely difficult and rare, and as we have mentioned, *because 0I → I1 is a Threshold, it cannot be crossed again*). But it remains "reladetly inverse as a compensating system." For this reason, the discourse, with its cult-like attributes, must cascade over the subject continually for fear of losing the Ix position to an I2 reset.

4) The "conditions of learning" are the attributes of the discourse itself, which is no monolith, but can be anything Dasein permits. After all, it is the voice of Dasein. Therefore, the hold can be weak or strong, the cultural cast can be religious or secular, the economic level can be high or low, the proficiency of the subject can be great or small, the orientation can be elevated educationally or modest. Here the "insensitivity" of Dasein is in play. It doesn't "care" (*caritas*) about the trivial details. What matters is the abduction into the universal anonymity of "no one." Again the mistake is to consider each position of abduction as a "progression" with a ratio, when in fact it is just iteration of

the same first move (0I → I1), but with a new *zone of proximal development* (a matter to be discussed later).[111]

During the CP, the mechanism of acquisition of DS might be called the "mirror" of the mirror stage. The device of the mirror remains intact throughout the life of the subject, forever an artifact of the dissonance between the "two I's": the specular and the real, which creates the unique sense of self consciousness in humans and is the forge of neurotic pathology. There must be a force and forge at work to form the social from the narcissistic — using the same mirror! These consist of "Evaluation, Potency, and Activity" according to Osgood, that "have a *response*-like character, seemingly *reflecting* the ways we can *react* to meaningful events rather than the ways we *receive* them [italics added]."[112] The critical words here are *respond, reflect, react, and receive,* which we might term the "four R's." The first three are in a class by themselves as a unitary process of development formulating the DS, whereas "receive" describes the cognitive communication infrastructure of the mind and its feeders in the form of social "activity." From this activity arise "pleasantness, strain, and excitement"[113] providing the *sturm und drang* needed to make an "impression" on the a priori Being-as-subject. Once initialized as the I2 position, the CP coils out as coming-into-Being until the child reaches adolescence and the brink of abduction.

4.2 Discourse at the position of *a posteriori*

As with T + S and t + s, as well as UG and DS and Self and self, there is the Discourse and discourse. (Though for the remainder of the discussion the two will be used interchangeably with a lower-case initial for simplicity.) In its native meaning, to discourse means to communicate a complete idea, though there is the collateral meaning of "discursive" communication, meaning both the adjectival form of discourse and "to wander at will." Both definitions are useful to us here.

---

[111] Vygotsky, L.S. *Mind in Society: The Development of Higher Psychological Processes.* Cambridge: Harvard U.P., 1978.

[112] Osgood, Charles. "Language Universals and Psycholinguistics." *Universals of Language,* 2nd ed. Joseph H. Greenberg, ed. Cambridge: MIT Press, 1966, p. 312.

[113] Ibid., p. 312.

Weinreich refers to any type of discourse when citing the "combinatory semiotics of connected discourse."[114] In other words, discourse has the unique property of conveying meaning that is *more than the sum of the parts of the words concatenated.* The mimetic property of listening and hearing the words contributes to the meaning that is not semantically in the words, but in the semiotic relationship between then. For example, the words horse and sword together evoke in the listener (using Zipf's Law) a *hierarchy* of associations which may or may not have been meant by the speaker. For instance, battle, war, the U.S. Civil War, a knight in shining armor, samurai, history, the past, and so on. Working on the syntactic level, the fault tolerance is high, especially in speech where feedback from the listener invokes syntax corrections from the speaker, providing a real-time heuristic not present in writing. (Phonemically fault tolerance is low for reasons already stated.)

To further define discourse, we return to de Saussure's idea of the phoneme as "sign," and therefore a semiotic entity subject to the representational and mimetic properties and associations of signs. "We will accordingly say that a language is a repertory of signs, and that discourse involves the use of these signs, seldom in isolation."[115] That they are not alone in their quest for hearing shows that phonemic signs exist not as particles but as parts of a whole which is in the end not *the* communication, but *a*communication because there is, technically, an infinite number of potential listeners who may or may not have the equipment to understand and even so, to varying degrees. Weinreich divides the discourse into *designators* and *formulators*. In the Chomskean sense, formulators would be considered generators in the creation of generative grammar, such as in the sentence "The cats fought all _____ long. Using Using Zipf's law, we would most likely fill in the blank with "night," rather than day, since we have a sense that cats fight at night not during the day. The word "day" remains the second possibility under the rules Osgood describes, where "night" is twice as likely to appear. Day is the most likely second choice because it is the inversion of night and therefore is the most likely alternate under generalization 3.

---

[114] Weinreich, Uriel. "On the Semantic Structure of Language." *Universals of Language*, 2nd ed. Joseph H. Greenberg, ed. Cambridge: MIT Press, 1966, p. 143.
[115] Ibid., pp. 144-5.

4.2.1 The Critical Period's contextual significance

At the end of puberty, the CP draws to a close. If a child has not learned listening and peaking by that threshold — without a preexisting pathology — there is little chance and almost no literature to support the learning of it successively. Workarounds of various sorts come into play to help the child negotiate with the world. In a normal child, though, the abduction process begins in ways we have already discussed. It is interesting to note that it is often adolescence when a subject (*subject* and *persona* are used interchangeably here) becomes interested in poetry, which is the deliberate synthesis of language and often devoid of analytic propositions. So too are the subject's commercial, sexual, romantic, and occupational interests awakened. Harkening to commercial appeals in the form of advertising and marketing, the subject learns about "lack," the emotion propitiated by the *acquisition, through commercial appeal,* of what one lacks. Sexual/ romantic interests may lead to "falling in love" where there is an instant leap from the centric to the eccentric in the spheres of experience. And finally, one may begin upon the formulation of a new core identity by joining the police, becoming a doctor, enlisting in the army, getting a college degree, or being ordained in a religion.

In all four cases one's proper name changes to "Officer," Doctor," "Sergeant," or "Father," hastening the undermining of the core identity built up during the I2 position phase and somewhat easing the conflict between the sense of "I" from the mirror stage and I2 from the socialization stage by introducing a third possibility: Ix, the abducted position. The attraction of the new core identity offered by the *sexual/romantic* and *commercial/occupational* discourses is more or less irresistible except in the most unusual of subjects. Process maps to the Big Five: government, church, schools, banking, and the media.

Artistic creation, often seen as some kind of "anti-discourse," in fact has its roots in the abduction which leads to the implantation of the discourse as the motor of the core identity, and which may be an excrescence of this new paradigm not its foil:

"The use of language can also deviate from the norm in the opposite direction [of the norm], so that the language becomes, as it were, 'hypersemanticized.' Such use of language is characteristic of much good literature, although it can be found in workaday life as well. There are at least two marks of hypersemenaticization: (1) The phonic vehicle of signs assumes an independent symbolic value (whether 'impressionistic' —

sound-imitative — or 'expressionistic,' i.e. synaesthetic); a special relation is imputed to sign with similar vehicles (rhyme, etc.); in short, incipient correlations between content and expression are exploited, in contrast to the arbitrariness of this relation in semantically 'normal' uses of language."[116]

5.1 The ontologies of discursive polyvalence

Which brings us at last to the matter at hand: Simultaneous Parallel Ontologies and ontic threads. Part 2 of this discussion is dedicated to this topic. However, we must first have scrambled up through the Preliminaries, through the scree of the concepts and literature, and on up into the height were we can see a larger landscape than before.

The coming-into-being of the traits of the senescent I2 position — in particular the sexual Being-as-subject — usher in the natal phase of the abduction position (Ix). A complex net of influences and interests now come to bear upon the subject/persona. First and foremost is what Socrates refers to as "self interest" and the "interests of the State." As we noted, speaking of the care of his children before his death, he urges his friends to guard over them lest they become self interested and abdicate to the State their personal sovereignty, and that his children should instead preoccupy themselves with *virtue* and *wisdom*. If they do not, then they should be troubled as he had troubled his friends and students. Of course, this death-bed admonition and *ad summum bonum* shows Socrates' fundamental distrust of the ready-to-hand world and the *usurpation/abdication* of the core identity by the *extrinsic/eccentric* powers of the state.

It is not so much the procreative power of sexuality as it is the romantic possibilities and the crafty interplay of bans, laws, and rules that come to bear upon sexual majority in the adolescent. Foucault sees a dual function of the discourse in the lives of those fully engaged with it in the Ix position. This function goes well beyond being an adjunct to the already-existing self; it is no less than a new *ontic* thread which then moves in parallel with coming-into-being, forming more than one *destinal* branch within the region of Dasein. "What is said about sex must not be analyzed simply

---

[116] Weinreich, Uriel. "On the Semantic Structure of Language." *Universals of Language*, 2nd ed. Joseph H. Greenberg, ed. Cambridge: MIT Press, 1966, pp., 147-8.

as the surface of projection of these power mechanisms. Indeed, it is in discourse that power and knowledge are joined together. *And for this very reason, we must conceive discourse as a series of discontinuous segments whose tactical function is neither uniform nor stable* [italics added]."[117]

True power (y), then, issues from the conjoining of the social (I2) and abducted (Ix) positions thus: (I2 + Ix) y. One needs some "power" to survive past the stage where one is taken care of by parents. That power may come, as it did for Mao Zedong, from the barrel of a gun, or it may come from the accumulation of capital. Again, Dasein is "insensitive" to these distinctions. They are trivial in comparison with the transformational Event that occurs when the core identity, in conflict with itself over the specular and real stages, at last finds a kind of peace in abduction into the social arch. The "social arch" is the architecture of the apparatus in which the discourse thrives "as a multiplicity of discursive elements that can come into play in various strategies."[118]

The multiplicity we will consider to be two threads in parallel. While there may be any number of threads, we know there will be at least two: the first being the original orientation of the Being-as-subject, and the second the Being-as-object of Dasein. Herein is the new conflict for the entity (though it need not *be* a conflict) to replace the old. The subject-object dichotomy arises in all its splendor to strut upon the stage of life, again creating the *sturm und drang* of the persona's personal opera (or operetta, as the case may be). In developmental psychology this would be considered one of the top phrases of development called "contextual relativism." Since what was once centric is now eccentric, and what was once eccentric is now the core, there is a clear sense of inversion, or being inverted. It is a brave new world for the persona.

"Discourses are not once and for all subservient to power or raised up against it, any more than silences are. We must make allowance for the complex and unstable process whereby discourse can be both an instrument and an effect of power, but also a hindrance, a stumbling block, a point of resistance and a starting point for an opposing strategy. Discourse transmits and produces power; it reinforces it, but also undermines and exposes it, renders it fragile and makes it possible to thwart it."[119]

---

[117] Foucault, Michel. "The Deployment of Sexuality." *The History of Sexuality: An Introduction,* Vol. 1. New York: Vintage Books, 1990, p. 100.

[118] Ibid., p. 100.

[119] Foucault, Michel. "The Deployment of Sexuality." *The History of Sexuality: An*

Discourse itself is subject to a *polyvalencence* of ontic threads. There threads run both in parallel and series in "discontinuous segments" that are sometimes parallel and sometimes not. At times they converge into one thread, or branch apart. We have discussed the topology of abduction at length. Here lie the dynamic winds and civilizations and tales and histories and destinies of the topology. The key is that it is "never completely stable."[120] This utter dynamic flux is the sinew of Dasein, in its indifference and insensitivity to Event, as an a priori without attribute (existence is not a predicate[121]). However, it is the power of Dasein, a power in which one may not participate without abduction. "In short, it is a question of orienting ourselves to a conception of power which replaces the privilege of law with the viewpoint of the objective, the privilege of sovereignty with the analysis of a multiple and mobile field of force relations, wherein far-reaching, but never completely stable, effects of domination are produced."[122]

5.2 The psychology of parallel ontology

Homo generator, then, must not remain naive to the *mutiverse* he finds himself in and which is written on the wall of every branch of science and mathematics today. It is a wonder that discoveries proven over and over in science and mathematics for a century are still, conceptually, no more a part of our world than were the discoveries of Galileo, Bacon, and Newton, which are are today the subject of comic strips and popular metaphor (such as in the admonition that "the world doesn't revolve around you").

The problem, perhaps, is the danger parallel ontic threads present to the apparatus of the camp, or what Foucault calls "one of the essential traits of Western societies (exploited the world over today)": war. *Dasein is Dasein.* Without attribute, there is not much to say about it by way of description (that has not been said by Heidegger!). The strategy of force, domination of the zero-sum game by a symmetrical brutality, is in constant danger of a new discourse running in parallel (and other directions) relative to the already-existing ontology. After two and a half millennia of development,

---

Introduction, Vol. 1. New York: Vintage Books, 1990, pp. 100-1.

[120] Ibid., p. 102.

[121] Ayer, A.J. *Language, Truth and Logic.* New York: Dover Publications, Inc., ND, p. 121.

[122] Foucault, Michel. "The Deployment of Sexuality." *The History of Sexuality: An Introduction,* Vol. 1. New York: Vintage Books, 1990, p. 102.

the Camp has come into its own as the politics and religion of the State (in Socrates' sense), "not out of a speculative choice or theoretical preference," but because "war, in every form of warfare, gradually became invested in the order [discourse] of political power."[123]

The Camp requires undivided, unitary, monofilament. The ontic thread must not be entwined with perhaps a contrary trend. First there is the matter of control; more than one thread is simply more complex to control. Second, there is the power of incipience and senescence, to begin and end. Third, there is the greater possibility of a reset to the I2 position by the abducted persona, or oscillation between the two positions (such as a poet who is also an academic but takes times off from his *exofficio* duties at the academy to write and give readings, or the person who is married yet from time to time has affairs).

Foucault cites the the old serial distinction between macro evolutionary stages of sexuality as first the "biological" and then the "historical," in other words, the libidinal expression of the uncivilized jungle versus the age of historical "civilized" repression described by Freud, who saw the former as repressed into unconsciousness by the latter. It would be better to see them as parallel, he says. "[W]hat is needed is to make it visible through an analysis in which the biological and the historical are not consecutive to one another [...] but are bound together in an increasingly complex fashion [...]."[124]

In the transformation of childhood polymorphous perversity into a kind of bestiary of pathologies in the 19th century, a schism was created where the ontic thread of childhood took on two distinct paths. "[T]here was formed the idea of a sex that was both present (from the evidence of anatomy) and absent (from the standpoint of physiology), present too if one considered its activity, and deficient if one referred to its reproductive finality; or again, actual in its manifestations, but hidden in its eventual effects, whose pathological seriousness would only become apparent later."[125]

---

[123] Ibid., p. 1202.
[124] Foucault, Michel. "The Deployment of Sexuality." *The History of Sexuality: An Introduction,* Vol. 1. New York: Vintage Books, 1990, p. 152.
[125] Ibid., p. 153.

5.3 The taxonomy of Simultaneous Parallel Ontologies

To begin, we must dispel the association that if there is more than one "ontology," or "being," there is more than one Dasein. There cannot be more than one "Being There." However, there can be more than one world (multiverse) present in the same discrete space (S), more than one time line (T), and one thing, by implication, can be in two places at once at the same time. Perhaps the multiple of 2 is not the limit, but for the sake of discussion 2 will suffice as n, representing any other number. We may say there are in fact n ontologies, but it is easier to discuss 2 because we can conceive of them in certain dynamic and pictorial ways. These ideas are well grounded in quantum physics in relationship to the position of particles and the location of waves, as shall be discussed later.

As such, we have a taxonomy of concepts and behaviors relative to Simultaneous Parallel Ontologies (SPO's), which we shall describe in their discrete form as "ontic threads." Their behavior and relationships are divided into direction, event, recursion, order, and principles. Direction indicates the arrow of the thread. Generally speaking, threads move in the same direction as the arrow of time: from left to right: $\rightarrow$. The difference is they do not move from past to future. That would imply ordinality and by extension the *progressive fallacy*. We would be constrained by ratio, and threads would have to be measured in increasing and decreasing units. Furthermore, the left-to-right ($\rightarrow$) movement does not indicate "progress" in the sense that right-to-left would indicate a retrograde movement ($\leftarrow$). Both directions are equal: ($\rightarrow \equiv \leftarrow$). Rather, we have the principle (borrowed from quantum physics) that *all points on the line of the ontic arrow are equal*. But as we are exploring more than one arrow, there are certain possible states the parallel arrows may be in:

1) Phasic: *Arrows ab move in the same direction at the same "time."*
2) Aphasic: *Arrows ab move in the same direction but with the index offset by x amount.*
3) Contraphasic: *Arrows ab move in opposite directions.*

It would be pointless to have an arrow that went in both directions at once: $\leftrightarrow$. The reason being that although we are looking at the heads of the arrows in diagrams, the second principle states that in fact *the arrow represents only the unraveling of events relative to the other thread and/or for the sake of the a priori* extensa *shows that there is "movement."*

An example of a *phasic pair* is when, for instance, core identity oscillates between the *ex officio* role (such as police officer, soldier, and so on), and the so-called "private life." Daddy may be the best killing machine in his sniper platoon, but he sure knows how to throw a barbecue for the kids on the weekend and to love his wife and go to church every Sunday. An example of *a-phasic ontologies* is when someone has *ex officio* duties but does not like them, and would prefer some other activity — and may even be engaged in another activity that is at least in kind with the first. An example of *contraphasic ontologies* is when *ex officio* is contrary to some activity, such as in the case of the politician who is "tough on criminals" and is elected on a "law and order" platform, but in fact is stealing public treasure, violating ethics rules, and frequenting prostitutes. In each case, one ontic thread must be an *ex officio* affiliated with production, maintenance, and defense of the Discourse — *often derived from the Big Five: government, church, banking, education, and the media.*

There are five types of Events along the threads: micro, ligature, recursion, bifurcation, and truncation. A micro event occurs on the thread, is independent of other threads, and follows Zipf's Law in its hierarchy of event types. For instance, brushing of teeth each day might be twice as likely as using mouth wash, which is then twice as likely as flossing. It determines the syntax of the thread, in much the way parts of speech determine how they are arranged in a sentence. The other events below are in the category of macro events. The syntax of the ontic thread should not be mistaken for the discourse, though it is a kind of discourse because it "tells the story" of it. As Foucault describes above, *"we must conceive discourse as a series of discontinuous segments whose tactical function is neither uniform nor stable."* What unites the segments and adds uniformity and stability to the discourse is the *fiber* of the ontic threads as folk tale (a topic we will explore in depth in Part 5).

In a ligature, two ontic threads, regardless of their direction, are bridged by a short thread which, for a moment, makes them one event (whereas multiple events could occur simultaneously otherwise, or only on on one thread, or none at all). The diagram looks like a short circuit, and indeed often ligatures have dire consequences, such as when a thief who works for a bank is caught helping himself to the funds he does not deserve. On the other hand, ligatures can have the effect of a breakthrough, as when

Archimedes decided to take a bath (thread a) and discovered a solution to the king's surface-area problem (thread b), shouting Eureka!

A recursion is sometimes called a "reset" when applied to certain moral, ethical, and developmental transformations. In a recursion there is a return to a previous state, which in biology is called "neoteny." There are two types of recusions in this system: a "clock" recursion and a "branch" recursion, each expressed thus: *If a then b, if b then c, if c then a.* We have "recurred" to a by a clock movement. Next, *if a then b; if b is x, then c; if b is y, then a.* We have recurred to a by a branch movement (provided b is $y \sim x$).

Bifurcation and truncation are in the same category. Bifurcation is when a monofilament branches into two ontic threads. A truncation is when the opposite happens (and is a negation of bifurcation): two ontic threads converge into one monofilament. If the monofilament is x, then its branches are a and b, expressed thus: $x = ab$, and the reverse for the truncation: $ab = x$.

Next is order. There are two orders: *series and parallel*. In series, b follows a, whereas in parallel a and b occur simultaneously. The principle here is that *in series, while every point on the line is equal to every other point on the line in terms of location, the movement or direction of the arrow is forward; it is progressive.* This progressive movement, rational and ordinal, is the root of the psychological sense of time and space (t + s).

5.4 Language, thought, and ontic threads

It would be a fair question to ask what ontic threads have to do with language per se. To begin with, they are made of what Foucault called "discontinuous segments whose tactical function is neither uniform nor stable."[126] Here we find the first similarity to language. As we have explored, language beyond the phonemic (with low fault tolerance), particularly speech, is subject to a lack of uniformity and stability — even in its phonemic variations! However, spoken language has a high fault tolerance because, as stated previously, it is 1) in real time, and 2) is subject to the heuristic of immediate feedback from the listener (would you say

---

[126] Foucault, Michel. "The Deployment of Sexuality." *The History of Sexuality: An Introduction*, Vol. 1. New York: Vintage Books, 1990, p. 100.

that again, would you speak more slowly, did you mean x, if not, then what did you mean). Furthermore, the complex subtleties of the thread mean that in the space of an hour two threads could branch from a monofilament, one could branch again, a ligature could occur between two branches (or three), the ligature could precipitate a truncation, there could be a recursion to a previous point on the line (which is the same as any other point), and then the whole thing could truncate back into a monofilament and proceed as it had before.

Generally speaking, though, the behavior of the ontic threads follows the rules of deep structure as presented by Osgood in section 4.1. In particular, Zipf's Law is in effect meaning that the micro events determine the syntax of the ontology, which in turn becomes an expressive semiotic discourse. *One's life as lived is the discourse.* Furthermore, the events of the life can be read like tea leaves by special priests called psychologists whose job it is to make sense of the micro events as well as the category of macro events which are the others already described. As described by Osgood above, "competing alternatives will be organized hierarchically in terms of frequency of occurrence."

As one ages, the story of the discourse changes, but more and more along the story lines provided by the apparatus or camp, particularly if there is a state of exception, where even the micro events are then determined by the State as in a concentration camp where each move throughout the day is choreographed, and each trivial activity — from urinating to drinking water — is regimented. Of particular interest is Osgood's third generality, that *"whenever there are competing means of achieving some criterion of communication performances, these competing means will be related inversely as a compensating system."* For example, if a man is unhappy with his marriage, he may maintain the marriage in as best form possible ("for the kids"), while also maintaining an almost marriage-like relationship with another woman who herself may have children as a "compensating system." Also, there will be competition and games within and between the ontic threads for advantage in work, social position, mate, friendships, career, accolades and so on. The competing means to the mainstream (for instance a desire to do nothing as opposed to working hard) will serve as compensatory ontic endeavor, spinning new branches and ligatures and other events.

What is most interesting, though is Osgood's fourth generalization: *"At all levels, the laws of language change (diachronic universals) will be found to reside in the principles and conditions of learning as they operate upon individual speakers and hearers.*" The "diachronic universals" indicate two threads of language operating simultaneously to produce a single effect, as in an SPO. That effect is Dasein, which is undivided, unitary, without characteristics, and *a priori*.

5.6 The undecidability of parallel ontologies

With the question of the a priori, we must also understand the provenance of Simultaneous Parallel Ontologies (SPO's) and their ontic threads. The consideration of Dasein and S + T as the a priorae, we see that parallel threads arise *a posteriori*. They are functions of the *polyvalence* of experience and exposure to Dasein. It is indeed an equation of addition when we consider space and time, for the two cannot exist without each other, and therein we discover the origin of the arising of SPO's. Space and time are not different; they are just the same thing seen two different ways, bringing us to the fundamental generalization made by Osgood above that "*At all levels of language organization, whenever there are competing means of achieving some criterion of communication performances, these competing means will be related inversely as a compensating system.*"

As we view an ontic thread as a concatenation of micro events, punctuated with macros and as a kind of "language," we find ourselves precisely in the same position as quantum physics where an atomic particle (e.g. an electron) can be viewed as a wave or particle, and furthermore cannot be located in space and time when viewed with light because light changes its position and state. S + T become "competing means of achieving some communication" with the rest of the arrow of ontology, and find themselves in a "compensating system" where one extends the other into infinity.

The situation is well described by the Schrodinger's Cat paradox.[127] As with Russell's paradox, this one presents two states that are only possible simultaneously (in parallel) and not in series.

A cat is placed in a covered box with a radioactive isotope. A machine monitors the decay of particles emitted by the isotope. If one atom decays,

---

[127] Schrodinger, Edwin. John D. Trimmer, trans. "The Present Situation in Quantum Mechanics." *Proceedings of the American Philosophical Society*, 124, pp. 323-38. Accessed 8 June 2011, pp. 7-8.

giving off particles, another machine poisons the cat to death. All the observer can know is if the isotope has decayed but not the status of the cat, though this can be assumed from the set up. The temptation is to open the box to confirm the death, which is the only positive proof. However, with the cat still in the box, at what point in the atom's decay do we say "The cat is dead"? This problem raises several issues (besides the humane one). First, when do we open the box? Second, how do we reconcile indeterminacy? Third, what veracity is there to our direct observation of the "state" of the cat as an analog to the state of the decaying atom? Fourth, in the "state"of the box, the cat at the moment of atomic decay is evenly divided between dead and alive, just as the atom is evenly divided between decadence and integrity. If we observe at that moment by looking into the box, we will attempt to observe a state that we cannot observe, and will conclude that the cat is either alive or dead but not both (but which is the actual case)!

This phenomenon in quantum mechanics is not unlike the modular solution to Fermat's last theorem where a kind of Dedekind psi-function is used based on the automorphic functions proposed by Shimura.[128] However, the likeness to Russell's paradox is more apparent when considering the Mobius inversion formula where a non-empty finite set contains equal quantities of odd and even subsets that sum symmetrically, just as in Russel's paradox where the set of all sets is symmetrically poised between containing itself and not containing itself — also an unobservable phenomenon that can be expressed and detected but not empirically perceived. "If one has left this entire system to itself for an hour, one would say that the cat still lives *if* meanwhile no atom has decayed. The psi-function of the entire system would express this by having the living and dead cat [...] mixed or smeared out in equal parts."[129]

The problem of such indeterminacy was taken up by Godel, particularly in his critique of Russell and Whitehead's *Principia Mathematica*.[130] His incompleteness theorem provides a way to observe the cat in both states, and, by analogy, a way for us to observe the parallel ontologies in the discourses of others and ourselves, for in observing others we observe the

---

[128] Shumura, Goro. *Introduction to the Arithmetic Theory of Automorphic Functions.* Princeton: Princeton U.P., 1971.

[129] Schrodinger, Ibid., p. 8.

130 Godel, Kurt. "On formally undecidable propositions in *Principia Mathematica* and related systems I." 1931.

cat in the box and decide on one particular state. Observing ourselves, we observe nothing but the specular self gazing back at us, *for we are nothing more than the gaze itself.*

Therefore, Godel has provided us with at least a theorem we can apply to observing states in metamathematics which will help us better understand the paradoxical state we and other are in. "From the remark that *Rq(q)* states its own improvability it immediately follows that *Rq(q)* is in fact unprovable (because it is undecidable). The theorem which is undecidable *within the systemPM* has hence been decided by metamathematical considerations. The exact analysis of this strange fact leads to surprising results about consistancy proofs for formal systems [...]."[131]

5.6.1 The ethics of the Categorical Exclusion

The quantum mechanics and *metamathematics* of Schrodinger, Shimura, Mobius, and Godel bring us back to the fundamental step in the Categorical Exclusion (CE): $(0 / 1) > (1 / n)$. The first step of $(0 / 1)$ represents for us the movement from the monofilament of our specular gaze to the dynamic interplay between parallel ontologies. It is not that at the point of branching into two ontic threads the bifurcation has *created* more than one thread. Rather, it is that the gaze has at last recognized that there is more than one thread *always already as the texture and topology of Dasein*, expressed semiotically as discourse. The gaze is constrained from recognition of the bifurcation just as the observer will find either a live cat or a dead cat in Schroedinger's box, but not a cat in both states, and just as either the set of all sets will be a set of itself or not — but never both (though is can only be a set of itself if it is not).

The leap then is a quantum leap (which is the smallest "leap" a thing can make, despite the use of the term in vernacular to mean "a great change"). A quantum leap is when an atomic particle such as an electron changes orbit and therefore frequency, which is what may happen when an atom is observed with light (or knocked out of orbit by a stream of electrons) and therefore we can never "observe" the atom in the state it was in unobserved — again the same paradox. We can use this leap, though, to serve as a *0 - 1* switch in binary mathematics to express the

---

[131] Ibid., p. 175.

encoding of instructions to a computing device. This is called "quantum computing." It also makes more than two (or three) states possible, dramatically increasing the efficiency and complexity of computing power.

What Schrodinger set out to demonstrate was not an already-known fact of quantum mechanics adequately demonstrated by Heisenberg, Bohr, and Planck. Rather, he was trying to show that an Event on the *nano* scale (decay of sub-atomic particles) corresponds to events in the physical, perceivable world. So too with the CE. The exclusion is a principle applicable to ethics as well as ontology. Examples in the physical world of experience, though not "proof" of anything (because they are empirical and therefore can only yield synthetic propositions), help us understand coming-into-being with more depth and clarity.

A subject may be said to have crossed a threshold — a categorical exclusion — when there is no possibility of reset to the previous state. Death comes to mind, but that is too obvious an example and does not expose a certain peculiarity of the exclusion, which is that is is ultimately metaphysical, though like the cat has observable analogues in Dasein.

A better example is a subject who commits crimes. Many crimes go undetected and unpunished. In the world without the progressive fallacy, it hardly matters if he kills one person or a thousand. (In fact, soldiers are rewarded for killing "as many" of the enemy as possible — perhaps tens of thousands — and yet are not said to be convicted murderers or even killers [though they in fact are] under the law *in the state of exception*.) We may say that he crossed a threshold when the subject committed the crime: from being innocent to being culpable under the juridical order. However, the more dramatic example is when the subject is caught and punished for the crime. The subject is now a "convicted criminal," and has entered into the ontology of being "a criminal" first, before being human.

This new metaphysical abstraction defines the subject's life as that person's discourse. But what of the previously innocent character's discourse? It does not "go away," but rather continues on as a parallel ontology because, excluding the progressive fallacy, the crime and conviction have always already occurred (since the ontic thread has no defined points just as we cannot locate a subatomic particle in a wave — meaning the particle is everywhere at once and nowhere in particular). At the same time, the persona's innocence is maintained because the persona always already never committed the crime or any other act. The only defining fact here is the gaze's recognition of the bifurcation as a macro Event (never mind the gaze and bans of the juridical and social systems). Furthermore, the particular nature of the Event is that once the persona has served the sentence, there is release. Has there been reset? No. Reset is not possible here, when it might be in other domains of action.

For example, a person who gains excess weight might be said to be "fat." Then that person loses the weight and is said to be "skinny." Both "fat" and "skinny" are synthetical propositions. Nevertheless, they have a function in the progressive, ready-to-hand world of ratio. *Compared* to this and that, these are descriptions of person X. As they are negations of each other, are synthetic, and have no ontological thread as micro events, we may say that once the person is "skinny" then that person was never "fat." There is no extant ontology of "fat." The same might be said for the criminal under a state of exception. Perhaps he killed an enemy. Perhaps the juridical system disappeared along with the State and chaos reigns. However, the state of exception is an *ontic rupture*, which cannot be marked as an event because the sovereign is always already in a state of exception. As the lawmaker/lawgiver, *the sovereign rules and makes the rules.* When the event of the state of exception occurs, it has already occurred just as the thief or murderer has already stolen or killed.

Crossing the threshold of the CE is a nontrivial event, whereas committing the same act *n* amount of times after is trivial. This helps explain somewhat the thinking of serial killers. What is more than one murder relative to not having murdered? It is a categorical exclusion, for which there is no reset. There might be a reset of the juridical consequences when they are removed, but the "bare life" act of killing is now immutable — even though it always already happened, for otherwise it could not have happened at all.

PART 3: THE DISCOURSE OF SPACE AND TIME

Transcendental Aesthetic cannot
contain anymore than these
two elements — space and time [...]
— Kant[132]

1.1 Dialectics as parallel ontologies

If we exclude psychological s + t, we are left with ontological S + T. While the psychological perception of time has significance here, it is not a priori and it is entirely subjective, being a kind of echo or imprint of the ontological sense as Kant expresses it. Explicit S + T, then, provide us with the primordial vectors of Dasein without having any attributes themselves but give rise, through coming-into-being, to the extensa. In as much as a thing "extends," it exists. So far we have discussed the extensa, their topology, and the ontic threads of discourse snaking through the terrain of each of our lives and all associated with them in more or less static terms except for coming-into-being. Now we turn to the dialectical movement of the discourse, which is an excrescence of the "facticity" (in the Heideggerian sense) of space and time. In particular, the subject-object dichotomy and how the two negations "communicate" the dynamic of Being, gives us insight into the workings of coming-into-being and being-as-subject and being-as-object in relation to time and space.

Hegel starts off showing that the two polarities are negations of each other and are therefore "the same." He uses the notion of Notion as the epistemological impulse of the output of dialectics. "[I]f we call Notion what the object is in itself but call the object what it is qua object or for an other, then it is clear that being-in-itself and being-for-an-other are one and the same."[133] Intrinsic "knowing" is not different from the assignment

---

132 Kant, Immanuel. *Critique of Pure Reason*. New York: Barnes & Noble, 2004, p. 13.
133 Ibid., p. 104.

of meaning to a thing or idea if and only if the common sign is what the Other also perceives it to be. While this is an ontological description, it applies to the fundamental premise of language according to de Saussure. The signified and the signifier must be a shared value — not in the obvious sense of practical necessity, which is obvious, but as recognition of the other as oneself at least in the domain of knowledge, thought, and communication. "Although signification and signal are each, in isolation, purely differential and negative, their combination is in fact of a positive nature, it is, indeed, the other order of facts linguistic structure comprises. For the essential function of a language as an institution is precisely to maintain these series of differences in parallel."[134]

The chief artifact in the social stage (I2) is the most significant characteristic of its predecessor: the specular mirror which is now used to gaze at the self in the form of self-consciousness, which is a kind of dissonance in relations with the Other, who is indulging in the same mechanism. Both self and other have the urge or tendency, derived from this dissonance, to dissolve the conflict of alterity in the abducted stage (Ix), which is the successor to I2. "But in point of fact self consciousness is the reflection out of the being of the world of sense and perception, and is essentially the return from otherness."[135] Self consciousness is derived from the a posteriori world of empiricism, with its psychological sense of $t + s$. But it is the facticity of Dasein that over-arches the movement, providing a starting point of bare life (0I) and working through transformational dialectics to the terminus at Ix. "In this sphere, self-consciousness exhibits itself as the movement in which this antithesis is removed, and the identity of itself with itself becomes explicit for us."[136] When it becomes "explicit," it is no longer the "arguable" being or presence of the synthetic proposition of the self-as-persona.

As with Schoedinger's cat, we cannot perceive the proposition of parallel ontologies until we create a tool (speculum) to view it which works at any stage of ontic transformation because it is explicit, not an argument, which the discourse always is (being based on empirical knowledge). Wittgenstein shows the dual nature of the explicit proposition and its functionality in the context of the epistemology of

---

[134] de Saussure, Ferdinand. *Course in General Linguistics*. Chicago: Open Court 2008.
[135] Ibid., p. 105.
[136] Ibid., p. 105.

the self. "The sense of a proposition is its agreement and disagreement with the possibilities of the existence and nonexistence of the atomic facts."[137] The "atomic facts" are one and the same with Agamben's "bare life," Heidegger's "facticity," and Kant's "explicit" propositions. They all point to the reality beyond the mirror, whether in the mirror stage or in I2 and Ix where its artifact continues to function as self consciousness (though somewhat mitigated in Ix by the implantation of the core identity of the apparatus).

Hegel describes the movement of the Unchangeable (bare life) through experience, with its accumulation of artifacts both psychological and within Dasein. The accumulation he calls "wretchedness"[138], and which Badiou calls "excrescence." The movement — through ontic positions in the transformational sequence, along the line of the ontic thread, from one thread to another in a bifurcation or ligature — is driven by what he calls "unchangeable consciousness" which remains unaltered no matter what thresholds are crossed. This is necessary to rein in the eccentric movement of all dialectical passes so that, in the end, it is a clock movement and not an extensa ad infinitum. The extensa ad infinitum,on the one hand, create an uncrossable divide between 0 and 1, and either an infinite progression of stages beyond Ix, or no "unchangeable consciousness" in the sanctuary of bare life. Throughout the whole process there is the irritation of self consciousness as artifact from the mirror stage ("wretchedness," "excrescence"), the vis-a-vis of the first sense of I in the mirror stage in mutual gaze with the social sense of I that looks at itself as others look at it. "For the movement runs through these moments first, the Unchangeable is opposed to individuality in general; then, being itself an individual, it is opposed to another individual," yielding a sense of separation and finitude in being-as-subject and its relation to being-as-object.[139]

At last Hegel states almost what we see in the modified Lacanian developmental stages of the sense of I, but in such a way that we can see the "self interest" Socrates warned about in the final or eccentric position of Ix. Hegel describes the 0I, I1, I2, Ix transformation as a "threefold

---

[137] Wittgenstein, Ludwig. *Tractatus Logico-Philosophicus.* New York: Barnes & Noble, 203, p. 61.
[138] Hegel, G.W.F. A.V. Miller, trans. *Phenomenology of Spirit.* Oxford: Oxford U.P., 1977, p. 128.
[139] Ibid., p. 128.

relation this consciousness will have with its incarnate beyond: first as pure consciousness [0I]; second, as a particular individual who approaches the world in the forms of desire and work [I1, I2], and third, as consciousness that is aware of its own being-for-self."[140]

However, we must also consider what Badiou says about the ordinality of the multiple which he calls "the backbone of all ontology, because it is the very concept of Nature." His discussion of natural multiples focuses on the duality of "two," which "formalizes natural existent-duality."[141] Of course, within the region of Dasein if there is a, then there is b, and if there is b then there is c, and if there is c, then c is related to a as an ordinal. From this formula arise the multiplicity of things which, as we said at the very start of this discussion, comes into being when it crosses a certain linguistic threshold where it may be said about this thing that it is. Badiou calls the relationship "the link between language and the sayable of being [...]."[142] as the multiplicity of related things in the coming-into-being, language necessitates differentiation of the name of one thing and the next, one idea and the next, so that there may be, as de Saussure puts it, "difference," and thereby discrete language in which to express our social being-as-subject. In this way the world of Dasein is "constructed" one multiple at a time arising from duality "as a program for the complete mastery of the connection between formal language and the multiples, whose existence is tolerated."[143] The "toleration" of multiplicity is non other than the forbearance of the "wretchedness" of consciousness and the endurance of the "excresences" of temporality and the extensa.

The wretchedness is not to be underestimated, nor are the pleasures and rewards of one's discourse. For herein is the very "motor" of Dasein, what makes its wheels turn and the drama of one's existence unfold for everyone no matter what. The only non-trivial distinction, then, is whether self consciousness has been augmented (or indeed replaced) by cognizance of the duality of existence, and how this duality is coextensive and cannot be seen directly but only perceived and sometimes felt. A ligature often provides an alert, for it brings one ontic thread into another, always precipitating a crisis of realization which often then returns to the wretchedness of the monofilament until the next event. It is a rare individual

---

[140] Ibid., p. 130.
[141] Badiou, Alain. Being and Event. London: Continuum, 2007, pp. 132-3.
[142] Badiou, Alain. Being and Event. London: Continuum, 2007, pp. 133.
[143] Ibid., p. 133.

who maintains the dualistic perspective and even exploits the possibilities of parallel ontologies (which are exploited anyway, but unconsciously and therefore at a disadvantage). Hegel sees consciousness as facing an "enemy" in the sleep of the ontic monofilament.

"In the struggle of the heart and emotions the individual consciousness is only a musical abstract moment. In work and enjoyment which make this unsubstantial existence a reality, it can directly forget itself, and the consciousness of it own particular role in this realization is cancelled [sic] out by the act of thankful acknowledgment."[144]

The "act of thankful acknowledgment" takes place at the point of abduction, which is by its nature a kind of forgetting, a relief, a trade of consciousness (as excrescence from the I1-I2 speculation) for the substitution of the interests of the State and the social arch. But again, this is not an "infinite" process. It follows a modularity, where the abduction is in itself an expression of the always already existing Dasein, in its most insensitive mode, and therefore the only possible way out of the trap created when the I1 and I2 stages gaze into each others' self consciousness. Hegel says that "this cancelling-out" is in truth a return of consciousness into itself, and, moreover, "into itself as the actuality which it knows to be true."[145]

1.2 Transcendental self consciousness

Readers of Hegel, however, have been criticized for taking the idea of self-consciousness too far into the transcendental realm of the spiritual. It seems enough that it can "directly forget itself" at the Ix position; it need not be an Emersonian "oversoul" or Jungian hive mind to represent the relief that comes to the wretchedness of the I1-I2 mind in its paralyzing self consciousness. Zizek in particular would draw a limit on the conception of self-consciousness by enclosing it in a pale of the psychological and ontological rather than the transcendental. "The crucial mistake to be avoided is a grasp Hegelian self-consciousness as a kind of mega-Spirit controlling our history. Against this cliche, we should ephasize how Hegel is fully aware that 'it is the finite consciousness that the process of knowing

---

[144] Hegel, G.W.F. A.V. Miller, trans. *Phenomenology of Spirit*. Oxford: Oxford U.P., 1977, p. 135.

[145] Ibid., p. 135.

the spirit's essence takes place and that the divine self-consciousness thus arises.' "[146] Zizek shows that depending upon our frame of view in assessing the relative freedom or incarceration of the abducted persona, we may see both states (like seeing the live and dead cat alternately). "For example, when we bracket moral and aesthetic concerns, a human being appears as non-free, totally conditioned by the causal nexus; if, on the contrary, we bracket theoretical concerns, he or she appears as a free autonomous being. Thus antinomies should not be reified — the antinomic positions emerge through shifts in the subject's attitude."[147]

This is a most telling passage. If it is possible to see both ontic threads, the best that could be hoped for as a simultaneous vision is a kind of parallax view. In other words, the kind of "broken reed" image in a still pond where water refracts the view of the submerged portion of the reed, making it look broken at the water line. There are two lines — one above and one below. But as Zizek describes, it is much more likely to be alternating and negating views of the consciousness.

Furthermore, we may view consciousness as an excrescence of space and time, from which it arises, as both s + t and S + T. The two are superimposed on each other in our experience, neither of them absolute. For what we know as S is only defined by the extensa. Remove the extensa, and there is no space. The same is true of time. Remove the measurement of it, whether by the rhythms of natural phenomana such as the rising and setting of the sun, or by articifical measurement, and there is little to hold it to a quantized phenomenon with the certain attribute. Also, if we look to the changes in the extensa, and in the furniture of the world, we may conclude that that too is an indication of time, but that is only if we do not take into consideration quantum mechanics and the impossibility of defining a particular point on the line of a wave, so that events which seem to occur in sequence in fact happen simultaneously but in a parallax view as Zizek describes it, forming the illusion of sequence. Kant concurs: "[T]hose who maintain the absolute reality of time and space, whether as essentially subsisting, or only inhering, as modifications, in things, must find themslves at utter variance with the principles of experience itself."[148]

As a priori, S + T contain everything but have no attributes, and are,

---

[146] Zizek, Slavoj. *Parallax View*. Cambridge: MIT Press, 2009, p. 65.

[147] Ibid., p, 50.

[148] Kant, Immanuel. *Critique of Pure Reason*. New York: Barnes & Noble, 2004, p. 12.

rather, parallax views of each other in that the extensa seem to need the "time" to extend and change, whereas time needs the extensa to be seen and heard. "[I]f they [...] make space and time into substances [...] they must admit two self-subsisting nonentities, infinite and eternal, which exist (yet without there being anything real) for the purpose of containing in themselves everything that is real."[149]

2.1 Space and time as synthetic propositions

Though S + T are a priori, are one, are not multiples, but contain everything, they are nevertheless synthetical propositions. In a sense they are the ultimate discourse because it is the extensa-as-language which create them and is in turn created by them. The subject-predicate (s-p) relationship in its deep structure (not its universal grammar) both mimics S + T and fabricates it in a cycle of coming-into-being, expressed thus, where →is, if then, (T + S) → (s-p). Kant's words on space apply to time as well: "Space is essentially one, and multiplicity in it, consequently the general notion of spaces, of this and that space, depends solely upon limitation. Hence it follows that an a priori intuition (which is not empirical), lies at the root of our conception of space."[150] The dependent limitation here is subjectivity in the form of its consciousness of multiplicity: "If we depart from the subjective condition [...] the representation of space has no meaning whatsoever."[151] Although what Kant says about space must necessarily apply to time, it is worth considering his verdict on the substance of time as a proposition: "Time is therefore merely a subjective condition of our (human) intuition (which is always sensuous, that is, so far as we are affected by objects), and in itself, independently of the mind or subject, is nothing."[152]

S + T provide us with the structure to create language, which in turn creates the "multiplicity" of S + T. This reciprocal process is the essential engine of discourse (or "the" discourse and all its threads). As each ontic thread is a discourse in and of itself punctuated with micro and macro events, the twining together of these monofilaments creates one Discourse,

---

[149] Ibid., p. 12.
[150] Ibid., p. 4.
[151] Kant, Immanuel. *Critique of Pure Reason*. New York: Barnes & Noble, 2004, p. 5.
[152] Ibid., p. 10.

though this story has no other name and cannot be written or pointed to because it is built entirely upon what Kant calls "nothing," and is a tale told by what Heidegger calls "no one." So then it is *nothing* told by *no one*. Therefore, all tales that are the stories of our lives, and the stories of the lives of peoples, and the stories of the religions and of the newspapers all arise as they do for the novelist and playwright: from nothing at all. The strangeness of a creative work to its own author attests to the "no one" behind it. It is as if, in beholding what we have created, we step back and ask where it came from because there is no feeling of possession — perhaps disappointment or awe, but not a sense of ownership. Which, on a larger scale, creates some serious concerns in societies based upon the idea that intellectual output is the "property" of its author when all that anyone can prove is that it was written, not where it came from in the forensic sense.

This "nothing/no one" is at the root of what Kant calls the "dialectical illusion." It should be pointed out now, as it was not earlier, that "dialectical" simply means "two speeches," as in "two lectures," though the prefix "dia" in this context also carried the implication of opposition, as in "diametric," or of two opposed values in inverse ratio. The diametric of the dialectical illusion is the use of the categorical distinction (sorting "nothing" into categories, which are "something" as both taxonomy and mathematical value), and *of what Kant calls the Transcendental Dialectic, which is, at last the critique of pure reason*, "not meaning it as an art of producing dogmatically such illusion [...] but as a critique of understanding and reason in regard to their hyperphysical use" which is further termed "sophistical illusion."[153]

2.2 Subject-predicate as space-time analog

What will now be explored is the predicate as coming-into-being. From the nothing/no one comes what Heidegger calls an "assertion" or a "pointing out"[154] For this purpose we will begin by looking at the German word *ragt*, meaning *projects*, towers over, or that it juts (*ragt heraus, ragt hervor*). If we conceive of S + T as xy vectors, with T(y) being the horizontal, *ragt* is the diagonal index projecting from the crux of the two in equal proportion

---

[153] Ibid., p. 28.
154 Heidegger, Martin. *Being and Time*. New York: Harperperennial Modernthought, 2008, p. 155.

to the extension of xy. What juts, is entirely dependent upon coming-into-being as the *excrescence* of xy. The *ragt* (z) juts from the crux of xy as the predicate juts from the subject of a sentence. The subject contains the S + T components in the form of the noun (extensa) and the verb (temporality), as in "John waits." Both John (n) and waits(v) can be measured, are sufficiently differentiated in the de Saussurean sense, and form a complete statement without predicate, and can therefore be expressed thus: [x(n) + y(v) = z].

Heidegger breaks the process of assertion into three principles:

1) The primary signification of "assertion is *"pointing out"* [Aufzeigen]
2 "Assertion" means no less than *"predication."*
3 "Assertion" means *communication.*[155]

Each of these propositions is based on the *xyz* vectors. Before they are explored, however, it is useful to say a few words about the subject-predicate relationship. In talking about "categories" we are inevitably constrained by Aristotle's categories of predication. Without going into detail here regarding the taxonomy of these categories in a discussion essentially of discourse, we may say that the predicate tells us something (a story) about the subject. The subject stands as "bare life," whereas the multiplicity of coming-into-being arises in the predicate. However, we may say that in fact the subject arises from the *pre*dicate (hence the prefix "pre") because the subject would not *ragt* from S + T were it not that there was something to "point out" about it. We have already seen that ordinality in the concatenation of parts of speech is trivial (as in S-V-O versus O-V-S languages). What is nontrivial is the relationship of the parts to make semantic "communication" through what Heidegger calls "predication." Lyon, quoting Sapir, says, "There must be something to talk about and something must be said about this subject of discourse [....] The subject of discourse is a noun [....] No language wholly fails to distinguish noun and verb [...]."[156]

It is not necessary to make much of a case for sentence grammar

[155] Heidegger, Martin. *Being and Time*. New York: Harperperennial Modernthought, 2008, p. 155-6.
[156] Lyon, John. *Introduction to Theoretical Linguistics*. Cambridge: Cambridge U.P., 1979, pp. 334-5.

following the path of formal logic, as we are surrounded by machines which interact with us through speech using this very relationship as the basis of their speech production. However, it is worth noting that from the predicate we "assert" the multitude of micro events along the ontic thread, as well as the macro events. Subject and predicate in fact create the "dialectical illusion" of space-time, in which they "then" arise as coming-into-being, leaping the threshold of the categorical exclusion $0 \rightarrow 1$. "They both made appeal to the Aristotelian doctrine of the categories of predication, which gave a philosophical basis to the view that the world *is populated* with individual persons, animals and things (substances) and that these substances are either the initiators or the victims ('agents' or 'patients') of *activities and processes*, are endowed with certain qualities, are *situated in particular places*, are *subject to change*, and so on [Italics added]."[157]

From the passage above it is not difficult to see the artifacts of S + T in the assertion of the predicate. In particular, the phrases "situated in particular places" (S) and "subject to change" (T) show the *ragt* of coming-into-being.

In this context, Heidegger's three propositions should be considered briefly. First, the "pointing out" as "signification" describes in de Saussurean terms, precisely what a sign is in its most fundamental form: a pointer, for example "verlassen" or "exit" or "way out" over a door. Second, Heidegger equates as material equivalents "predicate" and "assertion," and by association we may add *ragt*, as the predicate "juts" into the world from the subject-vector of n + v. Finally, he makes "communication" the equivalent of assertion, a word not often used in this context as much as "discourse." However, the word will be made good use of soon enough here. "Every predication is what it is, only as a pointing-out. The second signification of 'assertion' has its foundation in the first. Within this pointing-out, the elements which are Articulated in predication — the subject and predicate — arise."[158] As communication, then, the predicate comes into being by letting someone see with us what we have pointed out by way of giving it a definite character.[159] Often discussion of linguistics tends to forget that language is communication, and as such requires a transmitter (subject) and receiver (object). And of course the *response* is then a

[157] Ibid., p. 339.
[158] Heidegger, Ibid., p. 197.
[159] Ibid., p. 197.

negation of the first arrangement so that there is never really a subject and object but rather, as Kant asserts, "no one." The subject and object (predicate) of a sentence are related just as interpersonal proximities are related as subject-object. The correlation is nontrivial for the very reason Heidegger chooses the word communication over discourse (which technically does not imply an exchange of words, as do "dialectic" and "communication").

What gives the predicate its "pre" is that the content of the structure, following the noun-subject, is informed with mimetic impressions which are then subject to Zipf's Law, with the most frequently used and agreed-upon impressions expressed from a hierarchy of mutually-agreed-upon signs. "[W]e may define 'assertion' as a *'pointing-out which gives something a definite character and which communicates.'* " It is magnanimous of Heidegger to recognize the requisite interplay of the subject and object as living embodiments of the subject-predicate relationship. By doing so he also acknowledges the progressive fallacy in the sense that the linearity of S-V-O breakdown in the reciprocity of the subject and predicate, just as the linearity of progression breaks down in the subject-object relationship interpersonally, or in the "here-there" and "now-then" of space-time. "When an assertion is made, some fore-conception is always implied: but it remains for the most part inconspicuous, because the language already hides in itself a developed way of conceiving [space and time]. Like any interpretation whatever, assertion necessarily has a fore-having, a fore-sight, and a fore-conception as its existential foundation."[160]

What is needed to "see" the form-of-life as simultaneous parallel ontologies (SPO's)? First, the progressive fallacy must be grasped. If the predicate follows the subject (as it does in machines synthesizing S-V-O-languages), then there is a ratio between the two in an ordinal sense. The view can be expanded by zooming out so that we see, for example, a page of text with its paragraphs and pages (pages being the most arbitrary "limitation" imposed on discourse).

When we turn to speech, though, which is the sole concern of this discussion in the way of language production, the situation grows far more complex. As mentioned earlier, speech is subject to the vicissitudes of interaction, feedback, anticipation, signaling in every form from tone of

---

[160] Heidegger, Martin. *Being and Time*. New York: Harperperennial Modernthought, 2008, p. 199.

voice to physical gesture accompanying the speech-act. (Here speech is meant literally, by the way, and not as a catchall for writing too.) A speech-act is an act of speaking. Therefore, the speech-act is performative in the sense that the receiver actually creates the discourse, not the transmitter, by selective perception and subjective interpretation in the Heideggerian sense. It could not be any other way, for there is no verifiability in the speech-act, and there is no objectivity in the subject by definition in the moment of performance.

Next, in a related matter, we must be disengaged from the apparent linearity of discourse. This apparition is a hangover from the excessive imbibing of printed text which creates the illusion, because of our bias in the realm of relative physicality, of substance. Although speech also involves the physical universe in the form of billiard-like knocking about of molecules of air to *transduce* sounds articulated by vocal chords and other physical organs, it is still superstitiously regarded as inferior to text when in fact it is vastly superior in many respects and is the basis of text. This primitive bias is what Kant calls the "hyperphysical use" of understanding and reason (already quoted).

So the *combinatorics* of acknowledgment of the progressive fallacy and the assignment of linearity to text alone frees us to appreciate the form-of-life as having more than one ontic filament, with all the complexity in cognition which arises from that recognition.

2.3 *Ready-to-hand* as subject, *present-at-hand* as predicate

The subject of a sentence *does*. It is a noun *doing* something with something, even if that something is itself (e.g John waits). As such it is ready-to-hand, as a hammer is ready-to-hand for a carpenter. The predicate is not read-to-hand because it is not ready at all by itself. It lacks the necessary synthetic propositions of space and time as its *performative* context. "When an assertion has given a definite character to something present-at-hand, it says something about it as a 'what'; and this 'what' is drawn from that which is present at hand as such."[161] We may construct a sentence from this

---

[161] Heidegger, Martin. *Being and Time*. New York: Harperperennial Modernthought,

generative relationship using the subject phrase mentioned earlier: John waits (ready-to-hand) + for the train (present-at-hand [what]) + (adjunct) to Chicago, with the concatenation of $n + v + n + v + n$. Note the nature of the concatenation of parts of speech. As noted earlier, in number creation we may use Peano's formula of $n + 1$ to create any number, which would give us a concatenation of $n + 1 + n + 1 + n$ (etc.). According to Chomsky, English (and its relatives) is not a finite state language from the point of view of the Markov process.[162] Therefore, the repetitive structure of the language can be summarized by $(n + v)$. Again, we have a binary, not a ratio and not an infinitely variable structure, only an infinitely expressive structure which uses the same formation for all of its utterances. In short, herein we find what Chomsky and others have called Universal Grammar.

If we look at both formulas: $(n + 1)$ and $(n + v)$, we note that each side of each equation is conjoined by a symbol which might properly be called the copula, or something that couples the values. However, in speaking of the subject and predicate, the meaning takes on a new implication: that of generation, and is not isolated to a bare symbol of conjunction. Rather, it takes on the meaning of "to copulate," to generate something from, alas as Kant and Heidegger have pointed out, no one/nothing. The phrase, then, of $(n + v)$ may be taken as the copula generating the predicate (which is also concatenated as $[n + v]$). This is one aspect of "generative grammar" as it arises from the vectors of time (y) and space (x) as "z," the pro-predicate from which the next link in the concatenation then draws its generative power and so on. "When we consider this 'bond' [the *copula*], it becomes clear that proximally the synthesis-structure is regarded as self-evident, and that is has also retained the function of serving as a standard for Interpretation."[163]

So both the subject and predicate are "generative" in their structure, but only the subject provides the vectors xy to produce z. How can the "what" be generative too? It is in its basal deep structure, but possesses no a priori as does the subject, which "is." To "be," the subject must be a product of the a priori as coming-into-being, which the predicate is not. The predicate remains generative to provide for the next step, or iteration,

---

2008, p. 200.

[162] Chomsky, Noam. *Syntactic Structures*. The Hague: Mounton Publishers, 1975, p. 21.

[163] Heidegger, Martin. *Being and Time*. New York: Harperperennial Modernthought, 2008, p. 202.

of the schema. Adjuncts have no power to generate, and may be extended and elaborated upon *ad libitum* without affecting the chain. It is for this reason that incomplete sentences, though they may communicate some sense, are not generative, thereby breaking the chain, as in "The girl next door." We know precisely what this means in all its rich denotation and connotation, but there is not the slightest indication of what is to follow, what might follow, or how it is to be followed, creating a *non sequitur.*

3.1 Existential priority of discourse

Without making too fine a point about it, let it suffice to say that the coming-into-being of the subject-predicate as *"ragt,"* constitutes the "being there" of existence in its extension into the space of time. "[T]his phenomenon has its roots in the existential constitution of Dasein's disclosedness. *The existential ontological foundation of language is discourse or talk,* "[164]making abduction an existential necessity, and the state of exception an a priori as the sovereign is always already in such a state and no other state exists that is not in this state of all states. *"Discourse is existentially equiprimordial with state-of-mind and understanding"* because it is thought, and thought is language.[165] That Heidegger understands discourse as arising from the a priori is seen in the term primordial above. What we are looking at are the hydra heads of S + T as infinitely generative synthetic propositions, which is why Kant and others consider the synthetic proposition to be the generative engine of art with its conflation of the interpretive and literal.

In any case, existence itself, according to Ayer, is a synthetic proposition at least in its assertion in the Heideggerian sense, putting *existence-as-extensa* as always already a form of subjectivity, hence the origin in *no one/nothing,* for "there are no objects whose existence is indubitable," he says, "since existence is not a predicate, [and] to assert that an object exists is always to assert a synthetic proposition [...]."[166]

[164] Ibid., p. 161
[165] Heidegger, Martin. *Being and Time.* New York: Harperperennial Modernthought, 2008, p. 203.
[166] Ayer, A.J. *Language, Truth and Logic.* New York: Dover Publications Inc., ND, p. 121.

3.2 Discourse as language and thought

It is not necessary to make an elaborate argument regarding the nature of discourse as language and thought. However, it needs mention. In the end, this is the most significant finding of the investigation. That the very words before you, and the thoughts you have about them, are all part of the discourse that is both shared through the negation of the subject-object dichotomy, and individual through the origin or personality (in the technical sense) from the primordial state of 0I through the transformational states of I1 and I2. The final question of abduction (Ix) is a given: the sovereign is already in a state of exception. We are already within the set of all sets of the state of exception, both included and excluded in the basal structure of SPO, reading life as micro and macro events along as many filaments as we can discern in the progress of the story.

The Being which is "thrown and submitted to the world" as Dasein, is asserted (ragt) through language. What Heidegger means by "language" is not any part of it, sentence, speech, text, or any discrete dimension of communication but is, rather, the *facticity* of communication itself. "The way in which discourse gets expressed is language. Language is a totality of words — a totality in which discourse has a 'wordly' being of its own; and as an entity within-the-world, this totality thus becomes something which we may come across ready to hand."[167] It is not hard to see here that the relationship between discourse and Dasein is intimate, as discourse is a form of Dasein (which has no form) that asserts. What is asserted is something said, a reflection of multiplicity, and in this "something said," the discourse communicates.[168]

As the set of all sets which does and does not include itself, there is not much more we can say to describe Dasein, for it is without attribute (but contains all attributes about which we may say "this belongs to Dasein"). Discourse gives us the spectacular opportunity to explore its rich attributes, which is the ultimate object of this study, rather the way a scientists may look at a trace of a sub-atomic particle on a piece of photosensitive film, but cannot "see" it directly. This is entirely Schrodedinger's point in the cat paradox; as has been said, the paradox was already well known. Rather it was the demonstration of how nano events are reflected into the macro environment, just as discourse reflects Dasein in the same.

---

167 Heidegger, Ibid., p. 204.
168 Ibid., p. 205.

Heidegger, then, attempts to know more about Dasein by looking at its "cat paradox" in four ways. These are the "attributes" of discourse.

1) What is the discourse about (what is talked about).
2) What is said in the talk, as such.
3) The communication [itself].
4) The making-known.

In the first we are concerned with the attribute of the "story," for instance is the tale about who was at last night's event, what will be done soon, how something got the way it is. In short, we may say that 1 is concerned with who, when, where, what, why, and how. These six attributes (excluding the six basic actors — which we will discuss in Part 5), provide enough information about an event to know what it is "about." In 2 we discern the details of the tale, not so much what happened as what is the furnishing of the tale, the multitude of its content. In 3 there is the *facticity* of the message as a thing; for example, a speech, a postal letter, a dialogue or even dialectic, and its rhetorical form. In 4 there is the propagation, for there is no message without a receiver. The receiver *is* the message, not the sender, so if there is no receiver there is no message. In other words, everything about the communication (as thing) is determined by the nature of the receiver, from the semantic content to the national language in which the content is couched. Heidegger concurs: "Hearing is constitutive for the discourse."[169]

As such, then, Dasein (though in the transmitter too) is most attentive in the listener as the one who must understand, who determines everything about the message and without whom the message does not exist whether it is created or not. "Dasein hears because it understands, " says Heidegger. "As a being-in-the-world with others, a Being which understands, Dasein is 'in thrall' to Dasein-with and to itself; and in this thraldom it 'belongs' to these."[170] Dasein, being always already negative, is essentially understanding which is proximally alongside what is understood, so that it provides the springboard from which the subject leaps off [ragt] and finally arrives at the world.[171]

---

[169] Heidegger, Martin. *Being and Time*. New York: Harperperennial Modernthought, 2008, p. 163.
[170] Ibid., p. 206.
[171] Ibid., p 164.

3.3 The "making known"

Which brings us to the topic of propaganda in the sense of the propagation of messages. It is the the "making known," or fourth characteristic of discourse. As such it is categorically different from 1, 2, and 3 because it is not concerned with the creation of the message but rather the dissemination of it after it was created. There are two aspects to the propagation of messages: rhetoric and mass media. The first is the form or format of the message, and the second is the medium or channel through which the message travels. The discussion of propaganda also brings us to a modified definition of discourse: as the sum of a message and a medium. While it has been said here that the message is everything and the medium hardly matters, we must also consider that the medium — as with everything else about the message — was chosen not by transmitter but by the receiver. Choose the wrong medium and the message will not get through. A message that does not reach the receiver does not exist. Communication is an inductive process.

While the medium is not significant in and of itself (books have caused more revolutions than TV, film, and the Internet), combined with the message it creates a "semiogram," which is similar to a hypertext packet with its message and internet protocol bundled inseparably together; the IP address and the packet with its packet switching gets the message to where it is supposed to go, but does not necessarily determine the message's content (as some would have it). Rather, how a message is propagated will determine how well Dasein "hears" it, or whether or not it will hear it at all, which in the end is everything. "In language, as a way things have been expressed or spoken out [*Ausges prochenheit*], there is hidden a way in which the understanding of Dasein has been interpreted. This way of interpreting it [Dasein] is no more just present-at-hand than language is; on the contrary, its Being is itself of the character of Dasein."[172] Leading to the axiom: discourse which expresses itself is communication, and what does not is not.

4.1 Time as superimposition of states

Returning to homo generator and his priorities, we find that this persona is fundamentally different from his counterparts in the *everydayness* of the

---

[172] Heidegger, Martin. *Being and Time*. New York: Harperperennial Modernthought, 2008, p. 211.

world because he has lived and lives more than one ontology simultaneously. The subject-object dichotomy remains, but in a state oscillating with such rapidity that it seems to be one state that is both simultaneously just as it seems that motion in cinema is continuous when in fact it may be oscillating at 24 frames per second between nothing and something (yet another binary negation). As such, Godel's "incompleteness" theorem comes into effect where we may treat the discourse as Dasein, independent of the distinctions of transmitter and receiver, subject and object, time and space, becoming for the subject-persona "reality." Heidegger describes the indefinable incompleteness of Dasein: "It is still possible that one may give the problematic of Reality *priority* over any orientation in terms of 'standpoints' by maintaining the thesis that every subject is what it is only for an Object, and *vice versa*. But in this formal approach the terms thus correlated — like the correlation itself — *remain ontologically indefinite* [final italics added]."[173]

Homo generator remains at the point of Hegel's Second Negation, where the negation has been negated, yielding a positive assertion of what is in the world ready-to-hand and present-at-hand among the furniture of Dasein. We may equate the Second negative to the oscillation of the persona between positions I2 and Ix; one recursion (I2 → Ix, Ix → I2) is enough to invoke the Second Negation because Ix is a negation of I2 and vice versa, yielding the Second Negation expressed thus: (I2 → Ix, Ix → I2, I2 → Ix)Q, where Q is the Second Negation. Oscillation is expressed thus and contains n amount of negations: (I2 ↔ Ix)n, oscillation itself being a form of mediation. "The *mediated* relation constitutes the essence of the negative movement which in consciousness turns against its particular individuality, but which, *qua relation*, is *in itself positive*, and will bring consciousness itself to an awareness of its *unity* with the Unchangeable."[174]

In quantum mechanics, certain assumptions made in everydayness are suspended in favor of certain and uncertain axioms. Principal is the assumption that space and time are the same phenomenon seen in different ways. Why this is not the prevailing view is that other views with indefinite but greater history have priority as iconic views. An iconic or monolithic view tends to propagate like dead leaves blown from a tree, each essentially identical, easily establishing priority and holding on to it with a smothering

---

[173] Ibid., p. 252.
[174] Hegel, G.W.F. A.V. Miller, trans. *Phenomenology of Spirit.* Oxford: Oxford U.P., 1977, p. 136.

blanket of received "wisdom." However, the equiprimordial polyvalence of T + S (or S + T) is at the core of Dasein, Kant's a priorae, and the idea of SPO's.

In quantum mechanics, states are superimposed upon each other, eradicating the need for isolating an event in time or even the location of an event, which as has been mentioned before are on the sub-nano scale and may be considered "the smallest" or "the shortest" events possible.

"The quantum principle of superimposition states that any 'micro-objectual state' — or motion of particles that atomic systems are made of — may be considered as the superimposing of one or more states, leading to different results observable at different times (but not to a predeterminable, sole, objective result); hence one must no longer expect any model to exist, at least in the usual sense of the word."[175]

The questions we ask when speaking from Newtonian physics and its antecedents regarding (S + T) are 1) Did the event happen at point a or point b or at both points (ab), and 2) when did the event happen, at time a or time b or at both times (ab). The situation is more or less complicated for homo generator in the *Second Negation*, indicated as Q: "In quantum physics [...] the superimposition of the microstates A, B, gives as a result, now a, now b (but one cannot say in what order in *time*). This enables one to obtain a new objective condition (Q) giving the *result* in tn, sometimes as *a* and sometimes as *b*, *which nullifies all usual orders of time* [final italics added]."[176]

Here was have the makings of an existential crisis for the subject at the position of Ix, and it is precisely at this position the subject is in need of a new paradigm outside abduction, which we call Q. "Beyond" abduction makes no sense for Ix is a terminal state. But it is this very quality of a *cul-de-sac* that leverages the recursion resulting in Q, a "new objective condition." The fundamental rift in the discourse begins here (and note that "discourse" and "the discourse" are used interchangeably, as are "persona" and "subject") when *disjunction* (a ^ b) and *material implication* (a + b) are subverted by the new paradigm. "Since disjunction and material implication are basic structures in traditional logic, the quantum theory marks the beginning of a crisis in classical logic" and therefore in the structure of discourse.[177]

---

[175] Spisani, Franco. *The Meaning and Structure of Time*. Bologna: Azzoguidi, 1972, p. 9.
[176] Ibid., p. 11.
[177] Ibid., p. 13.

4.2 The metalogic of the semiogram

We may already know what the new paradigm is for quantum logic and Q, but then we can only guess at it. It may be called "metalogic" in the meantime as it is expressed mathematically, which has been done here and there throughout this discussion in looking at the Markov chain, the Galois lifting, and Tanayama-Shimura conjecture, Godel's incompleteness theorem, and homo generator's Q position of oscillation between I2 and Ix. It has taken a scramble up those foothills to be able to begin the search for a new form of language which we may have only glimpsed in poetry, certain fiction, the literature of philosophy, and most of all in mathematics. "Our goal is to establish the meta-ontological thesis that mathematics is the historicity of the discourse on being qua being," says Badiou.[178] According to Spisani, metalogic is a language that "presupposes a new form of logic working according to the autoreflection (*differentiating*) of the *identicalmoment* (a or b) and involving a special way of succession, in an objective time (Tn), as far as possible ignoring the observer's *subjective time* [tn] [...]."[179]

The "autoreflection" of the "identical moment" must preclude t (subjective time) in favor of no time at all (~T) at least in the practical ready-to-hand sense. This is not an amorphous "timelessness" sought after by spirituality. Rather, it is a modified, flexible, and non-absolute time resonant with Kant's pronouncement of T being a synthetic proposition and "nothing" at all. As language begins to reflect discourse disengaged from the Aristotelian paradigm of logic (e.g. the middle is no longer "excluded"), then a new paradigm arises in Dasein, though Dasein remains unchanged except for this. What changes is the topology of discourse, the furniture of Dasein replaced and rearranged, so that art, literature, history, science, technology, medicine, mathematics and even music enter a new plane of autoreflection which holds the object as its subject rather than the subject as its subject. "An operative plane does exist as a matter of fact, which can be objectified in time beyond the *observer*. It is not hypothesized, as being independent of classical inferential rules,"[180] for tn continues to "exist" as psychological time, and Tn remains as the excrescence of nothing (a priori). What changes is the monofilament of ontology, which now may exist in

---

[178] Badiou, Alain. *Being and Event*. London: Continuum, 2007, p. 13.
[179] Spisani, Ibid., p. 15.
[180] Spisani, Franco. *The Meaning and Structure of Time*. Bologna: Azzoguidi, 1972, p. 17.

phasic, a phasic, or contraphasic, states in the observable multiverse.

The semiogram — medium + content — is a topological feature of discourse which defines the gestalt of the message. While this gestalt may be received in different ways depending upon the frame of the receiver, it is nonetheless the whole of the communication once it is no longer the possession of the transmitter. Metalogic takes into consideration the semiotic power of the semiogram, for instance in the formula: $(m + c) \equiv d$, or medium and content are the material equivalent of discourse. As it is the receiver who determines not only the form but the content of the message — not the transmitter — the semiogram is at once how the message is transmitted and what the receiver expects that it contains.

It has been said that "the medium is the message," but that is not the case at all. Rather, it is the gestalt of the message that is what is ultimately received, and the gestalt is determined by the receiver. The semiogram makes it possible to transmit the message in a discrete packet, as in packet switching, allowing the quantization of messages to produce such marvels as film and video that are in fact quanta (24 frames per second, for example) and not "waves" in the sense that an electromagnetic oscillation is, ultimately, continuous, or that — perhaps more to the point — space and time are continuous and contiguous. Popper, quoted in Spisani, indicates a correlation in kind: "There exists but one rather elusive idea of '*correspondence between a statement and a fact.*' "[181] In the case of the semiogram, the statement is the medium and the speech act is the content of the message (*not* "the message" itself).

4.3 Indeterminability of p and q

Returning to Osgood's third generalization, that opposing propositions will assume a dominant and subdominant oppositional relationship[182], space and time, as the components of the semiogram, reduce each other in proportion to the distance between the transmitter and the receiver — and by "distance" here is meant not the physical distance but the semiotic distance to what degree the frame of the transmitter agrees with the frame of the receiver. If there is little agreement, then there is much negotiation

---

[181] Ibid., p 17, f. 17.

[182] *"At all levels of language organization, whenever there are competing means of achieving some criterion of communication performances, these competing means will be related inversely as a compensating system."*

in the interpretation of the message. "[G]iven two quantum *variables p* and *q* (the one relating to *time*, the other to *space*), the more the value of one of them is defined, the less can the value of the other be determined."[183] The reason is that the values are indeterminable, which is the adjective applied to the principle of Godel's incompleteness theorem. It seems impossible to assign an exact numerical value to values that are practically indeterminable. One concludes that when, in the case of *p* and *q*, the one is perfectly determined the other will be complete indeterminable.[184]

What makes the *determinability* such a concern in the communication is the ultimate success of what the discourse intends. For despite the fact that the receiver more or less determines what is in the message and how the message is transmitted, the concomitant fact remains that the discourse of the message, what is actually extracted from it, was in part crafted by the subjective frame of the transmitter. This subjective frame is none other than the conjunction of s + t, or the psychological sense of space and time, which is a posteriori. The a priori of S + T, which is the ultimate fact of the subject and object as transmitter and receiver, is the parent of the s + t child. The psychological sense of the vectors provides the "noise" which helps characterize the negotiation of the discourse, making no two messages alike as their frames upon receipt are in constant flux. Thus, "there is no available and adequate form of mathematics and logic, capable of explaining sufficiently the connection between (tn) and (Tn), or between *objective* space (Sn) and the *observer's space*, (sn) in which those 'contents' should move."[185] Nevertheless, says Spisani, the precise dynamic between *a priori* space and time remains mysterious, particularly in how it is expressed mathematically except to say that in communication the relationship appears to be inverse. What connection is there between objective *space* and *time*? To such questions the operational methods of *microphysics* cannot give an answer.[186]

The speechlessness of "classical mathematics and logic" in the face of homo generator's milieu begs for a metalogic. The discrepancy has much to do with the confusion over a priori and a posteriori T(t) + S(s) in the discourse extending from the assumptions made about our world and its physics and

[183] Ibid., p. 21.
[184] Spisani, Franco. *The Meaning and Structure of Time*. Bologna: Azzoguidi, 1972, p. 21.
[185] Ibid., p. 23.
[186] Ibid., p. 25.

technology. Phrases such as "in the future" belie the simplicity with which the frontier of epistemology is regarded. The affect on how discourse is generated and received pervades nearly every utterance, but in particular public discourse in the forms generated by government, the church, schools, banking, and most of all the mass media.

"From the simple attempts at abstraction and 'generalization' of common concepts — and of the speech of classical physics — spring uncertainties of calculus in *extra-empirical reality*, the confusion between *objective time* and *time* of the observer, the indeterminacy, in the spatio-temporal connection and [...] the crisis of *quantum mechanics* as a crisis in traditional *logic* and *mathematics*."[187]

Previously, utterances were subject to testing such as Aristotle's Rules of Thought, and positivism's *verifiability*. Now such testing is lost in the confusion over $S(s) + T(t)$, for when we peer into the box containing Schroedinger's cat, we end up in an epistemological argument over the state of the cat as living or dead, with at last a random difference of judgment or an equally random concurrence. The problematic here is the necessity of the true or false proposition which works well in conditional branching (*If a is true then p, if a is false then q*) in the design of applied logical systems such as computers, but stalls when we consider what kind of logic it is that can say that a is both true and false — not figuratively or because of a lack of information but ontologically so! Ultimately, the logic of the everydayness of discourse gradually falls out of descriptive synchronization with the realities of quantum physics, "in particular its relation to indeterminacy —, logic must be wrong (instead of simply recognizing the inadequacy of that type of logic which is called classical logic)."[188]

However, what the Rules of Thought and verifiability share in their suspicions about statements concerning the world is their disdain for the empirical. As Kant describes, the empirical statement rests upon t + s as psychological time, which is a posteriori and presumes the subject/object in the simplest sense. Logic seems to have been created to be used as a tool to escape from the gravitational force of empiricism. So why is the "scientific method" based on empirical observation even with the logical controls it touts? The reason is the priority of the "true" and "false" statement in relation to the hypothesis being tested. There is no end to the mayhem caused by this priority. For instance, the Nazis considered the proposition

---

[187] Ibid., p. 27.
[188] Ibid., p. 29.

"What is wrong with Germany is the Jews" to be true in the empirical, scientific, medical, ethical, economic, and juridical senses! And being at the time between 1940 and 1945 the greatest technologists on the planet, the applied sense of the empirical bore almost incontrovertable "proof" of its priority.

What is required for homo generator is what Spisani calls a "probabalistic turning point" meant to "resolve the antinomies of thought" that are "freed from overbearing empirical observations and from the Aristotelian-Galilean dogmatism of true and false —, an approach to logic which is neither traditional nor probabilitstic, aiming at new means of analysis in a renewed space-time definition."[189] What is being proposed here is a renewed space-time definition based on simultaneous parallel ontologies and the hardware and software that goes along with this definition. Spisani calls this correlation a binary correspondence that does not obviate classical physics and quantum theory, but that rather operates along two times — "and two spaces, calling for the parallel ontologies to be deduced to one only (α) to make a new calculus so that the process of self measure of its location in (Tn) may be evidenced."[190]

4.4 The simultaneity

Which brings up a new problem. But first it must be said that the idea of parallel ontic threads is not metaphoric but literal, as Spisani points out, since each thread is its own $T + S$ in what he calls the "objective" sense and what we have been referring to as the a priori. The problem dual ontic threads raises, though, is that of the mathematics. How are we to calculate in space and time with more than one track to account for? As has been mentioned above, that an ontic thread truncates or bifurcates is really an illusion, The collapse into a monofilament is merely another way of looking at ontology without the dualistic threads. It is rather like binocular vision which shows only one picture from two distinct images.

And this is a problem in thought, for what we make of existence is a matter of thought, which is the excrescence of language and the discourse. As things arise in the coming-into-being, they think of themselves as

[189] Spisani, Franco. *The Meaning and Structure of Time*. Bologna: Azzoguidi, 1972, p. 29.
190 Ibid., p. 31.

identity. If there is a teapot in an empty room it is still a teapot (whether it is "there" or not, or whether it is something else, is another matter). In other words, its "teapotness" is its identity. When it is regarded by the subject, it either remains a teapot or becomes something else — for instance "Mary's possession" or "something to boil water in with which I make anything but tea." Despite the rugged treatment it receives in the gaze of the subject, its objective identity remains intact. Spisani describes the object of thought as "identification," in that the object "thinks of itself" in the same way that the receiver determines the content of the message and the medium of transmission, and in its thinking of itself it retains its identity despite the subjective thoughts one may have about it. Is this not so? "The hypothesis can therefore be made that if point (α) 'thinks' of itself, it is able to identify itself, in a time which is it[s] own. That is, it moves in an objective time (Tn), the structure of which is independent of the *observer*."[191] Therefore, the T of the observed and the t of the observer are in *aphasic* relationship. The aphasia of space follows a similar path: "the identity of (α) where (α) corresponds to a change in time; and [with the] connection of the point with itself one arrives, also, at a different position in space."[192]

Although it would seem that *a priori* time would somehow be monolithic because of its primordiality, because of its synthetic nature (as described by Kant) T is only "a T," not "the T." The article is indefinite, the object of the article is indeterminate and undecidable.

"When the identity of (α) is denoted by 1 (one) and its *difference* 0 (zero), it is possible to admit that (α) has a dual behavior with respect to itself: the point (α), identical with respect to itself, is also *different*. Rather, it is so far as it is identical, that (α) is different, and this not only with respect to the result, but in the means of its indeterminacy."[193]

Here the conjunction of the categorical exclusion and the SPO's is clear. Spisani would collapse the binocular vision of the latter into a single value (α), but acknowledges that the thought-identity of the ontic threads remains a dualistic parallel as *difference*. The "dual behavior" could be described as 1(T1/T2) in its singularity and 0(T1/T2) in its *difference,* or Q in its totality as second negation.

The search for a metalogic, then, reaches a crisis when the observer

---

[191] Spisani, Franco. *The Meaning and Structure of Time*. Bologna: Azzoguidi, 1972, p. 33.
[192] Ibid., p. 73.
[193] Ibid., p. 33.

is determined to have inadequate ability to observe what is in the dualistic relationship, at least in mathematical terms (direct observation is not necessary but may occur, as long as it is taken for what it is: empiricism). The observer remains at the abducted, extrinsic position where the simultanaity of the relationship can only be perceived as difference. The question becomes: "Different in what ways?" And therein lies the need for a metalogic to describe it, a logic that is "proto" because it relies on the a priori as described by Kant rather than the *a posteriori* of the abducted observer at the eccentric position of Ix. What the observer fails to perceive in particular is that the positive (α) contains the negative position of $\sim$ (α), that is, the singularity of (α) is by its nature *not* a singularity. "The relation of (α) to (α) involves then $\sim$ (α), that is, the difference from (α), a difference that the observer does not detect in his result, because he makes use of a logic which limits investigation to the sphere of extrinsic relations"[194] which we can express by $[(\alpha) \rightarrow \sim (\alpha)]$, where ($\rightarrow \sim$) expresses *difference*.

So what is the indentity of the thingness of the thing in this equation for the observer? From the negation, identity *ragt* or "juts" from its 0I position across the spatiality of the threshold into the topology of the I1, I2, Ix concatenation. "If ($\sim \alpha$ stands for the difference from (α), then [$\sim$ ($\alpha\alpha$)] conveys the *difference* of the *difference*, that is the *identity*. If from (α) derives ($\alpha\alpha$) for the mentioned autoreflection, from ($\alpha\alpha$), differentiated though it may be, one returns to *identity*." In showing the thingness (identity) revealed by *difference, we* step into the territory of metalogic where it is possible to have two simultaneous singularities ($\alpha\alpha$). For homo generator, this territory is the second negation (Q). Therefore, we may express this intrinsic transformation as $[(\alpha) \rightarrow \sim (\alpha)] \equiv (\alpha\alpha)] \rightarrow Q$.

4.4.1 Intrinsic transformation as *pointing-out*

To say that a thing is, coming-into-being is necessary. There must be language to indicate this *coming-in*, which we call *pointing-out*. It has been mentioned above but is worth repeating here Heidegger's pointing-out of pointing-out: "[W]e may define 'assertion' as a '*pointing-out* *which gives something a definite character and which communicates*'."[195]

---

[194] Ibid., p. 35.
[195] Heidegger, Martin. *Being and Time*. New York: Harperperennial Modernthought, 2008, p. 199.

This definite character is what is called identity. Taking simultaneous singularities into account, though, another identity of pointing-out itself comes into being: pointing out as point, or position on the ontic threads. What is seen through metalogic, then, of the ontological nature of phenomena, is that it is always already intrinsic and therefore includes the extrinsic position but is always different in that it is not eccentric.

In the context of computing, identity would be called a "control point," or the point at which an operation is in the computational mode as a singular process. In modular mathematical theory, the point is the index of the equation where transformation occurs, sometimes even "splits" as in a Galois lifting. In quantum mechanics, though, it is an Event on the particle/wave that we may call the particle itself, or the "moment" when the particle changed its valence or orbit, or collided with another particle to product difference between states a and b. Without metalogic we will always think of this difference as linear, sequential, and both a predecessor and a successor to another state. In terms of Spisani's difference, though, these distinctions give rise to (α) as a singularity only, which turns the gaze from the possibility of parallel states. Therefore, the "point" takes on great significance as the locus of testing, testing of both reality and of our ability to perceive.

How we perceive it, then, determines everything about how we speak of the world. If how we speak of the world is not a reflection of what we know to be "true" about it from quantum mechanics and mathematics, how then can it be said that we speak of the world at all? What is it that we speak of then? As Kant shows, we then speak in synthetic propositions only, which would be fine except that we present these propositions as analytical, and in so doing drift into the dream of the eccentric, extrinsic, abducted position of discourse. "The identity of the point is, then, its difference from itself: the difference produced by the equal; but of an equal which endomorphically derives from itself the measure of difference. It does not establish it from the outside, but determines it in the inner "rhythms of its time and space."[196]

4.5 The meaninglessness of semantic meaning

Returning to language per se, we may say that the word is a "point" in the syntactic structure of the sentence. For, as de Saussure shows, what makes

---

[196] Spisani, Franco. *The Meaning and Structure of Time*. Bologna: Azzoguidi, 1972, p. 39.

a word a "word" is its discrete character or difference from other words; it is the difference from another word — semantically, graphemically, and phonologically — that gives it its unique identity as a statistically unique identifier or indicator of some particular idea. Nevertheless, on the morphological and syntactic levels, the word suddenly reveals its nature as a "part" of speech or a functionary in the concatenation of words. For example, in the statement "I am a teacher," what we are really saying, morphologically and syntactically is "n-v-n," or "noun-verb-noun" — Chomsky's basic unit of concatenation. As a proposition, we have A is A, Aristotle's fundamental truth of the Rules of Thought as tautology. While it yields us "a truth," it is certainly not "the truth." Description of the point using an indefinite article shows its generic nature or parts of speech alone, for we can question what is "I" and what is "teacher," even on the most basic level of "what kind of teacher are you?" or "are you a teacher who is teaching now, or one who used to teach?" These are worthwhile questions even in this context, which begin the unraveling of the point as anything definite, for, as Spisani says, "it is not possible to attribute precise material qualifications to the *point*."[197] What we are striving for here is what Spisani calls a logic (metalogic) that is profoundly contrary to traditional logic,[198] one that reflects the parallel singularities of quantum physics and the generality of Osgood in the behavior of parts of language. In as much as language's deep structure is logic, (*and, or, not, if/then*), we may wonder what this prological foundation of language would yield in terms of what is actually spoken. The guess is that it would far more approximate poetry (as speech in the works of Shakespeare serves as such but is in fact one long poem from first play to last).

5.1 The spatiality of discourse as topology

Tuan, also, finds expression of the intrinsic in literary and other works of art and the intellect. It seems that in the aesthetic of subject-object in the presentation of reality as the analyzed subject produces in the subject an acknowledgment of the its own subjectivity, imparting the emotion of truth. Since we cannot directly observe the true state of Schroedinger's

---

[197] Spisani, Franco. *The Meaning and Structure of Time*. Bologna: Azzoguidi, 1972, p. 41.
[198] Ibid., p. 41.

cat, we can at least feel the state as an intuition of the intrinsic position of the cat as being in simultaneous states. When we attempt to understand space, rather than time, extensa are no longer abstract. While time has its *extensa*(duration, incipience and senescence), they remain abstract because they are not "in space." Whereas the extensa in space seem "more real" because they can be pointed to. However, both space and time, as extensions of each other and the *xy vectors*of the same continuum and crux, are subject to the same rules only they are described differently, in particular in aesthetic productions. "[I]t is possible to articulate subtle human experiences. Artists have tried — often with success. In works of literature as well as in humanistic psychology, philosophy, anthropology and geography, intricate worlds of human experience are recorded."[199]

To talk about space and time (xy) in the same breath requires a sense of the aesthetic of the third vector (z), which is their product. It is aesthetic because the product is not directly one or the other but their output, their work, their artifice. Tuan also sees another principle at work in the construction of the aesthetic of space: emotion, which moves in a *contraphasic*motion from its inseparable companion thought. The goal of thought is conception, whereas the goal of emotion is the opposite: sensation, with a transitional region where thought and emotion intermingle like brackish water: perception. One may "think" that fire will burn the skin, but one must also "feel" that it will in the form of fear, otherwise, the chances of allowing oneself to be burned increase, never mind if one is also numb to the affect of fire, which is just a grosser "feeling" than fear. Therefore, emotion and thought run contrary to each other as SPO's in our perception of experience. It could be said that we neither think space nor feel it. Rather we perceive it, explore it, test it, think *about* it and feel *about* it . This singularity (α) is comprised of the duality of thought and emotion. "What can be known is a reality that is a construct of experience, a creation of feeling and thought."[200]

Tuan quotes Langer concerning the further duality of the conception and the sensation which lies at the root of thought and emotion. "The world of physics is essentially the real world construed by mathematical abstractions, and the world of sense is the real world constructed by the

[199] Tuan, Yi-Fu. *Space and Place: The Perspective of Experience*. Minneapolis: U. of Minnesota Press, 1977, p. 7.
[200] Ibid., p. 9.

abstractions which the sense organs immediately furnish."[201] What thought and emotion have incommon is their basis in abstractions which are arrived at through different mental organs. The difference is the same as that between time and space, as time is experienced through sensation (thought measured by clocks), and space is experienced through the geometry of topology, which is a rational and logical enterprise but nevertheless yields to the abstractions of the senses, which are all synthetical propositions (such as far-near, high-low, deep-shallow, beautiful-ugly). The evidence is in our aesthetical use of space (rather than time) as the basis of most figurative language — adding a synaesthetical quality to our interpretation of perception. We go *over* to someone's house, we *see* someone's *point*, we *dig* deeper into the matter, we *imagine* — a word strictly based on image alone and therefore the space-context.

Tuan uses the example of "taste," which is closely related in its concrete and abstract sense (as in "good or bad taste") to the aesthetical qualities of this or that. These points are trivial. What is nontrivial is the origin of such synaesthesia, which is in pre-Cartesian mythologization of space as "real" in the sense that abstractions are not. This distinction opens the door for things that are "not real" (such as a living Jesus or the Greek pantheon or the Norse gods or Heaven and Hell) to have physical reality by the very nature of the dividing up of experience in this way. Just as we may think of a monotheistic "god" as the reaction formation to the suppression of the Id, we may also see the physical reality of metaphysical beings and the places they inhabit as as reaction formation to the synaesthetic use of figurative language in literal speech — yet another example of using synthetic propositions in place of analytic. Even today there is much controversy over whether or not Heaven and Hell are "real places," and whether or not Jesus *and* God somehow inhabit that place peacefully. In the end, our language is interlarded with "geometrical terms" describing the topology of every nuanced emotion and thought. "The meaning of these geometrical terms is enhanced by their metaphorical use in the realm of taste."[202]

But these distinctions go farther then the everydayness of the speech act as performing these *a posteriori*transformational grammars of space and place. They are also at the root of formal geometry as it has come

---

[201] Qtd. In Ibid., p. 8.
[202] Tuan, Yi-Fu. *Space and Place: The Perspective of Experience*. Minneapolis: U. of Minnesota Press, 1977, p. 12.

down to us from Euclid, particularly in the use of that geometry in visual art where it must be formalized and enacted. The basis is in our own sensory perception, which may not be an approximation of the *microphysical* "reality" of the extensa. "Thus, sensorymotor and tactile experiences would seem to lie at the root of Euclid's theorems concerning shape congruence and the parallelism of distant lines; and visual perception is the basis for projective geometry."[203]

5.2 The difference between space and place

So far we have been talking about space more than place. A place, after all, is in a space. In the syntax of space perception, though, we may consider "place" to be the content of the transmission, and "space" to be the deep structure. Returning to the example of "I am a teacher," the nature of the pronoun as first person, and the designation of teacher (rather than, for example, police officer) are the content of the communication (transmission), whereas n-v-n, or better yet A is A, describes the deep structure. So we may correlate space (*deep structure*) with place (*semantic meaning*). "What does this place mean to you?" would not be a strange question to ask someone visiting her old neighborhood, and yet would delineate the distinctions just made. "It is characteristic of the symbol-making human species that its members can become passionately attached to places of enormous size, such as a nation-state, of which they can have only limited direct experience."

Underlying this passionate attachment is the urge, issuing from the Id, to protect and defend "the place." Ironically, this attachment is not really to "the space," as that space may vary as much as possible in character, from mountain to valley, from city to farm. The Nazi campaign of "*blut und boden*" had nice rhetorical and metaphorical resonance to a defeated, improverished Germany in 1933, but clearly little specific instructions about how to go about building a new nation. And yet that abstraction led to perhaps the fastest nation-building in history, in a surreal kind of speeded-up motion of reconstruction, destruction of other states, and self-destruction — all within twelve years!

In fact, it is the absurdity of blut und boden, and its strange

---

[203] Ibid., p. 17.

disconnection from space and fanatical devotion to place, that makes it so potent as propaganda. "Because the less people take thought seriously, the more they think in conformity with what the state wants."[204] This strange undertaking is what leads to what Deleuze and Guattari term the war machine. Thought, through the medium of space, generates the use-value and emotional attachment to place. To place thought in an immediate relation with the outside, with the forces of the outside, in short to make thought a war machine, is a strange undertaking because its creates a rift between the *thingness* of the space and the otherness of the place. Strangeness is an important principle here, indicating the estrangement of space from place.

This strangeness is no more literal and apparent than when an alien nation conquers a native one and "replaces" its values, for instance one god for another, or even one husband for another. Britain, after the struggles of Roman rule, fell to the Anglo-Saxons during the 5th century, and then to the Normans in the 11th. In both cases there was a change of religion, language, domestic custom, and most of all politics (from empire-monarchy to self rule). In the state of exception reigning after the conquests, contraphasic ontology ran rampant until it became the prevailing current — a process that takes at least a generation or two.

Once again, in the estrangement of two reciprocal principles (in this case space and time), we realize a contraphasic ontology. Such ontic threads moving in parallel but in opposite directions is characteristic of the abducted position which is itself an inversion of the I2 position, which is when people "think in conformity with the state." Thought itself feeds off of what is fed it. If the feeder is the state, then its meat will be made of the prevailing discourse of the state and its needs — whether they are in the best interests of the subject or not. "Thought is like the Vampire, it has no image, either to constitute a model of or to copy."[205]

Although we may have borrowed a great deal of our notation and operations from the Arabic-influenced algebraic world, the basis of Western and prevailing modern mathematics is Greek geometry and Greco-Roman calculus (influenced strongly by Indian and Egyptian theoretical mathematics). While the development of what we know today as mathematics evolved throughout the Middle Ages, it was not until

---

[204] Deleuze, Gilles and Felix Guittari. *Nomadology: The War Machine*. Cambridge: Semiotext(e), 1986, p. 44.
[205] Ibid., p. 45.

Newton's codification of the laws of gravitation and motion that we begin to see where the modern Notion of space begins, in parallel development with the nation-state-empire concept of place where citizens are vassals to the sovereign having sacrificed their own sovereignty for the good of the state in the form of *fealty and lucre.* "When greek geometrism is contrasted with Indo-Arab arithmetism, it becomes clear that the latter implies a *nomos*opposable to the logos: not that the nomads 'do' arithmetic or algebra, but because arithmetic and algebra arise in a strongly nomad-influenced world."[206]

Nomos serves as foil to the nation-state (place). Moreover, it serves as foil to the domination of the logos, or word, in the articulation of space. The nomad has no state, and therefore his sense of both space and place are entirely utilitarian, with use-value as the highest good. That is why when the nation-state comes to roost (like a Vampire) on the backs of the nomad, places with no water, poor ability to sustain crops, little or no wildlife, and scarce grazing land end up being "homelands" that they must later fight for, as if each unsustaining acre was a tile of paradise.

5.3 The basal ontology of space and place

But it is not enough to blame the state for the natal senses of space and time as they are ultimately configured in the adult. Of course, they arise prior to the state's direct or even effective influence which requires a more or less fully developed Language Faculty. "They grow out of life's unique and shared experiences," says Tuan. "Every person starts [...] as an infant. From the infant's tiny and confused world appears in time the adult's world view, subliminally also confused, but sustained by structures of experience and conceptual knowledge."[207] The first learned coordinates are ahead, behind, and sideways (a, b, c). Of course here lies the correlate to the discourse of time: future, past, and the moment (x, y, z). This knowledge arises from the linear sense of experience by "moving the body along a more or less straight line [...],"[208] giving us the correlates: ax, by, cz as our space-time continuum.

---

[206] Ibid., p. 63.
[207] Tuan, Yi-Fu. *Space and Place: The Perspective of Experience.* Minneapolis: U. of Minnesota Press, 1977, p. 19.
[208] Ibid., p. 20.

Furthermore, Tuan describes the sense of space at different stages of development that also correlate with Lacan's mirror-stage developmental positions. Of course 0I has an undifferentiated sense of S + T (in other words there is no s + t). At I1, the specular stage, however, "as infants, human beings [know] how it feels to live in a nondualistic world."[209] Dualism has yet to arise in two fundamental ways. The I1 infant knows of its own existence, but is not aware that others exist as it exists. Furthermore, it knows that it exists because of what Spisani calls *autoreflection*, which has not yet been subject to a new stage (I2) wherein its specular self will be in conflict with the social I, providing the pressure for change (dualism) which culminates in the abducted stage of Ix. The infant at I1 rests in the state of singularlity (α). In the next stage that singularity is transformed into a two-headed duality: (αα), one Janus face pointing backward at the I1 stage and the other pointing at the social topography present by context, often the parents. The first environment an infant explores is his parent, says Tuan. The first permanent and independent object he recognizes is perhaps another person.[210] The ideal stage of Lacanian socialization, though, is hardly a resting place, being present between two fundamental stages of higher development. Pressure is constantly on for abduction into Ix, for it is only through this process that one becomes homo generator after Hegel's first negation where thinking rests its gaze upon thinking itself in the I1 and I2 positions which are both dependent upon the mirror of thought. *The negation of negation* happens in a contraphasic transformation from (I1, I2) to Q(Ix). This stage Q(Ix) is self contradictory in that it is both an abduction/abdication of sovereignty, while also being the prerequisite for the self-determination of homo generator in the creation of new worlds. Tuan speculates that world-building beginning in the I2 stage as the child begins to acquire a sense of distance and direction through the need to judge where a grownup may be.[211]

5.4 The bringers of fealty and lucre

The nuances of space enter into play as the sense develops in all its complexity. Subject and object correlate to "here and there" — what

---

[209] Ibid., p. 20.
[210] Ibid., p. 22.
[211] Ibid., p. 23.

is "other" is always what is "over there," and what is here is intimate (proximate): "Of special interest [...] is the child's apparent concern with the remote and the proximate. He points to the horizon and plays with stones at his feet, but he shows little interest in the middle ground."[212] What is truly fascinating is the universal desire of children at the transitional phase between I1 and I2 to carry a *homunculus* around: a toy, a stuffed animal, a doll — anything that will somehow serve as a reassurance that the loss of the specular and sublimation into the social is not a dissolution of the ego. Time itself soon reassures the child that the ego remains intact in the socialization stage as it becomes clear that others in the social environment have egos too. "The young child distinguishes between 'home' and 'outside' as his play areas rather than 'my bedroom' and [the] garden.' The polar extremes are not understood equally well; for example, 'here' has greater significance than 'there.' and 'up' is more readily conceived than 'down'."[213]

In each of these developments, the space and place are what matter. Here and there are obvious examples. Subject-object is a bit less obvious except when we consider that the boundary of the two distinctions — for to have difference we must have boundaries — is considered to be the body itself, and, by extension, the possessions of the body just as the body itself is seen to be a kind of innate possession. Fear of socialization and later of abduction focus on the "strangeness" of the other, a category of being divided into two groups: The *Knowns* and the *Unknowns*. Even later, when faced with the Big Five[214], through *parasocial interaction* the subject begins first to know politicians, teachers, clergy, and media figures as Knowns. When presented with strangers, such as the enemy, or illegal aliens, or other pariah groups, these characters become the new Unknowns and are therefore subject to strangeness, a negative value that recoils into aggression and other avoidance behaviors and greater *fealty and lucre* toward the Sovereign. Universal grammar begins to appear at the incipience of the Language Faculty's development toward full power in the heart of the I2 stage. During the senescence of the I1 stage the child begins to make the sounds that indicate interest in the Other/Known. According to Tuan, first there are the wide-open consonants such as "a,"

---

[212] Ibid., p. 24.
[213] Tuan, Yi-Fu. *Space and Place: The Perspective of Experience*. Minneapolis: U. of Minnesota Press, 1977, p. 25
[214] Government, church, schools, banking, and the media.

and then later p or b (or m) made with the labia, producing "pa," "ma," "ba," and the other phonemes that are "the minimal consonantal system for all the languages of the world."[215] What does speech have to do with space? Foremost is the quality of speech to bridge the gap between self and other, between here and there. Often what the child wants is over there, and perhaps in a place where the child cannot get it. Therefore the adult must serve as the intermediary between what the child wants and the child's grasp, which is *having*. To have is quickly seen as the most desirable outcome to the communication, therefore it has been said that all communication starts out as a form of complaint, of *not-having*. The child, then, learns that there are two polar states for the ego: *having* and not-having, and that often it is the intermediary that *brings*. This *bringing* becomes the quality of the Other/Known, and is soon transferred to the Other/Unknown once the child discovers that Unknowns can bring too. But fealty remains with the Knowns simply out of probability: it is more probable that a Known will bring, therefore Knowns are cultivated, retained, acquired.

It is precisely this quality as artifact in the development of the adult that is exploited by promotional messages — whether from politicians or advertisers. They must enter into the adult's (child's) "place" and become Knowns in any way they can: TV, magazines, newspapers, the Internet. Just to be Known — even for nefarious reasons — is better than to be an Unknown because there will be little fealty and lucre coming the way of the Unknown due to the probabilistic thinking of the adult (child). The purpose of propaganda is to bring the subject into the set of all sets as a subset of the Other: to all selves in the set the subject is the object/other, but they all must becomes Knowns as the Big Five must be populated with Knowns to be considered bringers. Once the Big Five are considered bringers, then the subject becomes, as a subset of the Knowns, a bringer of fealty and lucre.

5.5 Naming and the assignment of semantic significance

As things are named for the child, they come into being. Until they are named, they are *present-at-hand* but arc not *ready-to-hand* for such simple reasons as the child cannot name the thing to inform the bringer to bring, or, in the more perceptive and ontological realm, the thing unnamed does not quite exist for the child. It remains the bare furniture of the world.

---

[215] Tuan, Ibid., p. 25.

The child sees that the Knowns and bringers have names for things and a kind of jealousy (which is the fuel of curiosity for a child in a position of narcissistic egotism) develops because to truly possess something it must be named. This having that others have, is a kind of threat to having for the child, and so the child sets about naming things using as a kind of leverage the naming of things brought by the Knowns. However, what concerns us here is not the naming of things, or of the furniture of the world, but rather the names of places and their classifications not as space but as place. "As soon as the child is able to speak with some fluency he wants to know the names of things. Things are not quite real until they acquire names and can be classified in some way. Curiosity about places is part of a general curiosity about things, part of the need to label experiences so that they have a greater degree of permanence and fit into some conceptual scheme."[216]

It takes about two and a half years, says Tuan citing Gesell, for the child to comprehend the idea of the location of a thing, person, or place. "He has no clear image of the intervening space between here and there, but he acquires a sense of place and security when his 'where?' is answered with 'home,' 'office,' or 'big building.' A year or so later, the child shows a new interest in landmarks. He recognizes and anticipates them when he is out for a walk or ride. Egocentrism is manifest in a tendency to think that all cars going in his direction must be going to his own place."[217] What is most interesting here are the words *security* and *egocentrism*. There is a tendency to think that young children somehow are innocent of basic human traits such as these when in fact infancy can be understood almost entirely in what adults see as negative traits. In his egocentrism all Knowns are prime bringers, and soon enough Unknowns become potential donors of what is brought. Moreover, it is when the wrong thing is brought or nothing is brought when something is sought that leads to tantrums of seemingly inconsolable grief and pain. These lessons linger thoughout the child's development, until they are transmuted, as it were, at the point of abduction into the universals of the set of all sets.

---

[216] Tuan, Yi-Fu. *Space and Place: The Perspective of Experience*. Minneapolis: U. of Minnesota Press, 1977, p. 29.

[217] Ibid., pp. 29-30.

5.6 A place in the world

As mentioned above, the child at first stops short of thinking of "here" as anything more than the body. The body is so "here," that everything must be stuffed in the mouth to be entirely "consumed" by the ego. Even objects as part of the teathing/oral fixation ritual are gummed into possession. It is not difficult to discover the possessions of a child, just as it is not difficult to discover the possessions of a dog or cat: in all three cases they are well chewed, drooled on, dragged through the dirt, and scented with hormones and other secretions from the endocrine system. Soon the boundary that is expanded to those things already marked for possession as it were, is expanded to the crib or sleeping area. From there the locus moves to the play area and so on. In the whole process the child is mapping out the world as it is known.

Throughout this process the body remains the chief possession, seemingly the one that cannot be taken away because it was not brought. Furthermore, it is the observatory through which the universe is observed ... a tower with a dome on top with binocular optics to survey, and memory to record and analyze. Moreover, the body has certain requirements of minimum space, air and water, terrain that is navigable, and sunlight for the part of the day when it is at work or play. The world must be organized to optimize these qualities and necessities given the available resources. We may always assume that the given resources are always maximized by the body to its best advantage, and thus the world created by humans takes its shape. According to Tuan, this shape depends on two principles: "the posture and structure of the human body, and the relations (whether close or distant) between human beings. Man, out of his intimate experience with his body and with other people, organizes space so that if conforms with and caters to his biological needs and social relations."[218] what is interesting is the variety of types of interpretations of what this world would look like. There are round dwellings, square, rectangular, towers, burrows, caves, and portable nomadic dwellings — all with one thing in common: enclosure. Unlike animals, humans enclose themselves in their living space, whereas only some birds do and the majority expose themselves to the elements when they could easily build a complete shelter or find a natural one to serve the purpose.

---

[218] Tuan, Yi-Fu. *Space and Place: The Perspective of Experience*. Minneapolis: U. of Minnesota Press, 1977, p. 34.

As for the relation of space and time, though, Tuan describes the orientation of the human body has designating space directly in front of the body as "sacred" space, with the horizon seen from the sacred vantage point as "the future." The space to the rear of the subject is "profane," and represents "the past" in all its morbid connotations. The directly up right from the body could be considered a "distant future" such as heaven, more sacred space in many divergent cultures. It is indeed the human body that Tuan and Kant point to as the cosmos incarnate only because what man can touch and manipulate will conform to the needs of the body (from elevators to windows to controls on a device), and what he cannot but only perceive — such as the stars — they will always be relative to the position of the body's basic orientation in space-time. Kant, quoted in Tuan, says, "Even our judgments about the cosmic regions are subordinated to the concept we have of regions in general, insofar as they are determined in relation to the sides of the body [...]."[219] The greatest navigators of the world still refer to the body in almost all forward commands of a ship: starboard (right) and port (left), always of the body facing forward. Kant says as much. "Similarly, our geographical knowledge, and even our commonest knowledge of the position of places, would be of no aid to us if we could not, by reference to the sides of our bodies, assign to regions the things so ordered and the whole system of mutually relative positions."[220]

Most curious of all, though, is the etymology of the word "stand," or "to stand." What makes the human being human in the physical sense is that the human truly stands. Otherwise, the organs and nervous system are not that much different from those of a frog (hence the use of frogs for anatomical dissection). According to Tuan, the word shares its root with "status, stature, statute, estate, and institute."[221] What is most interesting, then, is that it shares its root with the word *state*. The state stands as sovereign, and as the corporate and institutional prototype for the organizational structure of the church, schools, banks, and the media. As Agamben points out, the officio of the state derives its form from the medieval liturgia, as parent to child, though today the political state is the neoliturgical enterprise, even in a theocracy such as a modern Islamic state. It is nonetheless *a state*.[222]

---

[219] Ibid., p. 36.
[220] Ibid., p. 36
[221] Ibid., p. 37.
[222] Agamben, Giorgio. *Liturgia and the Modern State*. Lecture notes, European

But what does it mean to "stand" as the "state," and how is this related to the sense of the body before and after the threshold of abduction? To begin with, it is a common observance that fealty and lucre are often brought to the state (for the adult/child is now a bringer too) in a posture of obeisance, meaning in a bowed position or even prostrate before the sovereign. While this example is a bit archaic, its equivalent is the elaborate chair-sitting rituals engaged in today, such as no one can sit until the judge/legilator/boss/president/principal has been seated or asked them to be seated. The point of all these rituals, which vary with time and fashion, are that the subordinate is not standing. If we look at Tuan's choice of words above, most of them indicate elevation such as "status" itself, the juridical in "statute," the landowner in "estate," and the liturgical order in "institute" which means as a verb "*to establish in office*" and as a noun "*that office in which one was installed,*" the *ex officio* action or "place."

Standing or not is also associated with what is "high" or "low." It is not necessary to give examples of how these two words, as adjectives, transform the simplest words into social strata ripe with connotation despite lacking sorely in denotation, as this is a connotative affair in the end.

"Whatever is superior or excellent is elevated, associated with a sense of physical height. Indeed 'superior' is derived from a Latin word meaning 'higher.' 'Excel'(celsus) is another Latin word meaning 'high.' The Sanskrit brahman is derived from a term meaning 'height.' 'Degree,' in its literal sense, is a step by which one moves up and down in space. Social status is designated 'high' or 'low' rather than 'great' or 'small.' '[223]

It's not difficult to imagine the infant, who at first can only crawl, and who during this period spends much of its time prostrate like a propitiate before his master, will soon learn that standing is the source of *getting* and *bringing*. He learns, as do the "manimals" in H.G. Wells' novel *The Island of Dr. Moreau,* two legs are "good" and four legs "bad."[224] It is critical to the sovereign that the subject learns to get and bring, as it was to Roman rulers during the empire who required fealty and lucre from far flung possessions.

Graduate School, August 2009.

[223] Tuan, Yi-Fu. *Space and Place*. Minneapolis: U. of Minnesota Press, 1977.
[224] Wells, H.G. *The Island of Dr. Moreau*. New York: Bantam Classics, 1994.

6.1 The doctrine of Us and Them

At the foundation of the sense of here and there is, on the interpersonal level, the "us and them." For there to be these values at all there must be a strong sense of "I," though this sense can come in many shapes and is transformative in that its value changes morphologically as the structure of the position of development changes from 0I to Ix. Finally, it is a mistake to think that at the abducted, eccentric position there is no longer a sense of I. The only position that can lay claim to this distinction is the 0I, which is by definition a negation of I1, or the initial, first, primary sense of "I." If it were so that at the abducted position the state was left with a mob of personae bereft of the sense of personal identity, there would be no way to cultivate the Sovereign's most important weapon: the Doctrine of Us and Them, the "Them" being the outsiders who are either inside threatening stability, or outside threatening the peace. Either way, they are "Ausländerinnen," and help, by their otherness and alterity, to provide the cohesion lost when individuals are stripped/relinquish their sovereignty and a strong centralized power must hold them together. In fact, "Them" and "They" are reaction formations to the supression of the individual senses of destiny and determination. It is necessary to make such a distinction of Us and Them for the sovereign.

"A distinction that all people recognize is between 'us' and 'them.' We are *here*; we are *this* happy breed of men. They are *there*; they are not fully human and they live in *that* place. Members within the we-group are close to each other, and they are distiant from members of the outside (they) group. Here we see how the meaning of 'close' and 'distant' are a compound of degrees of interpersonal intimacy and geographical distance."[225]

Although the strongest manifestation of the Doctrine of Us and Them is found at the ripest stage of eccentric positioning, its origin is in the incipient stages of the I1 position when a child is, typically, about six months old. "Others" besides the parents or frequent care givers are perceived as "strangers" and are regarded with suspicion and dismay. Here is what is meant by "transformational." It would be an indulgence of the progressive fallacy to say that the being "develops" from one stage to the next, although it has been said here for mere convenience. Rather, there is a shift of position, sometimes backwards and permanent, of the index of

---

[225] Tuan, Yi-Fu. *Space and Place: The Perspective of Experience*. Minneapolis: U. of Minnesota Press, 1977, p. 50.

the "I." It is as if the world were first looked at through a red, then green, then blue lens. Despite the dramatic differences in tone, the world would remain the same. So too with the 0I, I1, I2, Ix concatenation. Another example is taken from Chomsky's idea of "transformational grammar." There are three basic sentence type in English: interrogative, declarative, and imperative (though sometimes exclamatory is added). The same basic sentence, nuanced only in purpose but not meaning, can be transformed in all three types as in:

Interrogative: Are you going to the circus?
Declarative: You are going to the circus.
Imperative: Go to the circus.

The "I" index simply moves from position to position depending upon the dynamic forces affecting it. One of the special qualities of transformational grammar, says Chomsky, is that it is part of Universal Grammar in that such transformations are made in all languages in the same way (with varying numbers of sentence types in this example). The same can be said for indication of position, such as in the German distinction of "diese," "das," and "jenes" (or this, that, those). "In many languages, spatial demonstratives and personal pronouns are closely related [and have] half mimetic, half-linguistic acts of indication. Personal pronouns, demonstrative pronouns, and adverbs of location closely implicate one another. I am always *here*, and what is here I call *this*. In contrast with the here where I am, *you*are *there* and he is *yonder* [*diese, das, jenes*]."[226]

These distinctions, although incorporated into a Doctrine by the sovereign for the protection of the state from *the auslander*, are biological in the cognitive orientation of the subject. "[I]f we assume that the speaker possesses as part of his biological makeup the general principles of transformational grammar, and is presented with some subset of the forms of the English auxiliary, then he would know, because he could deduce it, that these elements in other cases [...] would follow from the simplest permissible rule compatible with the given cases."[227]

---

[226] Ibid., p. 47.
[227] Chomsky, Noam. *On Language*. New York: The New Press, 1990, p. 111.

6.2 Discourse and the discursive

With all of this said about the discourse of time and space, we must also recognize (or remember) that Kant 1) considers T + S to be a priori, 2) both are synthetic propositions, and 3) "Space [and time are] not discursive, or, as we say, general conception of the relations of things, but a pure intuition."[228] This last statement appears to be a contradiction of 2, since how could something be "not discursive" (e.g. not subject to reason or argument), when it is argument that is one of the characteristics of a synthetic statement, at least according to Ayer? "For, in the first place, we can only represent to ourselves one space, and when we talk of divers spaces, we mean only parts of one and the same space. Moreover, these parts cannot antecede this one all-embracing space, as the component parts from which the aggregate can be made up, but can be cogitated only as existing in it."[229] Every set of spaces Sn is within the set of all spaces, which we can call, so that serves as the "set of all sets" which as space must also contain itself if it contains "all space." Therefore, the *paradoxology* of the nature of space precludes it from being *dianoetic, and, therefore, space is, as Kant indicates, to be grasped intuitively.* "Space is nothing else than the form of all phenomena of the external sense, that is, the subjective condition of the sensibility, under which alone external intuition is possible."[230]

---

[228] Kant, Immanuel. *Critique of Pure Reason.* New York: Barnes & Noble, 2004, p. 3.

[229] Ibid., pp. 3-4.

[230] Ibid., p. 5.

PART 4: **THE PSYCHOLOGY OF DISCOURSE**

*[T]he most significant moment in the course
of intellectual development [...] occurs when
speech and practical activity [...] converge.*

— Vygotsky[231]

1.1 The politics of space and time

Most of this discussion has been about space and time as the Kantian a
priorae. Despite being synthetic propositions, S + T are not psychological
per se. Rather, they are subject to the mind's intepretation as s + t, or
subjective space and time. This sense can vary enormously but not in any
way that can be measured, despite the seeming prevalence of the measuring
device of the clock. Rather, the clock itself enhances the subjective sense
of s + t because of its apparent objective position in the field of experience.
The mind thinks, "There is my subjective sense of time, and then there
is the objective measure of 'real' time by the clock." The same is true
for space, which is measured in the subjective sense as being near or far,
and in the "objective" sense as being X number of feet or miles or meters
or kilometers. The presence of forms of measurement only enhance the
appearance of s + t as somehow a priori and beyond that analytical in their
nature and therefore immutable.

But we have seen in quantum physics that on a macro or universal
scale there is no absolute measurement S + T (beyond the "speed of light,"
which is velocity and yields the illusion of distance measured in Earth
"years"), and that in fact they are the same thing seen two different ways
and affected by the warp of gravitational fields in the same was as the "same

[231] Vygotsky, L. S. *Mind in Society: The Development of Higher Psychological
Processes*. Cambridge: Harvard U.P., 1978, p. 24.

thing." What is significant here, though, is that the psychological sense of s + t shows the mental nature of thinking and thinking that something is so. "[C]onsciousness is a being that thinks, and that consciousness holds something to be essentially important, or true and good only so far as it is to be such."[232] Therefore, s + t are what Hegel calls Notions about phenomena. "For the object does not present itself in picture-thoughts but in distinct [...] consciousness being immediately aware that this is not anything distinct from itself."[233] The mind creates s + t with the assistance of the devices and policies developed to provide some kind of measure of these Notions. Why policies? Let us look at why they are measured at all.

In what Hegel calls the "lord and bondsman" relationship there are two values at work that make this relationship what it is: possession and work. We will think of the relationship first in agricultural terms, and then industrial. In the case of the lord, there is the landlord, or possessor of the land upon which the bondsman — held in a political bond with the landlord — both lives and works. While work is measures ultimately in its outcome (how much land cleared, how many sheep grazed, how many bushels of wheat harvested, how many pigs raised and slaughtered), it is the getting-there that is measured as the work, and it is measured in some seemingly objective form such as "from sunup to sundown" or from X o'clock to Y o'clock or "a good day's work." It is presumed that the outcome will, through the perseverance of the bondsman and the supervision of the lord, come to fruition eventually and in a timely way. So between the time worked and the quantification of the outcome, we may draw two values p and q. Furthermore, we may express the three possible values they may assume in their relation to each other 1) $p > q$, 2) $p \equiv q$, and 3) $p < q$. To the lord, 1 is the least desirable as it is the greatest amount of work with the least result, while it is the most desirable for the bondsman because there is more time to complete the work and more "work" to be done. For both lord and bondsman 2 is equitable, and that may be their contractual agreement (as in a union contract). For the lord, 3 is the most desirable because the most economical use of labor, which we may presume is "paid by the hour," yields the greatest outcome, but for the bondsman this is the least desirable for obvious reasons (unless the good will of the lord is a desirable value — though this is a two-edged sword since the lord may

---

[232] Hegel, G. W. F. *Phenomenology of Spirit*. A.V. Miller, trans. Oxford: Oxford U.P., 1977, p. 121.
[233] Ibid., p. 120.

have unreasonable expectations or place undue stress on the bondsman because of his apparent efficiency).

Ownership, naturally, is in the form of the land itself, which is owned by the lord and in fact is the reason why there is a lord. The bondsman on the other hand does not own anything, not even the "work" he puts in for the lord as that too is an extension not of the lord-bondsman relationship but of the land itself, just as it would be if the land were instead a factory or office tower. The land itself is space, and the work itself is time. But the relationship is purely psychological, existing only in the minds of the bondsman and the lord. The relationship is such only because it is acknowledged as such and is in no way ordained, fated, or any other part of natural law. The land is a function of space, and the work is a function of time. As Hegel says, "it exists only in being acknowledged [....] The detailed exposition of the Notion of this spiritual unity in its duplication will present us with the process of Recognition." The lord and bondsman are "recognized" as such by extension of space and time into the domains of their political association psychologically/spiritually.

The nature of their relationship, then, is independent of S + T except in as much as their relationship is within the totality of all *a priori* space and operates within the totality of all time. Otherwise, there is a constant interplay of the psychological values 1, 2, 3 as expressed above, each characterizing the relationship in its political psychology. "At first, it will exhibit the side of the inequality of the two, or the splitting-up of the middle term into the extremes which, as extremes, are opposed to one another, one being only *recognized* and the other only *recognizing*."[234] In other words, value 2 ($p \equiv q$) can on the one hand be equitable, or on the other hand draw the line between the recognized and the recognizing, which is itself an inequity and expresses the stress between lord and bondsman, management (who represent the owner by proxy) and worker.

The interplay of s + t and of lord (a) and bondsman (b) is a dialectic that, when played out through action, brings about being-for-self, which is the subjective sense of space and time. While both are experiencing s + t as subjective values, in relationship to each other the time worked by the worker is objective for the owner, and ownership of the land or the means of production is objective for the worker. "[A]ccording to the Notion of recognition this is possible only when each is for the other what the other

---

[234] Hegel, G. W. F. *Phenomenology of Spirit*. A.V. Miller, trans. Oxford: Oxford U.P., 1977, p. 112-13.

is for it, only when in its own self through its own action and again through the action of the other, achieves this pure abstraction of being-for-self."[235]

Just as the psychological sense of space and time cannot be escaped entirely, so too the lord-bondsman relationship which is a Notion just as s + t are, cannot be avoided, only exploited or engaged. In the dialectical movement of the relationship then, the recognition of *sp (a)* and *tq (b)* at least unequal two thirds of the time (at values 1 and 3), making value 2 a transitional threshold in the dialectical movement between the poles of inequality. And while the conditions of ownership versus work may be qualitatively different, what truly matters is that to the lord value 1 is "one-sided," and to the bondsman value 3 is so. Therefore, dialectically they are "equally unequal" in their paradoxology most of the time. "What the lord does to the other he also does to himself, and what the bondsman does to himself he should also do to the other. The outcome is a recognition that is one-sided and unequal."[236]

The significance of this dialectic becomes clear when we consider it in relation to the positions 0I, I1, I2, Ix. Indeed, it is the dialectic of s + t, in the psychological sense, that we count as "experience," for what is experience except what occurs in space and time as the thought of s + t not as it is in its unknowable form of the a priori (considering that what is "known" is therefore always a posteriori). What fuels coming-into-being is the dialectic which culminates in being-for-self at each (non-progressive) position of the "I" concatenation. The most significant for the lord-bondsman proximity is the oscillation between positions I2 (the social self) and Ix (abducted/abdicated self). "[J]ust as lordship showed that its essential nature is the reverse of what it wants to be, so too servitude in its consummation will really turn into the opposite of what it immediately is; as a consciousness forced back into itself, it will withdraw into itself and be transformed into a truly independent consciousness."[237] The necessity of the oscillation between I2 and Ix in a *pas de deux* is the formation of a "truly independent consciousness" through a clock cycle that conflates s +t into a sense of self or I.

Nevertheless, all transformational steps of the I remain part of the sphere of psychological values called "the self." As such they are not permanent because while they may be *in* S + T, they are

---

[235] Ibid., p. 113.

[236] Ibid., p. 116.

[237] Hegel, G. W. F. *Phenomenology of Spirit*. A.V. Miller, trans. Oxford: Oxford U.P., 1977, p. 117.

not *of* it. "[T]hat is the reason why this satisfaction is itself only a fleeting one, for it lacks the side of objectivity and permanence."[238] If there was not this lack, then there would be no free movement between what has become the dialectical polarities of the engine of coming-into-being. "For the independent self-consciousness, it is only the pure abstraction of the 'I' that is its essential nature, and, when it does develop its own differences, this differentiation does not become a nature that is objective and intrinsic to it."[239]

1.2 Being-for-self as freedom from the objective realm

The dialectic provides a chance to escape the tyranny of the objective through the psychology of the subjective. If objective space and time could be perceived by the subjective being, it would be an intolerable burden of impermanence and isolation for the I. The benefit of subjective time is most easily seen in the being's illusion of permanence and immortality. Since the being was not "born" a psychological entity, it cannot "die" as one. What dies is the organism attached (a priori) to S + T which, in the end, prevail. The psychological sense of s + t is so far removed from S + T that the subject is liberated from the relative reality of it. So too, then, is the bondsman liberated from his indenture and the lord from his Noblesse oblige as they are both equally in the same disadvantaged/advantaged position dialectically.

In this sense they deconstruct each other. "But for the subservient consciousness as such, these two moments — itself as an independent object, and this object as a mode of consciousness, and hence its own essential nature — fall apart."[240] And in their deconstruction of each other as merely psychological values of space and time, the being is liberated from objective S + T into being-for-self. Thinking is being-for-self, for the content of all thought is the same: "I am," the *cogito*, for that is why thought is called "cognition." "In thinking, I am free, because I am not in an other, but remain simply and solely in communion with myself, and the object, which is for me the essential being, is in undivided unity my being-for-myself [...]."[241]

---

[238] Ibid., p 118.
[239] Ibid., p. 119.
[240] Ibid., p. 120
[241] Ibid., p. 120.

1.3 Ennui at the point of abduction/abdication

However, at the position of Ix, the subject is not "in undivided unity" with itself, and is "an other." It is only in the recursion to position I2, and then in the oscillation between the two in dialectical fashion, that indenture and Noblesse oblige fall away into *being-for-self*. More might be said of the abducted position in the way of what is the motivation for the recursion. It could be said that the abduction/abdication is a loss of self, as the I2 stage is sublimated into the social arch of Ix. At the point of eccentricity, then, the being has lost its core identity, replacing it with the collective I of We. Motivation for recursion sets in at the dawn of what Hegel calls "The Unhappy Consciousness."[242]

The loss of self and the gain of the We is accompanied by a kind of mourning called *ennui* which creates constant pressure for recursion. This pressure is also found at the incipience of I at the 0I → I1 position where no core identity is replaced by a narcissistic sense of being-for-self. The ennui at this position is what drives the power to shift to the social I where the burden of hermetic self-consciousness is relieved by the social environment. At position I2, ennui sets in over the burden of self-reliance in the social environment in the forms of jealousy and competitions with other Selves. The lust for "We" sets in and abdication occurs at the very moment of abduction (*for they must be simultaneous for the Ix position to be of any use to the sovereign power*). "The Unhappy Consciousness itself is the gazing of one self-consciousness into another [I2 ↔ Ix], and itself is both, and the unity of both is also its essential nature. But it is not as yet explicitly aware that this is its essential nature, or that it is the unity of both."[243]

At both positions (I2 and Ix), consciousness gazes into the other position with a sense of longing for what lies over the threshold of the social Self and the We, unaware that it can only be both if it is to be aware of itself in a conscious sense through the oscillation between the two positions at least starting with recursion. "Consciousness of life, of existence and activity, is only an agonizing over this existence and activity, for therein it is conscious that its essence is only its opposite, is conscious of its own nothingness."[244] Being "unhappy," and "agonizing" over existence, are emotional and therefore psychological states. Furthermore, they are

---

[242] Hegel, G. W. F. *Phenomenology of Spirit*. A.V. Miller, trans. Oxford: Oxford U.P., 1977, p. 117.

[243] Ibid., p. 126.

[244] Ibid., p. 127.

brought about by peering into the abyss of the synthetical proposition of s + t, which is nothing but *a posteriori* excrescence, of "no one" in Heidegger's term and "nothing" in Kant's. Longing and desire, lust and grief, and the ever-present ennui of Being, permeate the shifts in the control point of the I in an eternal dialectical movement. The movement ushers the Self through the positions, not in a progressive way, but by necessity in a retrograde movement after the Ix position is first reached (otherwise one remains a bondsman forever).

Hegel describes the the three stages after 0I: "For the movement runs through these moments [positions] first the Unchangeable is opposed to individuality in general; then, being itself as individual, it is opposed to another individual [jealousy, competition]; and finally, it is one with it [We position]."[245] What is required is the Second Negation once the subject is in the Ix position. In the Second Negation (the negation of the First Negation of the negation of self), homo generator appears. Ennui remains as the excrescence of conscious awareness and the destabilizing "hoping" of the psychological medium of awareness. Therefore, t + s remain psychological positions in the advent of homo generator as a continuing process of the Second Negation, which is not so much an event as a process without beginning or end.

2.1 The speech-act and its consequences for the intellect

In this study we are concerned with the linguistics of speech alone, and perhaps text only in as much as it is a transcription of speech. The reason for this limitation is that thought as the sense of I arises before writing but only after speech. The sense of I, or the *cogito*, is not to be confused with intelligence — something we can detect by looking into a speechless infant's eyes or those of a higher animal. Vygotsky, citing Buhler's error, says that intelligence and thinking are often confused: "the beginnings of practical intelligence in the child ([Buhler] termed it 'technical thinking'), as well as the actions of the chimpanzee, are independent of speech."[246] But in fact they are entirely dependent upon it. This analysis postulating the independence of intelligent action from speech runs contrary to our

---

[245] Ibid., p. 128.
[246] Vygotsky, L. S. *Mind in Society: The Development of Higher Psychological Processes*. Cambridge: Harvard U.P., 1978, p. 21.

own findings, which reveal the integration of speech and practical thinking in the course of development.[247] The reason, he says, is that "speech plays an essential role in the organization of higher psychological functions,"[248] which we may assume include the sense of I and the perception of psychological s + t.

The cogito arises out of speech as the psychological apparatus of being-for-self and later, being-for-We, what Vygotsky calls "*one and the same complex psychological function.*"[249] The more difficulties are presented to the subject, the more developed the speech faculty becomes and, we may presume, intelligence and thought-complexity increase proportionally. The psychological sense of space and time arise out of the manual interaction with the environment accompanied by internal and external speech, producing a "discourse" about the world. "*[C]hildren solve practical tasks with the help of their speech, as well as their eyes and hands.* This unity of perception, speech, and action, which ultimately produces internalization of the visual field, constitutes the central subject matter for any analysis of the origin of uniquely human forms of behavior."[250] The speech-act then branches off into two forms: internal and external.

At first, it is only external speech that is used for communication, but as the child learns to write the internal speech becomes organized (eventually) in the grammatical and rhetorical graphemes that constitute that form of communication. Therefore internal speech, which Vygotsky labels as "egocentric," becomes the basis of thought. External communicative speech makes a poor system for the *cogito* because its entire organization is based not on innate structures (which are present in internal speech), but on the social apparatus of the sovereign and of the community of the sovereign which is in jealous competition with the Self. Therefore, external speech becomes a kind of competitive weapon or tool used in *bringing* and *getting* from the Knowns and Unknowns (or *Others*). It is only internal speech that serves as the image in the mirror for the mirror-stage. When one thinks, one "reflects." *The cogito is a reflection in a mirror, which brings on cognition in the form of thinking and recognition in the form of memory. The combination of thinking and memory is what we call "I."*

---

[247] Ibid., p. 22.
[248] Ibid., p. 23.
[249] Ibid., p. 25.
[250] Ibid., p. 26.

After ennui has motivated the phase shift from I1 to I2, the mystery of *bringing* and *getting* from the Knowns and Unknowns begins in earnest as the very structure of the social arch, or as it has been called, the Apparatus.[251] "The path from object to child and from child to object passes through another person. This complex human structure is the product of a developmental process deeply rooted in the links between individual and social history."[252] *Meantime, the sign comes into play as the Lacanian algorithm s/S: signified/Signifier.* (And by "signifier" is here meant a phoneme in the de Saussurean sense, not a grapheme necessarily.) At this moment in the phase shifting, when bringing/getting and Others come into play, the world explodes in a multiplicity of specular *percepts*. A *percept* is anything or anyone that has come into being for the subject. According to Lacan, what has come into being is, by definition, named, and therefore has been assigned a signifier (S) which casts its shadow upon the Signified (s), clouding perception of the *percept*. "It is to this object that cannot be grasped in the mirror that the specular image lends its clothes. A substance caught in the net of the shadow, and which, robbed of its shadow-swelling volume, holds out once again the tired lure of the shadow as if it were substance."[253]

Ennui begins with the clouding of the signified with the shadow of the signifier, a process in synchrony with the narcissism or egotism of the specular position where the image in the mirror (*as s*) is mistaken for the Self (*as S*). *"The system of signs restructures the whole psychological process and enables the child to master her movement. It reconstructs the choice process on a totally new basis."*[254] Of course what is the motivator in the process of ennui is what Lacan calls *jouissance*, a kind of joyful abandonment to the adjoining position, *in particular the fall/leap into abduction.* Again, the psychological sense of space + time is both the progenitor and the progeny of a manual or concrete "pointing-out" that goes on between signified and Signifier. When the signifier points to itself, there is ennui. When the signifier points to the Signified, there is

---

[251] Agamben, Giorgio. Personal conversation. European Graduate School, Saas-Fee: August 2009.
[252] Vygotsky, Ibid., p. 30.
[253] Lacan, Jacques. "Subversion of the subject and the dialectic of desire." *Ecrit: A Selection.* New York: W.W. Norton & Co., Inc., p. 316.
[254] Vygotsky, L. S. *Mind in Society: The Development of Higher Psychological Processes.* Cambridge: Harvard U.P., 1978, p. 35.

jouissance where "the signifier sends forth its light into the shadow of incomplete significations."[255]

2.2 Memory and thinking as the sense of Self

As mentioned above, the potent combination of thought and memory brings about the sense of self. It is necessary for there to be memories to define the self as one different from another self. This differentiation is similar to the naming that goes on as the child attached phonemic labels to the furniture of the world and its many animals. As de Saussure has said, what is necessary for a sign to be useful is that it is different from another sign. Otherwise, its being is arbitrary. Memory is also critical for the efficiency of the organism, not just its functioning in the manual senses of bringing and getting, but also in its development of a personal language — for in the end all languages are as personal as one's thoughts, particularly internal language.

The first form of thinking is remembering, says Vygotsky. "For the very young child, to think means to remember; at no time after very early childhood do we see such a close connection between two psychological functions."[256] The fundamental association between thought and memory is forged at this stage. While it remains, thought then develops into its vastly complicated apparatus that is, eventually, abducted. The furniture of the world becomes the furnishings of the mind. "The content of the thinking act in the child when defining [...] concepts is determined not so much by the logical structure of the concept itself as by the child's concrete recollections. *It is synthetic in character and reflects the fact that the child's thinking depends first of all on his memory* [italics added]."[257] The mind must be furnished with association, signs, connection, taxonomies, and categories. From these elements the structure of the mind (rather than the wet brain) emerges.

---

[255] Lacan, Ibid., p 152.
[256] Vygotsky, Ibid., p. 50.
[257] Ibid., p. 50.

2.3 Father as the signifier

If we think back on the origin of the Other, we will remember that it is first the parents (if present) and the immediate care givers who become the *Knowns* and the *bringers*. But "parents" are not an undifferentiated mass to the child. While the mother and father have more in common in the child's early development than they have to differentiate themselves from each other, the differences soon manifest. The father eventually becomes the Lawgiver, and by association is equated with the eclipsing shadow of the signifier in the specular solar system. The reason, in particular, is the mother is less of an "other" to the child than the father because the mother is always a little closer to being a Known than the father, who represents as familiar among the tribe of the Unknowns. Also, the mother, as the primary bringer, must maintain a level of trust with the child that the father need not maintain, therefore casting him in the role of the Lawgiver and emissary from the realm of the Others — the Others who at the position of I2 acquaint the child with the rules of both language, rhetoric, and behavior as a social being.

Lacan sees in the presence of the father-as-Lawgiver the precursor of both socialization and abduction. What is most curious is that socialization (and writing) always remain alien to the child as *alterity*, because the initializing role of the father can never be performed again, only duplicated.

"Let us set out from the conception of the Other as the locus of the signifier. Any statement of authority has no other guarantee than its very enunciation [at the position Ix], and it is pointless for it to seek it in another signifier, which could not appear outside this locus in any way. Which is what I mean when I say that no metalanguage can be spoken, or, more aphoristically, that there is no Other of the Other. And when the Legislator (who claims to lay down the law) presents himself to fill the gap, he does so as an imposter."[258]

At the point of abduction (Ix), then, the ersatz nature of the abductor as the authority (landowner, lord) who stands in place of the primal Father, become the source of *jouissance* for the subject (bondsman). The subject has now entirely stepped into the shadow of the signifier, which in the position of I2 brought ennui, but now brings the same response as full acknowledgment of the signified. The subject has entered the deathless world of the symbol, and feckless world of the governed. The sovereign,

---

[258] Lacan, Jacques. "Subversion of the subject and the dialectic of desire." *Ecrit: A Selection*. New York: W.W. Norton & Co., Inc., p. 310-11.

who was before taken as a symbol of the sun (son) now becomes the Sun itself. Lacan points out that this proposition is irresistable. "The work to which the slave is subjected and the pleasure that he renounces out of fear of death [...] will be precisely the way through which he will achieve freedom. There can be no more obvious lure than this, politically or psychologically. Jouissance comes easily to the slave, and it will leave the word in bondage."[259]

The paradoxology of the ersatz is most obvious in the mass media, where the jouissance of battle, fighting, vicarious sex, vast unthinkable possessions, and the magic powers of the fairy tale become realities. In exchange for his personal sovereignty, the subject now reaps the beneficence the Sovereign has to give as the *Bringer-par-excellence*. The ennui brought about by the duality of Signifier and signified is blurred in the shadow of the Lord — physical or metaphysical. Perhaps the Impostor position of the Sovereign is why the subjects are constantly hankering for the Lord's downfall in the forms of disgrace (which literally means fall from grace). And of course there is always the *jouissance* of revolution, where the decapitation of the King-Father frees the serf to become a king and Lawgiver in the forms of popular democracy and legislation "by the people."

But it would be inaccurate to focus merely on the sovereign who becomes what Lacan calls the "locus" of the signifier-as-law. The subject, too, besides in just his feeling-tone about the new position of Ix, has undergone an inversion just as the Other has (from Father/Other to Other/Other). Here is what Hegel calls a "double reflection" of the specular stage now transformed through jouissance into the incipience of the Second Negation. "[T]he truth of this certainty is really a double reflection, the duplication of self-consciousness. Consciousness has for its object one which, of its own self, posits its otherness or difference as a nothingness, and in so doing is independent."[260] We may now add "nothingness" to Kant's "nothing" and Heidegger's "no one." The signifier is *nothingness-nothing-no-one*. The signifier, as the discourse, is the emptiness of the shadow which does not contain the corpus, but only retains its outline depended upon a light source. The signifier is no more substantial as the negation of the signified than a finger pointing at an elephant is an elephant or a paycheck is a week's worth of work.

---

[259] Lacan, Ibid., p. 308.
[260] Hegel, G. W. F. *Phenomenology of Spirit*. A.V. Miller, trans. Oxford: Oxford U.P., 1977, p. 110.

3.3 Homo generator as maker-of-worlds

After all, what is the ultimate lure of the abduction/abdication? While the motive varies somewhat from the lord to the bondsman (for both must experience this phase-shift of position), it is the possibilities the Second Negation opens up for the making-of-worlds. While in the I2 position of competitive jealousy, the subject retains sovereignty but is overwhelmed with a dual ennui: the first as an artifact from the 0I → I1 shift, and the second as the dualistic conflict between Signifier and signified. As we have seen, jouissance lures the subject into the shift to Ix where ennui is inverted for the ersatz *renatalization* of experience. At the same time, though, the subject feels, after the shift, that there is a nostalgia or longing for personal sovereignty, precipitating the recursion to I2. After recursion, we may say that the negation has been negated (the first negation begins at the incipience of the I2 shift and ends at the senescence of the Ix position). When the Ix position has been negated, we may properly say that the Second Negation has occurred. Furthermore, we may say that here is the birth of Homo Generator (HG).

HG is foremost a fabricator, a maker of things and ideas, whose greatest achievement is the full deployment of symbolic languages — from speech and writing to mathematics (which is always writing). In addition, HG creates the great works of art and poetry and drama and fiction, the accumulation of scientific knowledge, and the spectacular feats of engineering. Ultimately, HG shapes the environment in a *nontrivial* way (how beavers shape the environment with their dams is *trivial*) as the *maker* of the environment and not just its manipulator. Therefore, homo generator is a maker-of-worlds, from the tribe of the Others, who speaks the language of the Sign. As such, this is what makes HG human and not just an animal. HG stands for the state, and understands, just as the signs "stand" for the signified as their material equivalent and even their superior for they are nothing at all and yet have ultimate power, whereas the signified is something but may have no power at all. "It may be said that the basic characteristic of human behavior in general is that humans personally influence their relations with the environment and through that environment personally change their behavior, subjugating it to their control."[261]

---

[261] Vygotsky, L. S. *Mind in Society: The Development of Higher Psychological Processes.* Cambridge: Harvard U.P., 1978, p. 51.

Ultimately, jouissance arises from the conquering of death. HG has conquered death through the agency of the Ix position of abdication (for it must be voluntary at the very instant of capture), and then negates the shift of position by recursion to the I2 position. By elevating the signifier above the signified, the subject first conquers death. Schirmacher describes the beginnings of the origin of homo generator's shaping of the world, beginning with the shaping of death where death becomes "nothing" but its signifier. Without this process we could not function. "The revolution of the artifacts is perceived as a negation of the natural body [....] Our culture is fascinated by the immaterial body which knows no aging process and may overcome even death."[262]

This is not to mistake the "postmodern" subject at the Ix position for homo generator in the Second negation. Both are makers. Only HG is a maker of worlds because personal sovereignty has been regained by negation of the abdication/abduction, while at the same time the topology of the Ix position has been thoroughly exploited. Most of all, HG "generates" a form of artificial life that benefits others without engaging the jealous competition characterizing the entire I2 position.

"What we as creators, participants, and observers can know about today's reality points to an immense shift: the emergence of artificial life as the reality for human beings [....] If biotechnology provides the hardware of artificial life, communication technology designs the software, which includes a postmodern culture. *It is within this cultural environment that we decide how we should act, what we hope for, and, finally, what it means to be a human being* [italics added]."[263]

4.1 The psychology of the tool of discourse

As is said above, the achievements of the subject in the Ix position are exploitative, are subject to the needs of the sovereign (and state), and embrace the signifier for the signified so that death is "conquered" through its eclipse in *jouissance*. However, what is retained from this experience is the use of discourse as a tool. We may imagine the mass media, the laws, the political speeches, the words in books, the lessons of teachers, the sermons of preachers, and the loans of banks as each in themselves just

---

[262] Schirmacher, Wolfgang. "Homo Generator: Media and Postmodern Technology." (1994.) European Graduate School articles. Accessed 15 June 2011.
[263] Ibid.

one interminable discourse which is not progressive. Rather, at any point in its ontic threading it is precisely the same function or message. In this way discourse is a tool, so that its content is more or less irrelevant (historians still argue over who was the greater mass murderer, the communist Mao Zedong, the Social Democrat Adolph Hitler, or the socialist Joseph Stalin, or the democrat Harry S Truman who ordered the dropping of atomic bombs on Japan, and so on).

What matters ultimately is the solving of problems along the ontic thread which gives us our Events such as ligatures, bifurcations, truncations, and recursions, all of which are psychological values. *An ontic thread is a posteriori, and is therefore both synthetic and a psychological topographic space.* "The invention and use of signs as auxiliary means of solving a given psychological problem (to remember, compare something, report, choose, and so on) is analogous to the invention and use of tools in one psychological respect. The sign acts as an instrument of psychological activity in a manner analogous to the role of a tool in labor."[264] It is easy to see how "to remember, compare something, report" comes close to the modes of rhetoric, such as narrative (remember), compare something (compare and contrast), and report (process analysis or division and classification). Rhetorical modes are the strongest tools of speech and are used in all aspects of public discourse (for example the interrogative-declarative-imperative pattern in advertising, or the ethos-logos-pathos pattern in speech making).

However, it is not accurate (or polite even) to say that a sign is a tool. That statement is tautological, pointing to nothing more then itself. Rather — and this idea is at the root of the media — it is "mediated activity" by the subject and cohorts that links the sign with the tool, such as rhetoric. For example, there is no rhetoric if there is no speech, and there is no speech if there is no mass media to convey it, and there is no mass media if there is no need for the speech, and there is no need for the speech if there is no apparatus which must communicate with the subject. Vygotsky quotes Hegel on mediation:

"That concept, quite justly, was invested with the broadest general meaning by Hegel, who saw in it a characteristic feature of human reason: Reason is just as cunning as she is powerful. Her cunning consists principally in her mediating activity which, by causing objects to act and react on each

---

[264] Vygotsky, L. S. *Mind in Society: The Development of Higher Psychological Processes.* Cambridge: Harvard U.P., 1978, p. 52.

other in accordance with their own nature, in this way, without any direct interference in the process, carries out reason's intentions."[265]

"Reason's intentions" here are to mean the intentionality of the rational thought in its making of worlds. The worlds do not get made if there is no thinking in the sense of effective or manifest thought. Manifestation of thought is a form of coming-into-being, only it arises from the subject who, in the best case, is homo generator. By these means, then, the "mediating activity" causes "objects to act and react," bringing about the intentionality of homo generator who understands the use of the media as the channel for discourse.

4.2 Sign use development

But of all homo generator's accomplishments, the use of signs is the greatest. From this creation flows all other strictly human output. Signs of course include the phoneme that is spoken and heard, as well as the grapheme that is written and seen. The line between the two is blurred with the growth of speech-to-text processing and text-to-speech in real time. Although we refer to both when referring to "sign use," the majority of this discussion, as mentioned earlier, is focused on sign-as-speech in the de Saussurean sense.

Critical to the development of signs is what Vygotsky calls the "internalization" of "a series of transformations." In particular, the transformation of external stimuli into internal memory in the form of symbols begins the process. For instance, if a bell were rung each time a child were fed, the ringing of the bell (and even the sight of the bell) would be associated with eating and the slaking of hunger. Eventually, food could be represented with a bell-shaped symbol (like an omega), or it could be morphized into the word "ding" to represent, in an onomatopoetic way, the sound the bell used to make. While there are "mental processes" occurring during the signaling for food, they are not what Vygotsky calls "higher" ones. It is the internalization itself that brings on this development. "Of particular importance to the development of higher mental processes is the transformation of sign-using activity, the history and characteristics of which are illustrated by the development of practical intelligence,

---

[265] Vygotsky, L. S. *Mind in Society: The Development of Higher Psychological Processes*. Cambridge: Harvard U.P., 1978, p. 54.

voluntary attention, and memory."[266] Even further, Vygotsky sees human psychology as unique in its ability to internalize external processes of great sophistication. Specifically the processes most often internalized are social and socio-historical, making homo generator, for all his creative independence, social at a level of intensity and deterministic freedom far greater than that of any animal. "The internalization of socially rooted and historically developed activities is the distinguisihing feature of human psychology, the basis of the qualitative leap from animal to human psychology."[267]

4.3 The dialectical historicity of discourse

What is of greatest interest here is the idea of the historicity of the internalization. History serves as an a priori to the child's personal history which is of course an accumulation uniquely belonging to the child. Therefore, the child's personal history is a posteriori to the social history he acquires directly. There is hardly a "story" in the child's life that is more of a discourse than the a priori history of his species, race, nationality, ethnicity, polity, community, and family. These six threads of discourse, whether convergent or divergent, reach an equilibrium among the Hearers. The Hearers are those who acquire the history *a posteriori* from the *Zeitgeist*. Among them, a consensus is eventually reached about, for instance, what the motives of the American Civil War were for the victor (North), and what were the crimes of the vanquished (South). Even for the divergent vanquished, the discourse reaches divergent and convergent Hearers alike and, one way or another, the discourse is embraced — even if with some reluctance. When a historical discourse reaches an unrevised equilibrium, we say it has become a "fossil" or is fossilized. "The fossilized form is the end of the thread that ties the present to the past, the higher stages of development to the primary ones."[268]

Vygotsky quotes Marx on the dialectical nature of historicity of change in the process of internalization. Of course the "transformation," as Vygotsky puts it, from external to internal is the greatest "change."

---

[266] Vygotsky, L. S. *Mind in Society: The Development of Higher Psychological Processes*. Cambridge: Harvard U.P., 1978, p. 57.

[267] Ibid., p. 57.

[268] Ibid., p. 64

Nevertheless, there is also change in the *Weltanshauung* of the subject when what was once the furniture of the world becomes the furnishings of the mind, as we have noted. As a Hearer, the subject is poised to change depending on the nature of what is internalized (born-again Christian or Hasidic Jew?). As was described earlier as the dialectic process of ennui-joussiance in shifting from one ontic position to another, the dialectic between the external and internal, between the historical and personal, fuels the *transformative* operation leading to the most extreme eccentric position and then the negation that brings the subject back across the threshold. "*To study something historically means to study it in the process of change*; that is the dialectical method's basic demand."[269] In the end, Vygotsky calls the process of the Hearers a *method that is "simultaneously prerequisite and product, the tool and the result of the study.*"[270]

Development should not be confused with progress. It is not that the child "progresses" through a hierarchy of stages. Rather, it is that each stage is a Zone of Proximal Development (ZPD), and is not relative to another zone. Each ZPD follows the same logic, and is relative only to the values contained within itself. By development Vygotsky means "transformation" of the same values from state to state, with no one state "better" or "more developed" than another. Despite the distinction of "primary" and "higher" states, he refers only to the level of complexity in terms of world processing dependent upon the Hearing of the world to the point where it is internalized at the new ZPD. The difference between the progressive development model and Vygotsky's ZPD's is the "method," which is dialectical, constantly iterating the same morphology with a new set of variables contained within it.

"We believe that child development is a complex process characterized by periodicity, unevenness in the development of different functions, metamorphosis or qualitative transformation of one form into another, intertwining of external and internal factors, and adaptive processes which overcome impediments the child encounters."[271]

---

[269] Ibid., p. 65.
[270] Ibid., p. 65.
[271] Vygotsky, L. S. *Mind in Society: The Development of Higher Psychological Processes.* Cambridge: Harvard U.P., 1978, p. 73.

5.1 The Zone of Proximal Development as transformational plateau

Discourse is transmitted to the child from the "very first day of life," says Vygotsky, in the form of speech, information, calculaic skill, and behavioral mimicry. Immediately a ZPD is established which has some characteristics familiar to this discussion. For instance, it begins in a 0-development state (despite what some parents believe about fetuses learning Mozart through the wall of the womb). The first ZPD is specular in that the furniture of the world is reflected in the "content-free" consciousness of the child (not necessarily a *tabula rasa*, which implies that it was somehow erased). In this way the child is both a *Seer and a Hearer* in the best senses of the world, with no limitation that does not arise from its own constitution. Once rudimentary language is learned, the child may move on to ask questions, which is the start of the analytic or critical mind. "[I]n the period of her first questions, a child assimilates the name of objects in her environment" through learning. Thefore, learning is what characterizes each ZPD as a learning plateau. It may be said that her learning "plateaus" in preparation for the next transformational event — and even entirely precipitated by the demands of the environment (e.g. if a child is not in need of speech she will not learn speech).[272]

However, our purpose here is to show that in each of the positions beyond 0I, there is structure within the state. So far we have described the interplay between ennui and jouissance as a dialectical process. Now it is time to consider levels of tension with the ZPD (which may be considered positions I1, I2, Ix). Vygotsky defines ZPD as "*the distance between the actual development level as determined by independent problem solving and the level of potential development as determined through problem solving under adult supervision.*"[273] Again we have another dialectical process with "actual development" at one pole and "potential development" at the other. What must be kept in mind is that after 0I, each actual development level was the former plateau's potential development level. Therefore, there is no "progress" from one level to another like a black belt in karate. "Potential" is not awakened unless there is environmental stimulus in the form of Others (adults). Vygotsky renames "potential," with its connotation of progress to "proximal," meaning that one zone's "actual" is another's

---

272 Ibid., p. 84.
273 Ibid., p. 86.

"proximal." That the transformation takes place with the agency of Others, and that it does not occur unless there is stimulus from the environment, shows us that it is a historical process in the sense Marx means it above. What is current for the learning child is history for the Other, and what is history for the Other is fossilized for the culture.

Socialization is sometimes seen, in the education of children, not as part of the learning process per se, but an adjunct because "they must live in society and be social." For Vygotsky, though, socialization *is* the learning process. And by socialization he does not mean the collective habits of animals. "*[H]uman learning presupposes a specific social nature and a process by which children grow into the intellectual life of those around them.*"[274] We may think of the dialectic of ennui-jouissance and the dialectic of actual-proximal as lying across each other, forming a cross, but functioning as simultaneous parallel ontologies (SPO's) in the development of the child from one position to the next. We may express this relationship thus, where x is ennui and y is jouissance, and where p is actual and q is proximal, and a, b, c represent I1, I2, Ix, and → the conditional "if, then":

$$ZPDn = \{a \, [(x \to y) \to (p \to q)], \, b \, [(x \to y) \to (p \to q)],$$
$$c \, [(x \to y) \to (p \to q)]\}$$

What is most expressive here is the iteration of structures in the concatenation of a, b, c. Again, there is no progress, only conditional "proximities" at each step. Without a structure of progression (for "a, b, c" is abritrary) there cannot be a need for testing.

5.2 Testing as enforcer of the Progressive Fallacy

For there to be a verifiable progression, there must be a test. A test ascertains the "level attained" of the subject within the context of the set body of knowledge and proscription. In as much as it is proscription, there is a defined canonic body of the knowing defining what is learning. At the position Ix, the canon becomes fossilized (as there is no next position, only recursion). All fossilized forms of knowing are in themselves

---

[274] Vygotsky, L. S. *Mind in Society: The Development of Higher Psychological Processes*. Cambridge: Harvard U.P., 1978, p. 88.

canonic and are subject to testing. Ronell describes the orthography of the canon. "While the test is a questioning act [indicating speculation and the specular "thus" (sic)], and while it may prompt the necessity of counter-examples, it already contains and urges a sense of the correct way to answer its demands."[275] Therefore, the test is merely an indication of the cohesion of its own orthography. Ronell divides epistemology into meaning and knowledge. It is one thing to know a fact, and another to know what the fact means (which is the problem with statistics). "The test attacks epistemological meaning with a kind of ontological fervor. The surprise passes for a shiver in ontology; something trembles in being."[276]

When there is developed a body of knowledge that must be learned, and when that knowledge becomes the entire purview of the system of personal development, then it may be said that the historicity of that knowledge, fossilized as it is, has become the dogma of the discourse. Dogma creates an immediate response for its opposite: non-fossilized, dynamic, and mysterious knowledge. It is no surprise that the great ages of mysticism (in particular the 20th century with its Alistair Crowleys, charismatic Christians, Hasidim, and Hindu swamis) coincide with great ages of rationalism and dogma subject to The Test, whatever it may be. "It was believed that by using tests, we determine the mental development level which education should reckon and whose limits it should not exceed [....] This procedure oriented learning toward yesterday's development, toward developmental stages already completed."[277]

The progressive fallacy, then, is the idea that, for instance, language skill, somehow becomes "better" as time passes, learning is administered (like medical therapy), and the results are tested on general-intelligence-loaded (g-loaded) testing systems. Once again, this is the fallacy that the "mere passage of time" is in itself the guarantee of improvement and increase. But what about those left behind in this race to nowhere? Those who "do not pass the test" are, ultimately, blamed for their inability to conform to the system of verification the Discourse has comprised as the measure of how much and what fossilized learning the child (or even adult) is capable of retaining and presenting or even using. Vygotsky claims that language is an effective "paradigm" for the dichotomy and dialectic

---

[275] Ronell, Avital. *The Road Test.* Chicago: U. of Illinois Press, 2005, p. 186.
[276] Ibid., p. 186.
[277] Vygotsky, L. S. *Mind in Society: The Development of Higher Psychological Processes.* Cambridge: Harvard U.P., 1978, p. 88.

between development and learning. "Language arises initially as a means of communication between the child and the people in his environment. *Only subsequently, upon conversion to internal speech, does it come to organize the child's thought, that is, become an internal mental function* [italics added]."[278]

If we take this process in three basic stages, we can see how discourse becomes thought. First, there is the Utility of communication. A Utility by its nature and definition has not meaning as such. It is used; it does not mean. A screwdriver does not "mean" in any way except the most exotic and fanciful. However, when language becomes the vehicle for the transmission of fossilized historicity (not "history," but the sense of history, for history itself is a collection of facts), it is subjected to testing. *All testing must have incentives and coercives.* Through this system, the utility of language diminishes and the rise of it as the socket of connection between the *Hearers* and the *Sayers* jumps into the foreground, and we are left with the internalization of the discourse as thought. The thoughts become the resonance of the discourse, the test is passed, and step by step the Hearer becomes more of a *Sayer*.

6.1 What the child needs from itself and others

There are then two forms of discourse: one more or less codified as a canon of knowledge and behaviors, and the other referring to its primal roots as the mode of communication on a utilitarian level. It seems intuitive that the second would contain less pathology then the first, at all. It is hard to find what might be pathological in the use of language to communication, and as we have already discussed, to use language to address *lack* or fundamental need of something from the Bringers. We may concatenate the path of this utilitarian communication like this: Transmitter/Lack (TL[p]), message (m), message channel (mc), Receiver/Bringer (R/B[q]), feedback channel (fc), transmitter/Receiver (t/R), Grasping/Having (G/H), no Lack (~L). Which would yield this schema:

$$(T/L[p]), (m), (mc), (R/B[q]), (fc), (t/R), (G/H), (~L)$$

---

[278] Ibid., p. 89.

Although this schema has a feedback channel by which the Bringer brings to [p], by reversing [q] for [p] we have the same schema by satisfying the lack expressed by [q] rather than [p]. Again, as with the schema of the ZPD, [p] ≡[q] and [q] ≡ [p]; they are material equivalents and therefore their concatenation follows the same pattern.

However, when we refer to the codified form of discourse, there arises the concern of what the content is because the content is static not dynamic. Now both the content of a free discourse and a codified one are subject to the same arbitrary population. However, a significant difference is that the population of the free discourse is based on lack, or needs as they are presented in the environment. Whereas in the case of the codified discourse, content is determined by fiat, which may or may not be in the best interests of the subject. The sovereign and the sovereign's helpers determine what will be on the test, what is worth testing, what is important, and how the subject will behave toward the sovereign and others. In this situation the subject may show pathological behavior because of the nature of the fiat (e.g. the fiat says to kill members of group Y without clear provocation). In such a situation, then, the subject will show pathological behavior. This behavior will manifest as either the sociopath, the psychiatric case, or both.

6.2 The background of developmental ontology

Before we can explore what might be pathological in the psychology of the abducted, in particular that species which has never returned from the Ix position for recursion, it is necessary to look at how the personal is formed in the first place by innate as well as social forces. In exploring the development of the sense of "I" during the 0I →I1 we are primarily discussing the Critical Period (0-12). This process seems to run in this pattern of subphases as expressed by Mahler, et al.:

> 0. Separation-Individuation (Autistic-Symbiotic)
> 1. Differentiation + Body-Image Development
> 2. Practicing
> 3. Rapprochement
> 4. Emotional Object Constancy + Consolidation of Individuality[279]

---

[279] Mahler, Margaret, et al. *The Psychological Birth of the Human Infant: Symbiosis*

Subphase 0 (0I → I1) is considered to be a transition from the Normal Autistic Phase of infancy at birth to the incipience of the sense of individuality through separation from the birth mother. This state is described as a "sleeplike state" that far outweighs "state of arousal." This is a common observation made by parents of newborns. Freud, quoted in Mahler, et al., describes the state as a "neat example of a psychichal system shut off from the stimuli of the external world [...]"[280] Moreover, this stage is also characterized by the lack of cathexis with the Bringers, who bring without prompting from the infant or expression of lack. Soon though, the infant's bahavior "centers around his continuous attempts to achieve homeostasis" through crying, making pleasing noises, gesturing, and thrashing about. Soon a view of the world enters the symbiotic phase where the dialectic begins in earnest between "pleasurable/good" and "painful/bad," establishing the fundamental dichotomy of the Pleasure Principle.[281]

The period is characterized in part because of the "holding behaviors" of the mother during this period and what affect they have on the child's emotional development. There is a "normal" level of symbiosis that can be defined by negation, meaning that, obviously, *not* holding and *abusive* holding are detrimental to the child's development. Here is the first source of possible pathology, related to the discourse of affection from the principal Known: the mother. Although it is not thought out in words, it is discovered as a feeling-tone with the content "comfort and security come from the Known." A disruption of this discourse at so fundamental a phase is often disastrous.

6.3 Differentiation + Body-Image Development

In the first subphase (I1), by necessity and as part of the child's development (and the Known's development as a mother), there is a pulling away, a separation, particularly as new behaviors such as crawling lessen the need for carrying and walking for holding. At this moment of pulling away, of differentiation (which is binary, not progressive), the child immediately takes on a *transitional object* such as a stuffed animal or a baby blanket.

---

and Individuation. New York: Basic Books, Inc., Publishers, 1975, p. v.
[280] Ibid., p. 41.
[281] Ibid., p. 43.

The infant uses the object as a substitute for the touch of the mother, particularly around the face and mouth.[282] At the same time, the object is a reaction formation the heightened sense of which comes with the mother's differentiation. The transitional object becomes the Other that the child, in mimetic self dramatization, now Brings to itself, the mother, and the environment, giving the child its first taste of being a Bringer. At this moment too the child grasps the *cogito*, the "I am" discourse, of course not in words but in feeling tones and without the social content.

Another characteristic of this phase is the "checking back" with the mother. The father has not entered the scene with the same force as a Known that the mother has, making her The Sovereign. The father has yet to become The Lawgiver, which is necessary at the social position. The mother serves both functions now because she gives and takes away, in her juridical capacity. Mahler, et al. also say this phase serves as a transition to the exploration of strangers as the child ventures out from the safe zone near the mother to explore what lies beyond — a beyond which, by degrees of distance, contains more and more Others. "The baby begins comparative scanning. He becomes interested in 'mother' and seems to compare her with 'other,' the unfamiliar with the familiar, feature by feature.' "[283]

It seems that at each stage of development the point at which a new discourse is discovered is also a point at which a new pathology can be manifest through maladaptation. The painful/bad, pleasurable/good perception of the infant's tiny world must make "sense" to the infant, which is clearly an innate sense in the most fundamental meaning of the word. Differentiation from the mother must be binary and without trauma or ambiguity, and must be accompanied by reinforcements such as the transitional object. The checking back phase must be juridically appropriate and must be both protective and permissive to have its desired effect. Finally the exploration of the Other as the stranger marks the incipient stage of the transformation. It is at this stage that seeds can be sown for psychopathology in the form of the sociopath, misanthrope, or other maladaptation. It all seems to depend upon the discourse associated with the presence of Unknowns.

Body-image development is of the child's place in the world as a solid, living entity. There is the tacit sense that others are so too. There

[282] Mahler, Margaret, et al. *The Psychological Birth of the Human Infant: Symbiosis and Individuation.* New York: Basic Books, Inc., Publishers, 1975, p. 54-5.
[283] Ibid., pp. 55-6.

is an awareness that the body is the locus of pain and pleasure, and that it has needs that are imperatives. The child also develops a sense that it is someone in particular, because it is given attention by the Knowns and Unknowns alike that reinforce this sense.

The child "turns with more or less wonderment and apprehension to a prolonged visual and tactile exploration and study of the faces and the gestalt of others [and seems to] check back to his mother's gestalt, particularly her face, in relation to other new interesting experiences."[284] The step from 0I to I1 is binary, and the step from I1 to I2 is binary also. There is no gradiation, no progression between the two, though they are related and dependent upon each others as Zones of Proximal Development. They are proximal to each and therefore one depends as much as another as the other does on it. In reality, the child does not progress through the stages just described; rather, the stages are interdependent, and continue to be values in the persona long after the child has reached adulthood, for what, after all, is the adult made of but childhood experience, gates, thresholds, and zones of development!

6.4 Practicing and rapprochement

Phases 2 and 3 are grouped together because of the reciprocity and similarity. In Practicing the child learns (more or less on its own, by the way) "crawling, paddling, climbing, and righting" itself.[285] There are dozens of other skills, more subtle, that are also practiced. This period culminates in full bipedal movement forward with direction and purpose (the "standing" that is at the root of the state and participation in the state and the juridical order). In Rapprochement, the child adapts to the consequences of the culmination of Practicing with a "stage of cognitive development that Piaget (1936) regards as the beginning of representational intelligence (which will culminate in symbolic play and in speech) [...]."[286] In this stage, says Mahler, et al., "the toddler reaches the first level of identity — that of being a separate individual entity."[287]

---

[284] Ibid., p. 56.
[285] Mahler, Margaret, et al. *The Psychological Birth of the Human Infant: Symbiosis and Individuation.* New York: Basic Books, Inc., Publishers, 1975, p. 65.
[286] Ibid., p. 76.
[287] Ibid., p. 76.

We jump to the second year of life for the child. There is greater domination of the environment. But what is most significant is not a decrease in anxiety regarding the environment, but rather an increase of fear over what is called "object loss." As the child becomes more like the adult, and the binaries of 0I and I1 harden, separation from the parents (but in particular the mother) becomes more of both a reality and an irrational fear. In the child's fundamental adaptation as I1, and having seen the horizon of I2, a gulf develops between the child's essential security (provided there is no real reason to be insecure) and the imagined separation from the best-known Knowns who are foundational for the security base of the child's venture into the world of strangers and Others.

What interests us, here, is the opportunity for neurotic and irrational fears. Here begins the first "storytelling" of the child's emotional life. Later in life the story will become much more elaborate, to be exploited by psychologists who earn their living listening to these stories and commenting on them rather like literary critics. Once again a binary ensues but on the sub-position level of I1. Just as the child at last stands up and begins exploring the world as a fully bipedal creature with hands free and eyes forward and off the ground, it is also confronted with the angst accompanying freedom, for it is a kind of freedom to be so disposed. Anxiety becomes associated with freedom, so that there is a contrary desire for freedom to go away even if it means forsaking the thrill of bipedal locomotion. *It is this emotion alone that is exploited at the Ix position by the sovereign in the abduction process.*

"With the spurt in autonomous functions, such as cognition, but especially upright locomotion, the 'love affair with the world' begins. The toddler takes the greatest step in human individuation. He walks freely with upright posture. Thus, the plane of his vision changes; from an entirely new vantage point he finds unexpected and changing perspectives, pleasures, and frustrations. This is the new visual level that the upright, bipedal position affords."[288]

What we are particularly concerned with here are his "pleasures and frustrations" as the analogs of the dialectic of jouissance and ennui, and their relationship to the dialectic of the ZPD between the actual and proximal. The dialectic is what propels the subject toward the abduction position and back through recursion. What is there in this "two legs

---

[288] Ibid., p. 70.

good" perspective that initializes cognition and brings about a sense of social frustration and fear of freedom? First it is considerable that the hands are free and the sense of space has radically changed. Previously the head was the leading and most dexterous organ, being the central "vacuui" of the world for the child as the place where food and water go and where substances are tested for their tactile nature much as most mammals would test the world. But with hands and arms entirely free to interact with the world and others, there is great potentiality for manipulation of the environment, for the exploration of materials, for the Getting and the Bringing.

But there is also the sense that the old Bringers are not needed as much, which *brings on* a kind of morbidity in the *looking-back* of personal history. This *looking-back* brings on nostalgia for the oblivion of the 0I position and the tender care of the I1. Also, recall that the ennui is brought on by the conflict between the specular self and the social self, with the social self indulging its gaze in the looking-back, and the specular self frustrated at having to share its narcissistic pleasures with a world of demanding Others and the great task of Bringing to oneself and eventually and inevitably to others. "[T]here is a noticeable waning of his previous imperviousness to frustration [....] Increased separation anxiety can be observed: at first this consists mainly of fear of object loss [....] As the toddler's awareness of separateness grows [...] he seems to have an increased need for [the love of the] mother [...]."[289]

The Rapprochement stage culminates, as might be expected from the above, in an existential crisis creating the second great psychosomatic trauma of the child's life, the first being the birth trauma. Near the end of the child's second year, there is a critical fear of the loss of love.[290] This phase is sometimes known in the vernacular as "the terrible twos." In this position the child exhibits the kind of behavior that, in adults, is considered to be mental illness: an alternation of omnipotent grandeur and prostrate dependence upon the primary Bringer, the mother. The father's Lawmaking comes into the foreground as he attempts to assist the mother in "laying down the law" about such behavior. Here we have the social foundation, of the Diagnostic and Statistical Manual (DSM-IV) which neatly codifies what in a two-year-old is considered normal but in a

---

[289] Mahler, Margaret, et al. *The Psychological Birth of the Human Infant: Symbiosis and Individuation.* New York: Basic Books, Inc., Publishers, 1975, pp. 76-7.
[290] Ibid., p. 95.

32-year-old is diagnosed pathology. "Conflicts ensued that seemed to hinge upon the desire to be separate, grand, and omnipotent, on the one hand, and to have mother magically fulfill their wishes, without having to recognize that help was actually coming from the outside, on the other."[291]

There is much more to this third phase that we cannot go into here, such as the start of gender identity, the beginning of empathy, obtaining an optimal distance from the mother (and father), and the development of a variety of emotions. What we have been particularly interested in here for the sake of this discussion is the growing integration and disintegration of the personality, and the certain thresholds it crosses in this positional phase shifting. Of special interest is the fear of freedom and the set-up for the later threshold of abduction at the Ix position. Finally, we looked at the role bipedal locomotion has in the formation of the cogito and its social components as manupilation of the environment of Unknowns and in self Bringing. Now it is time to turn to the matter of emotional object constancy.

6.5 Emotional Object Constancy + Consolidation of Individuality

The significance of this stage to the exploration of the psycholinguistics of discourse is in the development of "object constancy" where the mother (in particular) is virtualized in the abstract emotional imagination of the child. This occurs with other objects as well (for instance the father has a stronger object constancy in a female child). Without this first analog of what will later be adult love of an exagomous object, no happy relationship is possible. Furthermore, the relationship with the exagomous object in the end permeates all relationships in the adult's life, and therefore is primal. The consolidation of identity/individuality poises the subject to feel a degree of autonomy, which has been called sovereignty, and is indeed the origin of the sense of self possession. An unstable formation of indentity/ individuality, and the inability to hold objects constant in the mind when absent from them, are the basis of some of the most intractable psychiatric disorders classed among the "personality disorders" of the DSM. Both malformations contribute to abduction into the discourse at the position

---

[291] Ibid., p. 95.

Ix, but tend to block the recursion back to I2, making the Second negation impossible.

What is most interesting about this phase, generally in the third year of life, is that in both males and females the father takes a greater role as the Maker of the Law. Lessons begin with what is "good" and "bad," so the child, who at this stage is fully lingual, encounters his first synthetic propositions and is told that these propositions are more "important" than the imperatives he has known. (It is perhaps this inversion that led Kant to formulate an alternate system of good/bad in the form of the Categorical Imperative as a remediation.) The constancy of the object "implies the unifying of the 'good' and the 'bad' object into *one whole representation* [italics added]. This fosters the fusion of the aggressive and libidinal drives and tempers the hatred for the object" when the mother or father is absent.[292]

The phrase "one whole representation" shows how a discourse is created. This one could be called "The Doctrine of Meek and Mild," where volcanic libidinal forces are tamed by the juridical implied threats of the father and of the social environment of The Law. There are many ways to express the law, such as that Jesus wants his followers to be meek and mild, or that "bad" behavior will be punished and good rewarded. Is it that the rewards are insufficient that bad behavior is so difficult to avoid, or is it that bad behavior is so pleasurable it is too difficult to resist? Or is it that synthetic statements, by their basis in "nothing/nothingness/no one" do not have the prohibitive power of the more aggressive forms of interference?

What is certain is that the object constancy affects all aspects of development and surely will affect the outcome of the Ix →I2 inversion/ negation/recursion. "The slow establishment of emotional object constancy is a complex and multidimensioned process involving all aspects of psychic development [....] Numerous other factors are involved, such as innate drive endowment and maturation, neutralization of drive energy, reality testing, tolerance for frustration and for anxiety, and so forth."[293] The list just indicated covers nearly all categories in the DSM.

The most critical achievement, which does not come about without object constancy, is the emergence of the personality as a sovereign individual. It is from the vehicle of language, platformed on the emotional

---

[292] Mahler, Margaret, et al. *The Psychological Birth of the Human Infant: Symbiosis and Individuation.* New York: Basic Books, Inc., Publishers, 1975, pp. 110-11
[293] Ibid., p. 110.

stability of object constancy, that individuality and personal sovereignty are founded at least in their incipience. All language flows from the subject phrase of the cogito: "I am," which also is the framework which *ragt*or juts into the predicate of the world of synthetic appearances. The child's first experience of this jutting is with analytic phrases such as, I am a boy, I am a girl; I am a son, I am a daughter; I am a brother, I am a sister; which are then extended to synthetic propositions such as, I am a good boy, I am a good girl, and I am a good boy who loves his mommy, and so on. "During the period of normal symbiosis, the narcissistically fused object was felt to be 'good' — that is, in harmony with the symbiotic self — so that primary identification took place under a positive valence of love,"[294]but now is left behind for the gesture toward exogamous objects beyond the love of the mother which, ironically, is only possible if the mother is virtualized and internalized as an essential component of the core identity. A bungling of this transition by the parents — either through neglect or over dependency — causes trantrums and maladaptation which of course manifest later in life as psychiatric pathologies. The emergence of the sovereign self is a process that expresses itself autonomically — if and only if the object constancy of the mother (and father) was facilitated, which means, in essence, not interfered with as an organic process.

This is a period of the deployment of the sovereign personality in its nuanced and colorful complexities as well. Children seem almost generic in early childhood in their behavior at the OI stage, which makes sense considering that their sense of "I" is limited to their nervous system and its imperatives, reactions, and autonomic processes. However, at this the binary crossing of the I2 threshold, the child blossoms one way or another, including sexually. "Thus, the fourth subphase is characterized by unfolding of complex cognitive functions: verbal communication, fantasy, and reality testing."[295]

The details of the unfolding — both in its normal mode and pathological mode — are worth exploring, but not here as they belong more to the realm of developmental Freudian psychology. However, it is worth noting what dire consequences there are for the subject at this stage, and how social fiat discourse can contribute to the undermining of the devlopment, which is what the next part of this study will be concerned

---

[294] Ibid., p. 117.
[295] Mahler, Margaret, et al. *The Psychological Birth of the Human Infant: Symbiosis and Individuation.* New York: Basic Books, Inc., Publishers, 1975, pp. 117.

with. "The principal conditions for mental health, so far as preoedipal development is concerned, hinge on the attained and continuing ability of the child to retain or restore his self-esteem in the context of relative libidinal object constancy."[296] As we shall see, "self-esteem" begins with the juridical father at this stage, but ends with the Big Five: government, church, schools, banking, and the media.

1.1 Ontology of the abducted position

As mentioned, the consequences of abduction (abdication) are felt as pathology when there is no recursion to the I2 position from Ix. Failure to recur could be a function of a threshold, where the subject is imprisoned because of a war, a crime, or persecution. In this case, there is no return to personal sovereignty, only a repetition of the circumstances the prisoner finds himself or herself in. Another situation is where the subject volunteers to remain at the Ix position (abdication). It should be mentioned again here that abdication is not the primary function of the I2 →Ix phase shift. While there is no abduction without abdication, there would be no opportunity for abdication without abduction. It would seem that in the prisoner's situation of course the subject would not have "wanted" to be abducted into the criminal justice system with its jails and prisons.

However, there was the volitional impulse (the abdication) to commit a crime for which the prisoner knew there were consequences (the abduction). What about the case where the prisoner was unjustly imprisoned? Whatever the circumstances, there could have been what is called an "involuntary abdication." In other words, it might be some de facto quality of the subject that also leads to the abduction. For instance, the Jews of the Warsaw Ghetto; it was their Jewishness that was their abdication, though they did not *choose* Jewishness but were, by definition, *Chosen* to be Jews. So there is an active and passive, dynamic and static, volitional and involuntary abdication. As we shall see, the implications of the fatalism of the latter are rather frightening, for there is no possibility of movement from Ix →I2 as recursion.

What we are left with are three possible pathologies that are discrete, but also appear in combination (of which there are 9). We will look at these pathologies as *modes*, and in their discrete modes.

---

[296] Ibid., p. 118.

1.2 Etiology of abduction pathology

Referring back to Mahler, et al., we see that object constancy around the age of 3 is a critical period in the child's development in that the inability to cultivate the constant virtual object in the psyche reverberates in at later stages of live as personality disorder. It is not so difficult to see how without the consant virtual object there would be separation anxiety when the object (of the subject) was not present, and even when the object was present – with the implied negation of not being present at some point which is an absolute inevitability.

As the psyche is more or less the core of the identity of the subject, the lack of the presence in the psyche of the object creates an eccentricity. The psyche is a centric position. Its content is what anchors it in personality. It is really inaccurate to say that so-and-so has no core identity or that core identity is present or not present. Core identity is as inevitable an organ of the mind as the heart is an organ of the body. If we say, metaphorically, that someone is "heartless," of course we do not mean he or she has no living, beating heart! However, if the container of the core identity is not filled with the virtualized furniture, personas, and objects of the world, it becomes eccentric in its *cathexis*, that is its attachment to external versions of the same.

The need for abduction then grows inordinate. It stops being a course of natural development in the phase shifting toward the recursion to the Second Negation as homo generator. Rather, it becomes an end in itself (not including forcible abduction where there is only passive abdication). Furthermore, the dialectics of ennui/jouissance and actual/proximal become corrupted, so that ennui becomes a *demotivator*for recursion. Actual development is seen as progression and, in a progression, who wants regression? Often individuals are accused of being "immature" when they recur because they seem to return to what Gardner calls a child-like state of play.[297]

Unfortunately there is no evil doctor from the Island of Dr. Moreau commanding the abduction of souls. Rather, much of the responsibility can be laid at the altars of the environment and its social and cultural components, which Kreisman and Straus say include, "fast-paced, fragmented societal structure, destruction of the nuclear family, increased divorce rates, increased reliance on nonparental day care, greater geographical mobility, and changing

---

[297] Gardner, Howard. *Creating Minds*. New York: Basic Books, 1994.

patterns of gender roles [...]."[298] We may bristle at this list, since it is almost a description of the modern social order, but then we must also bristle at the dramatic increase of personality disorder as a diagnosis and its increasing importance in the DSM. For instance, "changing patterns of gender roles" might be a way of avoiding a personality disorder, and certainly is a recursion from an abducted position.

However, it is not this for everyone. It takes only a handful of severely disordered personas in a community to create a disturbance in the fabric of the social arch. And while the social arch more often than not needs disturbance (as the agent of abduction and often then enforcer of the prohibition against recursion as retrograde), there is a problem when an ever-increasing amount of its finite resources are devoted to therapeutic efforts, interdiction, and psychopharmacology – all of which only aid the abduction process and in the end inhibit recursion. It is also a mistake to think that Kreisman and Straus claim that these are "the causes" of personality disorder. They are at least only antagonists and should be considered in our discussion. There are also biological factors, such as genetic traits that determine brain chemistry in the neuroendicrine system: "These neurotransmitters also affect the balance of adrenaline and steroid production in the body."[299]

Futhermore, before we recoil at the indictment of the prevailing liberal social order we must remember Freud's position at the *fin de siecle* of the 19thCentury. What was considered to be the social structure – with all its hypocrisies and flaws so apparent in retrospect – is now characterized as "repressive," as to be almost iconic (as in the word "Victorian" used as a synonym for "repressed"). Is this fair? If we also consider the political reforms of the time, both in the forms of representational parliamentary government and the dawn of alternatives such as communism and socialism, it becomes more difficult to indict 19th century Europe as somehow more repressive than monarchy. Also, in comparison to the great dictatorships and totalitarian governments of the 20th Century, the 19th seems like a liberal paradise.

In psychology, the epidemic among the demographic Freud treated as a clinician were afflicted with hysteria or obsessional neurosis or both.

---

[298] Kreisman, Jerold J and Hal Straus. *I Hate You – Don't leave Me: Understanding the Borderline Personality.* New York: Perigee, 2010, p. 60.

[299] Kreisman, Jerold J and Hal Straus. *I Hate You – Don't leave Me: Understanding the Borderline Personality.* New York: Perigee, 2010, p. 61.

We know that there are new diagnoses in the DSM for what ailed some of his patients. Even with this knowledge, we must conclude that there were symptoms the extremely observant Freud documents that today seem not to exist or are certainly rare and not common as they were for him – even among the same bourgeois demographic. Kreisman and Straus attribute at least part of the malformation of the ego to a "disintegrating culture." We must consider what Freud hypothesized – that repressed instincts may lead to neurosis in certain individuals – and then consider what pathologies might arise when they are "permitted" in a selective fashion as they are today. "Now, over a century later, aggressive and sexual institincts are expressed more openly, and the social milieu is much more confused. What it means to be a man or a woman is more ambiguous in modern Western civilization than in turn-of-the-century Europe. Social, economic, and political structures are less fixed. The family unit and cultural roles are less defined, and the very concept of 'traditional' is unclear."[300] This is not to say these facts are "bad." Rather, the point is that they must be taken into consideration when exploring the origins of personality disorder, which it is the hypothesis here is the chief obstruction (barring involuntary abduction) to the recursion to the I2 position from Ix and the formation of homo generator at the Second Negation.

Foucault calls the Victorian myth the "Repressive Hypothesis." We see that the progressive fallacy (that the mere passage of time brings improvement) is at work here. It is assumed by the liberal ideology – which is fundamentally progressive in nature and even calls itself progressive at times – that the apparent permissiveness of modern European culture is a remedy and improvement of the "repressed Victorian" period when social mores somehow created a few generations of emotional and psychological cripples. Foucault focuses on the institutions of education in his critique of the treatment of sexuality in modernity. He starts with the 18th Century, showing that if there is any progression at all it is toward the repression of sexual libido and id and not their liberation as liberals would have it.

"On the contrary, since the eighteenth century [the pedagogical institution] has multiplied the forms of discourse on the subject; it has established various points of implantation for sex; it has coded contents and qualified speakers [....] causing children themselves to talk about it, and enclosing them in a web of discourses which sometimes address them, sometimes speak about them, of impose canonical bits of knowledge on

---

[300] Ibid., pp 77-8.

them, or use them as a basis for constructing bits of science that is beyond their grasp – all this together enables us to link an intensification of the interventions of power to a multiplication of discourse."[301]

In other words, modernity imposed the old liturgical order on the apparent freedoms of the modern age with its very greatest invention: the confession. The priest was replaced by the psychologist, who is at once the soothsayer who extrapolates the folk tale of the etiology (which is in part what is being done here now) and the prognosis, while at the same time listening to the pathological "bad things" the patient has done and wants to not do and be forgiven for ("I'm getting help for my problem").

Deluze and Guattari describe at least one of these stories, taken from the plays of Sophocles: the iconic Oedipus Rex. "Structural interpretation makes Oedipus into a kind of universal Catholic symbol, beyond all the imaginary modalities. It makes Oedipus into a referential axis not only for the pre-oedipal phases, but also for the para-oedipal varieries, and the exo-oedipal varieties."[302] Most significant is for the "pre-oedipal phases," since the damage is done during the period in the child's life 0-4 during which the positions of 0I, I1, and I2 have their first iteration. In the analysis of the pathology emanating from that first period of the Critical Period, there is a retroactive reassignment of Oedipal complexities which are later confessed to the psychologist who leads the subject into what Foucault calls above "an intensification of the interventions of power to a multiplication of discourse." Furthermore, Foucault invokes an imperative applied to the formation of the complex as discourse: "Not only will you confess to acts contravening the law, but you will seek to transform your desire, your every desire, into discourse. Insofar as possible, nothing was meant to elude this dictum [...]."[303]

Mass media has helped propagate – through propaganda and its organs – this imperative or dictum. Confessions from serial killers to politicians who stole money or had sex with someone they should not have abound. It is even an industry. The result, though, is the malformation of the centric ego from the constant eccentric pressure of the milieu, the *in*

[301] Foucault, Michel. *The History of Sexuality: An Introduction (Vol. 1)*. New York: Vintage Books, 1990, pp. 29-30.

[302] Deleuze, Gilles and Felix Guattari. *Anti-Oedipus: Capitalism and Schizophrenia*. Minneapolis: U. of Minnesota Press, 2008, p. 52.

[303] Foucault, Michel. *The History of Sexuality: An Introduction (Vol. 1)*. New York: Vintage Books, 1990, p. 21.

media res, of the environment. "The flooding of technical advancement and information that swept over the late twentieth and early twenty-first centuries, much of it involving computers, PDA's, cell phones, and so on, often requires greater individual commitment to solitary study and practice, thus sacrificing opportunities for real social interaction."[304]

7.3 Economic pressure on the developing ego

It would be a mistake to imagine that economic pressures are not critical in the malformation of the ego to the point that the core identity is not furnished with the content necessary to anchor it in the psyche. Such pressure includes the imperatives of the Big Five: the taxes and other financial demands of government, the tithing and pan handling of the church, the property taxes and tuition of schools (and the necessity for certification to be admitted into certain economic echelons), the interest rates of loans (and the necessity to borrow to, for example, go to college or buy a house), and at last the commercial appeals of the mass media. Finally, the Keynesian business cycle stirs the pot of economic stress to the point where it is almost a dialectic for abduction and for the back pressure against recursion. "Periods of economic uncertainty, exemplified in the roller-coaster boom-and-bust scenarios, have become the rule not the exception [....] Some of these changes may be related to society's 'failure to achieve a kind of social rapprochement.' " In Rapprochement, as has been mentioned earlier, the child adapts to the outcome of Practicing with a "stage of cognitive development that Piaget (1936) regards as the beginning of representational intelligence (which will culminate in symbolic play and in speech) [...]."[305]

The critical phrase above is "representational intelligence," or the ability to *virtualize* the object as the furniture of the core identity in the psyche. In the eccentric position (Ix) the centric position is abducted by the shadows of the divisive media, which, as the terminus of the concatenation of the Big Five and its lingual mediator, serves the previous four in a unique way as "symbolic play and [...] speech." The psyche, in its dumb autonomy, accepts the shadows for the relative substance of the virtualization of such critical

---

[304] Kreisman, Jerold J and Hal Straus. *I Hate You – Don't leave Me: Understanding the Borderline Personality.* New York: Perigee, 2010, p. 79.
[305] Ibid., p. 76.

real-world values as "mother." Sex, knowledge, political value, economic priority, and critical understanding soon follow from the abdication of their value in the Freudian sense as "psychic energy." "Disruption of the rapproachement cycle often results in a lack of trust, disturbed relationships, emptiness, anxiety, and an uncertain self-image – characteristics that make up the borderline syndrome."[306]

The inverted state resulting from the abduction of the core identity without recursion leads to linguistic confusion where signified is inverted from signifier, causing thought to subvert itself in a way that precludes critical thinking, analysis, and epistemological truth testing. This state of mind is extremely useful in creating "useful idiots" and other forms of malleable masses that can be exploited as needed for economic gain by a powerful elite or to engage in wars for the protection of their interests. Ultimately, the content of the core identity reflects the environment as the effect of the mirror stage. "Like the world of the borderline, ours in many ways is a world of massive contradictions," say Kreisman and Straus. "We presume to believe in peace, yet our streets, movies, television, and sports are filled with aggression and violence."

The result is what they call a "mythical polarity" of "black or white, right or wrong, good or bad" reinforced by the juridical protocols and imperatives seen as the core of the core of the social arch. "The legal system, built on the premise that one is either guilty or not guilty with little or no room for grey areas, perpetuates the myth that life is intrinsically fair and justice can be attained […]."[307] The "myth" is the prevailing discourse which becomes a vacillating substitute for dialectics. The result is the erasure of *homo generator* in favor of *homo industrialis*. "Creativity and intellectual diligence are sacrificed to convenience and precision."[308]

7.4 The social order of abduction

Most of our discussion has been about abduction in the context of personal psychology. But what of the collective psychology of the social order? This is a topic for another book to treat with depth, but it must be mentioned here. Nowhere does the abducted social order make itself more apparent

---

[306] Kreisman, Jerold J and Hal Straus. *I Hate You – Don't leave Me: Understanding the Borderline Personality.* New York: Perigee, 2010, p. 81.
[307] Ibid., p. 83.
[308] Ibid., p. 83.

than in the colonial order, where an entire population is, as it were, abducted by an invading power. With little exception, if there was no an outright war between states where one emerged the victor, then the association between the orders is one of abduction and abdication. What leads a whole population to dismiss its own sovereignty in favor of an alien system (such as Christianity or Islam)?

Before discussing colonial order *per se*, let us look at the possible psychology of abdication. We may post a few axioms about it: 1) No people gives up sovereignty when there is hope, and 2) Hopelessness is the prerequisite for full abdication. The best work on hopelessness as a syndrome has been done on laboratory animals. Seligman cites the work of Richter where rats died from hopelessness in controlled situations. The first part of the experiment a rat was placed in a vat of water with no escape. The animal would swim for up to 60 hours before giving up from exhaustion and drowning. Then, the rats were held in the investigator's hand until they ceased struggling, and then were placed in the water. They died much sooner than the first rats. At last they had their whiskers trimmed and were again held. These rats could be said to have died sudden deaths. What might this mean for us? "Richter reasoned that being held in the hand of a predator like man, having whiskers trimmed, and being put in a vat of water from which escape is impossible produces a sense of helplessness in the rat."[309]

How do these data correspond to our axioms? In the first, "No people gives up sovereignty when there is hope," we see the seeds for a material equivalency or tautology. Hopelessness is the giving up of sovereignty. Abdication is the gesture of impotency in the face of the Potentate or Sovereign. The tautology also satisfies the second axiom. In this case we have the material equivalent A is A. What this means, though, is something particular. Richter furthered the experiment by holding the rats and then saving them. After returning them to the vat they also swam for 60 hours; their hopefulness was restored by the saving gesture, even if in the end they were not saved. Finally, some were put into the water and removed several times. These rats too swam for 60 hours before drowning, with the expectation that they would at some point be saved.

What does this look like on a human scale in the colonial environment? First there must be some correlations. The "vat" corresponds to the native

---

[309] Seligman, Martin E. P. *Helplessness: On Depression, Development, and Death.* San Francisco: W.H. Freeman and Co., 1975, p. 169-70.

land of the colonized subjects. Very often they were "drowning" in their own economic, social, epidemiological, environmental or internecine crises, often with an almost intolerable combination of one or all of these ills. Nevertheless, the social order persists, often with terrific efforts to right the situation or part of it in any way possible. Eventually, though, the call goes out to an interested power to intervene (the hand). How this power intervenes varies as does the touch of the researcher's hand on the rats. Sometimes the colony is "saved' outright (e.g. from an outbreak of the plague, as in Camus' *The Plague*). Sometimes the colony is held in immediate military subjugation, herded into "refugee camps," where as a culture they die immediately and as individuals they die piecemeal as they did in the Warsaw Ghetto or in Palestinian refugee camps on the Gaza Strip. Sometimes the colony is alternately held and released, held and released, allowing them hope but ultimately letting them drown when the colonial power pulls out of a place where it should never have been in the first place.

In each case, though, the individual subjects must have their sovereignty as individuals removed so that their sovereignty as a people will not survive the colonial onslaught. At the same time, to show that they are not conquerors but rather are present to help the colonists, the propaganda of the sovereign power must extol individuality above all, and construct schools and courts and jails and police and media infrastructure to communicate this idea that abduction is freedom from the ills the people originally were suffering when the colonial powers arrived on the scene. "The colonized intellectual learned from his masters that the individual must assert himself. The colonialist bourgeoise hammered into the colonized mind the notion of a society of individuals where each is locked in his own subjectivity, where wealth lies in thought."[310]

Prima facie this looks like the urging of sovereignty on the part of the Sovereign power, but the very nature of the idea itself shows its contradiction. There can be no sovereign power when there is pervasive personal sovereignty. It is a contradiction cloaked in egalitarian language. The giveaway is the phrase "locked in his own subjectivity," which is an adequate description of the idea in Kreisman and Straus of the isolated core identity wrapped in its own world of inherited ideas, desolate, bereft of the paradoxical exogamous relationships the centric personality has and choking in the incestuous neurosis of the eccentric. Furthermore, the subjectivity is

---

[310] Fanon, Franz. *The Wretched of the Earth*. New York: Grove Press, 2004, p. 11.

of the nature of the pleasuring the mass media – with its panels of shadows – imparts to the subject as a substitute for the domestic furniture that would otherwise inhabit the core. It is only when social connections are made and the subject begins to come out of the narcissism of the eccentric position, that the liberation process begins anew. "But the colonized intellectual who is lucky enough to bunker down with the people during the liberation struggle, will soon discover the falsity" of the doctrine of individualism as narcissism purveyed by the colonists.[311]

7.5 The pathology of social abduction

On the contrary, vilification of the colonized is needed to justify the moral superiority of the sovereign power which, either directly or by proxy, rules over the subjects of the colonized "vat." The result is always that at some point the colonists feel "hopeless," at which point they either rebel or drown in the sovereign's usurpation of their abdicated fate. Whether their abdication is active or passive, the result is the same: they are faced with a bifurcation of ontic threads: either fight and win a new self-sovereignty (or death in a lost battle), or give up and accept the rule of the sovereign and perhaps also suffer a fate they would not wish for themselves (sudden death from hopelessness). They may also choose to continue on in a parallel ontology, undermining while cooperating, for no people is so simple that every group wants the same thing. So as a people they may end up both fighting and accepting, producing as these threads continue, a *contraphasic* movement where opposite ends are being striven for.

"Challenging the colonial world is not a rational confrontation of viewpoints. It is not a discourse on the universal, but the impassioned claim of the colonized that their world is fundamentally different. The colonized world is a Manichaean world. The colonist is not content with physically limiting the space of the colonized [through refugee and prison camps], i. e. with the help of his agents of law and order. As if to illustrate the totalitarian nature of colonial exploitation, the colonist turns the colonized into a kind of quintessence of evil."[312]

The psychiatric impact of the process of vilification leads to a reaction from the colonized. Often the Manichaean elements running

---

[311] Fanon, Franz. *The Wretched of the Earth*. New York: Grove Press, 2004, p. 11.
[312] Ibid., p. 6.

on contraphasic ontological threads clash, creating a ligature Event in the form of civil war. Such wars are often characterized as the most bloody if for no other reason than the fact that both armies are already on the same territory, know it equally, and see no other outcome except annihilation of the other. This annihilation is already present psychically as the negation of the Other as the "quintessence of evil" – the true lesson taught by the colonial power to the group which acquiesces to its juridical imperatives. "Because it is [through] a systematized negation of the other, a frenzied determination to deny the other any attribute of humanity, colonialism forces the colonized to constantly ask the question: 'Who am I in reality.' "[313] The question belies the eccentric position (Ix) of the colonized.

Life at the eccentric position is fundamentally at odds with Dasein. While it is in Dasein and of Dasein, its is a contraphasic impulse. The result is psychiatric disorders (such as we have already discussed) manifest in the adult and in the class of adults under the same regime. As a class this juggernaut has much more power than the sociopathic individual. Eventually the personality disorder gets collectivized and codified into the Doctrine of Cruelty, discourse at its worst, where the subjects autonomically carry out the juridical imperatives of the Sovereign. The borderline personality begins to show the symptoms of psychosis. Fanon, a psychiatrist, describes his patients who suffered from the trauma of a civil war in a colonized African nation. "We believe in the cases presented here the triggering factor is principally the bloody, pitiless atmosphere, the generalization of inhuman practices, of people's lasting impression that they are witnessing a veritable apocalypse."[314]

---

[313] Ibid., p. 182.
[314] Fanon, Franz. *The Wretched of the Earth*. New York: Grove Press, 2004, p. 183.

PART 5: **MORPHOLOGY OF ABDUCTION (ABDICATION)**

It is as if another soul had entered into the body and thenceforward subsisted there, in place side by side with the normal subject.

– Traugott Oesterreich[315]

1.1 What is possession/a possession?

There are two basic meanings of "possession." The first is something one owns, and the second is "being possessed," meaning under the control of something alien to oneself. The first seems simple enough but is not, and the second seems complex and strange and is. When someone possesses something, a subtle change has come over the person or thing. How one or the other is possessed is of interest as well. For example, sometimes a person is possessed like a thing is, meaning that person can be bought and sold, modified, and disposed of. It also may mean that that person is not accorded the same rights and privileges as the owner. We say of this person so possessed that he or she is "a slave." The owner creates a new category for this person who is "not free" as the owner is. Therefore, the relationship is binary, expressed thus as negation: if p equals "free," and owner and slave are a and b, and → is "if, then," then: $x \equiv (a + p) \rightarrow (b + \sim p)$.[316] If q is the positive expression "slave," then the symmetrical relationship is thus (as the negation of x as y): $y \equiv (b + q) \rightarrow (a + \sim q)$.

The owner and the slave, then, are in a mutual relationship of *abduction and abdication*. The slave abdicates not because he or she wants to (voluntary abdication), but based on membership to a class of potential slaves as designated by the slave owner, the slave owner's cohort, and

---

[315] Oesterreich, Traugott K. *Possession, Demonaical & Other Among Primitive Races, in Antiquity, the Middle Ages, and Modern Times.* Hyde Park, N.Y.: University Books, 1966, p. 17.
[316] The symbol $\equiv$ is meant as "material equivalent," whereas $=$ means simple "equals" as in $1 + 0 = 1$.

the *social arch*.[317] In perfect symmetry, the owner belongs to the class of owners or possessors. As long as the relationship is maintained and not inverted, the social arch remains intact. Invert it, and the arch crumbles and a new one must be erected in its place.

What change overcomes those who are possessed as things? There is a vast literature of slave narratives and analysis of various forms and eras of slavery. One element that this literature has in common is the apparent *helplessness* and *ennui* of the slave. No matter what the brain or brawn power of the slave, often the condition is characterized by extreme passivity toward the masters which is often misinterpreted as sympathetic reaction to a benevolent regime. Rather, it is what Seligman calls "learned helplessness." The possessed subject learns that his sovereignty has been entirely usurped (often from birth) and that there is no alternative except the "House of Pain" or death. Freedom is not even a concept because the subject's *Weltanshauung* is hermetically sealed off from the proposition of the negation of slavery. This view is *learned* because it is *taught*. It in no way reflects Natural Law nor even the Law of the Jungle. It is the foundation of the social arch. Its weapon is ennui, which fatigues the possession to the point of dehumanization.

Seligman may give us some insight into the psychology and mentality of the possession. He has identified six criteria which correlate to "learned helplessness." Furthermore, the six symptoms are the same for clinical depression as they are for learned helplessness:

1) Lowered initiation of voluntary responses.
2) Negative cognitive set (difficulty seeing cause and effect)
3) Time course (repetition of the lesson increases helplessness)
4) Lowered aggression
5) Loss of appetite
6) Physiological changes (lowered norepinephrine)[318]

This last physiological effect is of particular interest. Possessed creatures (such as animals in a zoo) are often characterized by a certain listlessness.

---

[317] By "*social arch*" is mean the structure or architecture of a particular society or culture.

[318] Seligman, Martin E.P. Helplessness: On Depression, Development, and Death. San Francisco: W.H. Freeman and Co., 1975., p. 82.

The complaint about captive animals is that they "sleep too much" to be entertaining for the audience. So it is with the "shiftless" captive human – either as a slave where the subject is possessed privately, or in prison where the subject is a public possession with an investment in keeping him or her "off the streets." Norepinephrine affects the amygdala, where attention and response is managed. Most of all, it affects heart rate. Lowered levels cause a slower heart beat and therefore less excitement and agitation. In the "flight or fight" scenario, there is increased norepinephrine. Therefore, a chronically low level will help to preclude flight or fight, which is most useful in a possession (we do not want our dogs running off).

The impact of being a human possession stretches across the board from energy level to intelligence quotient (IQ) on the Stanford-Binet Intelligence Scales. "Lowered response initiation may also be the cause of a variety of other so-called intellectual deficits in depressed patients. For example, the tested IQ's of hospitalized depressives drop during the disorder, and their ability to memorize definitions of new words deteriorates."[319] This, too, is of particular interest, especially the deterioration of the "ability to memorize new words." This means that the helpless, depressed slave is more resistant to the development of writing and reading, which might inform and embolden his speech and thought. This is of certain interest to the "abdication" of the possession, for if we examine the root of the word we find the same root (dic) as in "diction," "dictator," and "dictation." In effect, *abdication cuts out the tongue of the slave*, precluding a return to the I2 position of loquacious generation. Unable to network, bereft of education, listless and depressed, with no fight or flight left, the possessed subject never recurs to the I2 position from Ix. A threshold has been crossed from which there will be no return.

This is what Heidegger would call a "problematic," though, for the ontology of the modern possessor. There is no cotton to pick that is not picked by machine. The person who drives the machine is a well-paid and skilled operator of heavy machinery, and if the driver also owns it, then is also a strategic manipulator of capital. Rather, the slave is needed in the tower blocks of offices where the word is king. In this environment, the cutting of the tongue slices in a different direction. The modern slave is highly educable and trainable. Special polytechnic schools have been created to vet the subjects *trainability* and suitability for office work

---

[319] Ibid., p. 83.

requiring the sophisticated creation of messages and the manipulation of the office machine: a computer. As a necessary adjunct of the office machine, the worker is placed in a cubicle that serves as the container of human effort in its interface with the machine and the other *cubiculos*. The worker may feel lethargic, listless, and helpless, but there are drugs to combat these feelings that act directly upon the same neuroreceptors that the norepinephrine acts on. Fear takes care of the increased "fight or flight" response: fear of losing one's job, fear of not being able to pay a mortgage, fear of not being able to support a family, fear of becoming worse than a slave. And there are anti-anxiety drugs for this response too, if fear is not enough or becomes too excessive.

1.2 Possession of the core identity by the social *Arch*

There is a vast and curious literature about demonic possession. Most of the earliest and most copious accounts are taken from Christian literature of the Middle Ages where even entire abbeys and monasteries were possessed by "demons." However, the record goes back to the old testament and even to the early writing of the Sumarians, Egyptians, and other early civilizations. In more modern times, accounts once abounded to the point where there is an ancient and venerable lineage of shamans and necromancers who assisted in situations where possession was detected and unwanted and required removal and other abatement (e.g. Aleister Crowley, Madame Blavatsky). So why is it then that at a certain point in the development of a civilization such accounts of possession and shamanism *vanish* (except as anecdotes of anthropology from far-flung and atavistic civilizations)?

   We may conclude that the subject possessed by the demons of yore is now "possessed" by a clinical pathology identified in the Diagnostic and Statistical Manual (DSM-IV): schizophrenia. The *psychologization* of the natural phenomenon of possession (whatever it is) pervades the entire clinical structure even for pathologies which are not severe such as the ones mentioned above that are the symptoms of helplessness and depression – both quite common ailments today.

   Deleuze and Guattari describe the reinvention of the possessed persona as the schizophrenic who must become part of the industrial *officio* as *homo industrialis* and not *homo generator*. "What the schizophrenic experiences, both as an individual and as a member of the human species, is not at all any one aspect of nature, but nature as a process of production

[….] It is probable that at a certain level nature and industry are two separate and distinct things: from one point of view industry is opposite from nature; from another, industry extracts its raw materials from nature […]."[320]

Even if the schizophrenic is not the producer, he or she is the object of the productions of medicine. In fact, we may say that medicine is *caused* by the schizophrenic, which is the intention above of Deleuze and Guattari in describing the pathology as "nature as a process of production." The analog to the shaman and the subject who is possessed is exact: the possessed person caused the shaman, the rituals, the medicines, the treatments, the therapies and the cultural bond existing between the shaman, the subject, and the community of individuals (who desire to be rid of the possessing spirit).

We can perhaps believe that furnishing the core identity with the possessions of the sovereign will create an abducted persona. It is more difficult to see that the schizophrenic – cured or not – is the modern transformation of the traditional individual possessed by a demon. The desire expressed to cure the persona of the possession is a community decision because the persona is *non compos mentis,* more or less incapable of making the decision. This is not the case with the ennui and listlessness felt by the abducted slave, who is capable of making decisions and is therefore in more of a position to be assigned voluntary abdication. Therefore we may say that the depressed person is a victim of voluntary abdication and the schizophrenic of involuntary.

More needs to be said about voluntary abduction. The temptation mechanism of voluntary abduction is desire. Desire is the abdication, what Deleuze and Guattari call the "desiring-machine." Its mechanism hinges on an appeal to the *id.* For instance, a subject may desire the thrill of gambling, but cannot afford to lose money. So the subject steals the money from an employer and is caught, leading to a lengthy jail sentence for embezzlement. The subject has crossed a threshold of no return by abdicating through the desire to gamble. There is also the desire for the bourgeois lifestyle which requires certain sacrifices which may last a lifetime as an abdication ("I always wanted to be a poet but went into advertizing because it paid well"). "It is at work everywhere, functioning smoothly at all times, at other times in fits and starts. It breathes, it heats, it eats. It shits and fucks. What a

---

[320] Deleuze, Gilles and Felix Guattari. *Anti-Oepipus: Capitalism and Schizophrenia.* Minneapolis: U. of Minnesota Press, 1983, p. 7.

mistake to ever have said *the* id. Everywhere it is machines – real ones, not figurative ones: machines driving other machines, machines being driven by other machines, with all the necessary couplings and connections."[321] While Deleuze and Guitarri make it clear they mean "real machines," we can guess that they also mean *soft* and *hard* machines, computer software and an automobile manufactory in China. The curious exclamation, "What a mistake to have ever said *the* id" italicizes the word "the" meaning not that it is not the id behind desire, but that there is no locus of the id, no focal point in head or heart. Desire is the machines, the machines exist because of desire and not the other way around. In this situation, desire is the *a priori*. As such it is, in itself, the machine it created.

1.3 Demonic possession and its analogs

According to Oesterreich, another analog for demonic possession in modern times is the hysteria of Freud's day.[322] Hysteria is not a diagnosis in the modern DSM. In fact, it is after the Enlightenment and during the period of rational investigation during the 19th Century that the demonically possessed and the shaman who treated them began to vanish like unprotected endangered species. It is curious to note that during the Roman Catholic Church's attempts to explain and treat possession there was little luck in doing so and at time almost an epidemic of cases. And yet modern medical practices and ideas and perhaps the social environment that comes with it served to all but extinguish possession in a matter of decades.

Oesterreich sees two kinds of demonic possession which pass for abduction/abdication. The first is where the person possessed seems to be occupied by two separate individuals. The second is where the "two individuals" merge into one with a dramatic personality change. The first type shows evidence of *simultaneous parallel ontologies* (SPO). The second shows *linear serial ontologies* (LSO). Both find their way into the creation of the *desiring-machine* at the position of Ix. Therefore,

---

[321] Deleuze, Gilles and Felix Guattari. *Anti-Oepipus: Capitalism and Schizophrenia.* Minneapolis: U. of Minnesota Press, 1983, p. 1.

[322] Oesterreich, Traugott K. *Possession, Demonaical & Other Among Primitive Races, in Antiquity, the Middle Ages, and Modern Times.* Hyde Park, N.Y.: University Books, 1966, pp. 85, 125, 128n, 171, 196-7, 240, 249n.

abduction may take the form of SPO or LSO. Which is the more efficient one for the purposes of the apparatus? It seems that either will do *provided there is no recursion.* In the first state "the original personality vanishes and in its place comes the second which was hitherto a mere compulsive state." The second "seems to occur in the modern 'demoniacal fits' of highly hysterical persons."[323] It might be said, then, that the more "modern" state of a blending of personality would be prevalent and the more desired for the machine of the apparatus. It is more desirable because it is integrated and not so subject to the Events of an SPO such as *ligatures* and *truncations,* yet remains vulnerable to a reversal in the form of a *recursion* and a *bifurcation* into an SPO.

The driving engine is desire in both cases, but the coupling mechanism, as Oesterreich points out, is the compulsion toward something. Media's role in this process is to present the subject with commercial appeals to 1) create *Lack* and 2) to satisfy *Lack.* Baudrillard considers "lack" to be the modern acquisitive ethos: "It used to be, 'To each according to his deserts,' then 'to each according to his needs,' and later, 'to each according to his desire.' Today it is 'to each according to his lack.' "[324]To obtain what the subject lacks, the subject will make the abdication, bringing along all training and education so that the apparatus has a trained worker for the machine. What pinions the subject to the Ix position is the obsessional desire (neurosis) which then becomes the personality through the agency of abduction/abdication and the furnishing of the core identity with what Levi-Strauss calls the "bricolage" of the Sovereign. "Generally speaking, all states of emotional compulsion have a strong tendency to become the true nature of the individual."[325]

Nevertheless, possession is hardly gone from the landscape, though now it is couched in clinical terms. "Naturally the present time does not show a complete absence of states akin to possession. Possession has appeared to us as a particularly extensive complex of compulsive phenomena, [....] But these processes do not now develop with the same ease as formerly when the autosuggestion of possession intervened."[326]

[323] Oesterreich, Traugott K. *Possession, Demonaical & Other Among Primitive Races, in Antiquity, the Middle Ages, and Modern Times.* Hyde Park, N.Y.: University Books, 1966, p. 85.
[324] Beaudrillard, Jean. *Fatal Strategies.* Angeles: Semiotext(e), 2008, p. 50.
[325] Ibid., p. 85.
[326] Oesterreich, Traugott K. *Possession, Demonaical & Other Among Primitive*

That autosuggestion is not much of a part of inducing possession today shows that 1) it is not necessary, and 2) the cultural context has changed so that the meaning of the suggestion, such as the invocation of a pagan god, has no emotional force today and therefore may not serve as a catalyst (though hypnosis may, and it *is* a rather modern phenomenon).

To go any further, we must conceive of the Sovereign and the apparatus governed as having a certain kind of "personality." This is not so difficult when we recall the origin of the sovereign as God the Father. It is possible to tell children in religious families (not Muslim or Jewish) to "draw God." There will be an old man, virile, with a long white beard, a full head of white hair, and a bold Aryan nose – a Norse leader like Beowulf. To "draw a King" results in a generic "king" with ermine robe and crown and often, a beard. The command to draw the President will result in an attempt to draw a realistic portrait of a certain individual, and of the pope usually his ecclesiastical robes.[327] The sovereign may also be abstract such as drawing the sun for Louis XIV (the "Sun King"), or Akhenaten "Son of the Sun" and the first monotheistic ruler of Ancient Egypt. The crucifix will suffice for a representation of Christ just as the *Magen David* (Star of David) will suffice for the image of King David. The Great Seal of the United States entirely represents not the American people, but the president alone. The swastika did not represent Germany, but Hitler, and not Hitler per se but his power and its wellspring the "*blut und boden*" of the Aryan race for which he was the sole channel. The sovereign has a personality. And we may say that after 1933 the people of Germany, who had between the wars been treated by the victors as more or less slaves and were therefore in a state of ennui and helplessness, were ready to abdicate and be abducted into the power of the swastika just as a subject would be possessed by a demon. *Hitler seemed well aware of this, cultivating a mysticism around the phenomenon.*

According to Oesterreich, possession takes outward physical form in three ways:

1) The possessed takes on a new physionomy.

2) Change of the voice in various ways.

3) *The subject speaks from the point of view of the possessor.*[328]

Races, in Antiquity, the Middle Ages, and Modern Times. Hyde Park, N.Y.: University Books, 1966, p. 124.

[327] Personal observation in classrooms, 2000-2011.

[328] Oesterreich, Ibid., pp. 17 – 21.

Now in the case of the demonically possessed individual these effects are dramatic. The face is contorted, the voice alien to the person (different gender, pitch, or language), and the "I" is assigned to the intruder and not to the host. What of the abducted/abdicated persona? Obviously there are not these symptoms as described above. However, this comparison is not meant as metaphor, but as a "real one, not a figurative one," to echo Deleuze and Guattari. In fact, the changes in the abducted position may be far more dramatic. There may be a uniform, rituals, sacred texts, required facial hair styles, ornaments, scarification, piercings, tattoos, certain kinds of dwellings or lifestyles, sanctioned recreational activities, and a belief set that must be adhered to. The abducted persona may be required to look a certain way, speak a certain jargon or in a subservient tone, and to speak for the corporate will and not for the subject's self. "But the most important particular in which 'the invasion of the organism by a strange individuality' is manifested, is [the] new voice does not speak according to the spirit of the normal personality but that of the new one. Its 'ego' is the latter's, and is opposed to the character of the normal individual."[329]

2.1 Morphology of the metastructure of discourse

So far we have not left the subject-predicate (SP) level of discussion regarding discourse. All SP structures are contained within the context of the rhetorical framework of the discourse which itself is expressive independently from the SP. For example, a process analysis explaining how something is made or done will have an entirely different structure than a persuasive appeal that will follow either the interrogative-declarative-imperative (IDI) pattern if a commercial appeal, and the ethos-logos-pathos (ELP) pattern if an ideological appeal. Within the IDI or the ELP pattern there will be concatenations of SP expressions, but they will be organized by sentence type and position based on their best use in the presentation of the appeal.

Which brings us to an interesting correlation to Schrodinger's Cat Paradox paper. The question for us here and now is how are these SP diads organized in the metastructure? The hint is above: *in the best way*

---

[329] Ibid., p. 21.

possible. But there must be some governing principles that define the "best way." Of course, there is always the refuge of orthodoxy or "how it is done," but that will not help the creative effort to persuade, inform, analyze, classify and so on. The criteria must not be arbitrary and they must be able to be encoded, meaning that if we were to make a machine that composes metastructures, it would follow certain algorithms based on certain ideas. (The reason for constructing such a machines is proof of concept). Those ideas are awareness, observation, and measurement, which are the three parameters of analytic epistemology in science. "We are told that no distinction is to be made between the state of a natural object and what I know about it [....] Actually [...] there is intrinsically only awareness, observation, measurement. If through them I have procured at a given moment the best knowledge of the state of the physical object [...] then I can turn aside as *meaningless* any further questioning about the 'actual state' [...]."[330] It should be added that Schroedinger does not believe this to be the whole truth (which is why he wrote the paper). *When there is a "change of state" then the perception of the object will change too.*

This change of state may be applied to the change of position between 0I, I1, I2, and Ix, . While the structure of the core identity remains essentially the same, and while the furnishings change with T + S as the "impressions" of the world, the shift in state means that what can be known by awareness, observation, and measurement changes in various ways too, such as relative proportion or in the final outcome of a sample analysis (model) on the ontic thread(s). The problem is, "Reality resists imitation through a model. So one lets go of naive realism and leans directly on the indubitable proposition that *actually* [...] after all is said and done there is only observation, measurement [....] [W]e must now explicitly *not* relate our thinking any longer to any other kind of reality or to a model."[331]

---

[330] Schrodinger, Erwin. John D. Trimmer, trans. "The Present Situation in Quantum Mechanics." *Proceedings of the American Philosophical Society*, 124, 323-38, ND, p. 8.
[331] Ibid., p. 8.

The reason is that a metastructure is "meta" (*maha, mega*), beyond the physical, and therefore confounds *awareness* of its scope but not of its properties of being observable and measured. As we shall see, *metastructure is a 'pataphysical property*. Which raises the question of where the morphology of the structure arises from, what it is, and how it works.

The closest that anthropology has come to answering these questions is in the work of Propp concerning fairy tale morphology. His thesis is that all "fairy tales" follow certain patterns that can be expressed symbolically and be codified. In other words, the discourse of the folk tale (in this case Russian) can be deconstructed into components that are assembled in different ways but can be classified and analyzed for their common elements. For example, there are six (or 7) basic characters in the folk tale: *the hero, the hero's helper, the villain, the object sought, the donor of the object, and the receiver of the object.* (A seventh serves as an auxiliary character – the false hero — when there is that particular twist in the plot.)[332] These characters can be used in any tale while not affecting the uniqueness of the tale as a discrete story. "Tales possess one special characteristic: components of one tale can, without any alternation whatsoever, be transferred to another."[333]

Propp sees the morphology of the tale as a form of syntax which must be known to *speak about* the metastructure of the experience of the folk tale. "Is it possible to speak about the life of a language without knowing anything about the parts of speech, i.e., about certain groups of words arranged according to the laws of their changes?"[334] A leap will be made here to attempt to equate the metastructure (morphology) of the Russian folk tale not only with folk tales from around the world, but also with the structure of discourse itself as a syntax of discourse. "[Q]uestions relating to the study of tales lead to the solution of the highly important and yet unresolved problem of the similarity of tales throughout the world."[335]

An example of the six characters in a typical commercial appeal can be seen in an advertisement for a personal care product such as deodorant. The hero is the product itself, the hero's helper is the friend of the man with

---

[332] Propp, Vladimir. *The Morphology of the Folk Tale.* Austin: U. Texas Press, 1988, pp., 79-80.
[333] Ibid., p. 7.
[334] Ibid., p. 15.
[335] Ibid., p. 16.

body odor who advises use of the product, the villain is (of course body odor), the object sought an is inoffensive body smell (or the love of those who do not like body odor), the donor of the object is the manufacturer of the product, and the receiver of the object, by objectification and negation, is the character with body odor/the audience for the commercial appeal.

We also see this pattern in literature, such as in Shakespeare's *Hamlet*. The hero is Hamlet, the helper is Horatio, the villain is Claudius, the object sought is Justice, the donor of the object is the mummers who frighten Claudius into revealing himself in public, and the receiver of the object is Hamlet's father's ghost. We may take this one step further and look at a news broadcast structure of a military action. The hero is the country fighting the enemy, the helper is the ally who assists ably in the fight, the villain is the enemy, the object sought is victory, the donor of the object is (often enough) God/fate/providence (*inshallah*), the receiver of the object, ostensibly, are the people of the victorious nation – or maybe some abstraction too such as justice or peace. For instance, in the Jesus tale Jesus is the hero, the disciples (except Judas) are the helpers, Judas is the villain, the object sought is beatification in the form of salvation, the donor of the object is God the Father, and the receiver of the object is humankind. *Judas "abducts" Jesus by kissing him to identify him to the Roman authorities who then take Jesus into custody, or "abduct" him into the Roman/Sanhedren realm of justice.*

2.2 Abduction and testing in the folk tale

A Russian folk tale[336] almost always involves an *abduction* of an innocent party necessitating rescue or escape, and the *testing* of the hero or some other hero-related character. Of course the abduction is perpetrated by the villain usually as the main motivator of the plot. "This function is exceptionally important, since *by means of it the actual movement of the tale is created* [italics added]. Absentation, the violation of an interdiction, delivery, the success of a deceit, all prepare the way for this function, create its possibility of occurrence, or simply facilitate its happening."[337] By "absentation" is here meant "abduction": "the villain abducts a person (A1) [a notation which will make more sense later]. A Dragon kidnaps the tsar's daughter, a peasant's daughter; a witch kidnaps a boy; older brothers

---

[336] "Folk tale" and "fairy tale" are used interchangeably.
[337] Ibid., pp. 30-1.

abduct the bride of a younger brother."[338] These interesting examples of abduction underscore the critical role it plays in the generation of the plot of the discourse of the tale.

Abduction plays precisely the same role in the "plot" of the life of the subject. The great drama of life is to be abducted and then be rescued or escape. At the abduction position of Ix life begins in earnest. The petty conflict between the specular image and the real image vanishes. A new conflict arises between the original Self, and the abducted self as if the corpus were possessed by a demon. As mentioned earlier, the occupation of the subject takes place at the position of the core identity, but is manifest either as an SPO or as an LSO. This irritation causes a destabilization of the abduction so that a recursion to the previous position of I2 is possible. If all goes well (in the fairy tale), the subject recurs and the Second Negation follows, bringing to life *homo generator*.

There is also the matter of *Lack*. For there to be *lack* there must either have been nothing there in the first place, or what was there was seized just as the subject was abducted. What is there or not is the furniture of the core identity as it was acquired through experience. In the folk tale not only are characters abducted, but objects of interest or value are taken away (stolen). A battle for their return ensues. It is this lack that is exploited by the message of discourse from the Big Five. "We conclude from this that lack can be considered as the morphological equivalent of seizure [....] Insufficiency, just as seizure, determines the next point of the complication [....] This lack can be compared to the zero which, in a series of figures, represents a definite value [cf. Peano]."[339]

As with the subjects in Seligman's studies of helplessness, not all heroes of a tale are successful axiomatically. "*Banished, vanquished, bewitched, and substituted heroes demonstrate no volitional aspiration toward freedom*, and in such cases this element is lacking [italics added]."[340] As with the slave who has learned helplessness from the masters as their form of "benevolence," the defeated hero also lacks the motivation to "flee or fight," or may have crossed a threshold (barring death) such as prison, where there is no chance at freedom anyway.

---

[338] Ibid., p. 31.
[339] Propp, Vladimir. *The Morphology of the Folk Tale*. Austin: U. Texas Press, 1988, p. 34-5.
[340] Ibid., p. 38.

2.3 Magical agents make the impossible possible

One of the lures of the discourse as presented by the sovereign is the promise of the magical reward or solution. In the case of the "sun kings," their divinity was implied in their nick names. With all sovereigns, however, the magic is promised and sometimes delivered when they "work miracles," sometimes feats of engineering and sometimes great victories in war. It might even be the more literal miracles of Christ who never has a chance to build a bridge or fight a foe, but raised Lazarus from the dead and helped a blind man to see. Again this is a binary negation of what is not magical. The proximity of the magic to the non-magical inserts the subject into the objectivity of a new 'pataphysical world offered by the sovereign where anything is possible. Propp calls this magical property an "agent" because it propels the plot in strategic ways. Also, it is in the 'pataphysical world where the hero and the villain at last have their decisive battle.

The agent, which is often donated by the sovereign or his or her proxy (the court wizard or neighborhood witch), serves as a vehicle to both lure the subject into abduction and to remove him from it into some kind of preferred state. Furthermore – and most important – the magical agent gives the subject special powers to obtain what is desired and what cannot be obtained without the agent. It can be transferred, pointed out, prepared, bought, found by chance, revealed, consumed, seized, or gained by the assistance of others.

The magical world revealed by, for instance, media products or the political apparatus, dazzle the subject who now has an even weaker incentive toward the freedom of homo generator who must do everything manually without the assistance of magic as a "maker" in the sense of *poesis*. Like the vanquished hero above, the enchanted hero (subject) is in thrall with the abducted world and abdicates again and again when the opportunity is presented to seize back sovereignty.

The world of mass media with its fantasies lived out by actors and scenery and events made realistic by computers, as well as the live spectacles where vastly moneyed players battle with each other for a position in the progressive march toward an ultimate distinction (World Cup, Stanley Cup, Superbowl, World Series, and so on), make the magical world irresistible. The promises of politicians of desirable outcomes (often in four short years) are equally magical. These include promises of peace, prosperity, more freedom for the bourgeois electorate and less freedom for those who threaten it, and synthetic and progressive propositions such as "better" government, improved schools, "good" roads and highways, stricter justice, and affordable health care for all.

In commercial appeals deodorants are the catalyst for falling in lifelong love, age wrinkles vanish, beer and cigarettes are associated with freedom and the outdoors, dogs specify which brand of food they prefer from a can or a bag, heroes fly through the air to save a housewife from a dirty bathroom, cars go twice the speed limit without getting tickets, children grow up in thirty seconds, commoners marry royalty, subjects meet their fantasy celebrities hawking products and services, and politicians make their impossible promises. *The magic 'pataphysical world is without limit, and it is for this reason that at the I2 recursion it becomes the world of homo generator too, but with HG as a maker (poesis) and not a subject.* The magical thinking of the subject in the abducted state inverts perception of possibility and probability, so that it seems more is possible and a positive outcome is more probable if, and only if, the subject is abducted, not freed into the Second Negation where at least there is potential to create as homo generator. Which path the subject-hero chooses determines the story: "The morphological significance of the hero is […] very great, since his intentions create the axis of the narrative."[341] The axis determines the ontological "direction" of the narrative.

As most of the magical appeals emanate from the Big Five to support their interests, their names and identifications are critical for the recognition of the magical powers they can impart. That is why branding is so critical, both of the "donor" of the object sought and the object itself. The origin of branding, too, comes to us as a borrowed plot vehicle from the folk tale. "A brand is applied to the body. The hero receives a wound during a skirmish. A princess awakens him before the fight by making a small wound in his cheek with a knife. A princess brands the hero on the forehead with a signet ring; she kisses him, leaving a burning star on his forehead."[342]

---

[341] Propp, Vladimir. *The Morphology of the Folk Tale*. Austin: U. Texas Press, 1988, p. 50.
[342] Propp, Vladimir. *The Morphology of the Folk Tale*. Austin: U. Texas Press, 1988, p. 52.

2.4 Entering into an SPO/LSO in the folk tale

Confusing matters further for the subject, there is the presence of simultaneous parallel ontologies (SPO) that branch out in bifurcations and close down into truncations (LSO) as the tale progresses. For instance, in the tale, if a child is abducted a bifurcation is created since there are now two stories: 1) the tale of the abducted child, and 2) the tale of the abducted child's rescuers. Both must endure their ordeals, and pass the tests that come along, for the child to be rescued and, possibly, for justice to be done to the abductor. When there is an SPO, each branch is called by Propp a "move." "This phenomenon attests to the fact that many tales are composed of two series of functions which may be labeled 'moves' (*xody*). A new villainous act creates a new 'move,' and in this manner, sometimes a whole series of tales combine into a single tale."[343]

Once there are two moves, they too either run in *synchrony, asynchrony, or contrasynchrony.* A ligature may help close down a parallel ontology, such as when a villain is pardoned by the juridical authority. "In parallel with this we sometimes have a magnanimous pardon (U neg.)."[344] One ontic thread may close down because of a ligature event such as a marriage, or the foiling of a marriage, which is close to the very definition of ligature made or broken. "If a new act of villainy interrupts a tale shortly before a wedding, then the first move ends with a betrothal, or a promise of a marriage."[345] But it must be affirmed that SPO's are not unrelated or even independent, but in any form of movement are always on the same axis with no progression just as there is no one place where a subatomic particle is at any given time. "They all belong to a single axis and not, as has already been mentioned, to a number of axes," which is what Propp calls "the double morphological meaning of a single function,"[346] adding that, "Functions constitute the basic elements of the tale, those elements upon which the course of action is built."[347] Propp labels these functions using a complex system of notation (such as the "U neg." above) to produce a concatenation of functions which describe the action of the folk tale. For example, the driving force of most plots is villainy in the form of abduction,

---

[343] Ibid., p. 59.
[344] Ibid., p. 63.
[345] Propp, Vladimir. *The Morphology of the Folk Tale*. Austin: U. Texas Press, 1988, p. 64.
[346] Ibid., p. 64-6.
[347] Ibid., p. 71.

which, attestinting to its primary spot in the drama, is indicated by the letter A. The letter B is mediation or a "connective incident" which has been called here a ligature. C is a consent to counteraction, and so on. The letters are then *superscripted* with numbers to show their permutations and variations. A letter represents a class of action; the superscript numeration represents variation of objects in the class.

A simple tale may follow this schema:

$$\alpha A^1 B^1 B^2 CHB^3 U = w0$$

In this little tale, there is the initial action α, the family and the place and so forth, and then the incipient action, which is A1, the act of villainy in the form of abduction. A call for help is issued at B1. The help is dispatched at B2. There is consent to counteraction (seizing the abducted party) at C. At H the hero (rescuer) struggles with the villain (abductor), gaining release of the captive at B3. There is punishment of the villain at U, and a monetary reward for safe return of the abducted at w0. "This is a classification by structural, interior features, and not by features which are external and changeable."[348]

The significance of this schema for us is that it gives a structural view of a discourse. Although Propp examines only *Russian* folk tales, he makes a strong case for the universality of not only the 6 (7) characters, but also how the modules of the schema interact, describing nearly every form of ontology we have explored here so far. After all, once a tale is broken down into a schema, it is then just a structure or architecture (arch) that may also describe a story in a vastly different time and place. The goal of structural anthropology is to find what humans have in common more than it is an attempt to flush out the difference which are often trivial or what Propp calls "features which are external and changeable."

---

[348] Propp, Vladimir. *The Morphology of the Folk Tale*. Austin: U. Texas Press, 1988, p. 103.

2.5 Testing as a plot motivator and determinant of discourse

In every tale the hero is tested. We could attribute this to the need to show that the hero is indeed heroic and not just labeled as such. Often the reward the hero attains for his heroism is the hand of the princess (for it is almost always a male as hero), or money, or royal land or all three in a jackpot story. Other characters, such as the helper and even the one in need of rescue/escape can be tested too. *So what the tale has in common for a variety of characters is the testing apparatus which stands between the desiring and the desired.* The mechanical relationship between the two and the mechanism of testing is what Deleuze and Guattari call the Desiring-Machine (DM). The DM's fuel is testing, not desire. Desire is the static element in the story and the testing is what moves it along after αA. "Morphologically, a tale (*skazka*) may be termed any development proceeding from villainy (A) or a lack (a), through intermediary functions to marriage (W*), or to other functions employed as denouement."[349]

Often the "moves" of the tale are precipitated by a test. For example, in the "Tale of the Swan-Geese," a series of tests starts, continues, and ends the story. This story is not unlike the hypothetical one in the schema above. The incipient event is when the parents tell the daughter to "watch your younger brother," and not to "leave the courtyard" (α). There are two tests here, one of the daughter who is given adult responsibility, and another for both who must not give in to the temptation to leave the courtyard (γ). The daughter fails the test (M) and the villainy begins when the swan-geese abduct the little boy and fly away (A1). The daughter, distraught, seeks the boy and goes through a series of tests. First a magic stove (of all things) withholds the child's whereabouts until the girl eats rye cake, which she does not want to eat. She fails the second test (E neg.).

After encountering a magic hedgehog, she tests the animal herself by asking the whereabouts of the child (§). The animal points out where the swan-geese took the child and she comes upon a hut resting on stilts made of chicken legs — a common object in many folk tale traditions but called the *baba-yaga* in Russian ones. The sister rescues the boy and must undergo testing again by the same characters but in reverse of the original order (↓, Pr1). At last the girl arrives home with the boy (Rs2). The entire tale, with its parallel ontic threads, is expressed thus[350]:

---

[349] Propp, Vladimir. *The Morphology of the Folk Tale*. Austin: U. Texas Press, 1988, p. 92.
[350] Ibid., p. 99

$$d^7E^7F^9$$
$$\gamma^1\beta^1\delta^1A^1C\uparrow\{[DE^1 \text{ neg. F neg.}]\}G4K^1\downarrow[Pr^1D^1E^1F^9 = Rs^4]3d^7E^7F^9$$

It is not necessary to understand all of the symbols. There is enough of the story described above to give a sense of how the symbols represent the structural elements, including the second ontic thread. What we are interested in here is where the instances of testing occur and how they fit into the overall scheme of the discourse.

Propp defines the discourse of the fairy tale thus: "[A] fairy tale is a story built upon the proper alternation of the above-cited functions in various forms, with some of them absent from each story and with other repeated."[351] For the first time we begin to get a panoramic view of discourse as it appears structurally in schemata, rather than in the *ragt* of the SP and its copula. While, as Propp observes, some parts of the tale are not always present and others are repeated, the general consistence of tales, their number of tests, the basic characters, and the outcomes are boldly consistent. A discourse is a discourse.

But this question of success or failure of the tests is quite interesting. In the Swan-Geese story above there are at least three failures in a short time by the daughter, who actually *abdicates* her little brother by placing him outside the house near the road and then going to play there herself, violating the restrictions set by the parents for good reason (we may presume: to avoid what then ensues). He is then *abducted,* at which point, after failing the first and most critical test, she becomes the hero! Even as hero she continues to fail critical tests in her journey to find her brother, who could be anywhere since she only knows that it was the swan-geese that did the abducting. Yet she manages to get the child back and bring him home and all is well. What is it about *failing* tests that is heroic? Ronell, quoting Nietzsche, *describes the method of the true philosopher [hero] as a path of failure.*

"The genuine philosopher scores failure time and again. The crash course is party of the deal struck with the game of contract for which the genuine philosopher has signed on. This figure 'lives "unphilosophically" and "unwisely," above all *imprudently*, and feels the burden and the duty of a hundred attempts and temptations of life — he risks himself constantly, he plays the wicked game –.' "[352]

---

[351] Propp, Vladimir. *The Morphology of the Folk Tale*. Austin: U. Texas Press, 1988, p. 99.
[352] Ronell, Avital. *The Test Drive*. Urbana: University of Illinois Press, 2005.

3.1 The epistemology of the discourse of art

The final question is that of art. What is in the subject-object relationship between a work of art – poetry, fiction, sculpture, painting, music – and the persona, whom we may no longer call the "subject" because the persona is both subject and object.[353] Adorno sees this as the essential question in modern aesthetics. "Variously the controversy may focus on the conclusion drawn from the subjective reactions to art work, in contrast to the *intentio recta* toward them, the *intentio recta* being considered precritical according to the current scheme of epistemology."[354] The current scheme of epistemology, in analytic philosophy, is, as Schrodinger described: awareness, observation, and measurement. This method is calculated to produce the most objective data. How well does it work with art?

As we have seen above, the objective part of the story a work of art tells can be turned into schemata. The scheme is wholly objective; in fact, it can read as a story, and as a certain story, but at the same time its nuanced idiosyncrasies are lost. As has also been said here, the work of art is itself the generator of the method of seeing, the need for appreciating, the desire to experience. *"The strongest buttress of subjective aesthetics, the concept of aesthetic feeling, derives from objectivity, not the reverse* [italics added]."[355]

Inasmuch as art is a form of communication, it is subject to the same rules of communication as we have set down here: the expressive work itself is the receiver of the transmission. Everything about it is entirely in the phenomenological frame of the audience. The choice of color, the shapes presented, the harmonies chosen, even the length of sentences on the page are all part of the development of the work of art from the objective characteristics of the persona whose gaze falls upon it, or whose aural "gaze" absorbs it into the fabric of the subject that is shared between both the work and its audience. "Aesthetic feeling is not the feeling aroused: It is astonishment vis-a-vis what is beheld rather than vis-a-vis what it is about; it is being overwhelmed by what is a aconceptual and yet determinate, not subjective affect released, that in the case of aesthetic

---

[353] Until here, the word "subject" was meant to indicate either the subject of a sovereign, or the subject (as in topic) of the discourse.

[354] Adorno, Theodore W. *Aesthetic Theory.* Minneapolis: U. of Minnesota Press, 1997, p. 163.

[355] Ibid., p. 164.

experience may be called feeling."[356] As has also been discussed, the distinction of subject-object, particularly in the appreciation of the feeling of the aesthetic experience, is a specious one, just as making a distinction between "here" and "there," where there is magically transformed into here when the two positions are tactically reversed. A schema of the subject (s) and object (o) relationship is thus:

$$s \rightarrow o$$
$$o \leftarrow s$$

In terms of ontic threads, the proximity of s and o is contraphasic and reciprocal. That they track on the same axis but in different directions on that axis makes them SPO's. While the entire frame of the viewer is generated by the work of art, the work of art, independent of the viewer, was generated in turn by the aesthetic feeling of its generator, which, though *a priori* to the work of art, is nonetheless *a posteriori* to the audience. This concatenation of audience-artist-art-audience-artist-art [(a, b, c) → (a1, b1, c1)] and so on is an LSO. "Kant would like to ground aesthetic objectivity in the subject rather than to displace the former by the latter," says Adorno. Then, quoting Kant on using reason to track aesthetic feeling, "I have used the logical functions of judging to help me find the elements that judgment takes into consideration when it reflects (since even a judgment of taste has reference to the understanding). I have examined the element of quality first, because an aesthetic judgment about the beautiful is concerned first with it."[357]To sequence subject and object as one having priority – in anything – over the other would be to create a progression, which would be a fallacy even if there is first a = s → o, then b = o → s and vice versa. They can only be expressed simultaneously, showing the organic necessity of the SPO. "If, however, these two elements are harnessed together in the intelligible realm then Kant's doctrine for it fits its content [*Inhalt*]."[358]

Therefore, it is through the reciprocity of the work's being as subject and object that it becomes a "work," a whole, unitary Event in the ontological sense. The subjectivity of it is in the execution, and the

---

[356] Ibid., p.164.
[357] Adorno, Theodore W. *Aesthetic Theory.* Minneapolis: U. of Minnesota Press, 1997, p. 165.
[358] Ibid., p. 165.

objectivity in the laws it obeys as what it is and that make it what it is. "[T]he reciprocity of the subject and object in the world, which cannot be that of identity, maintains a precarious balance. The subjective process of the work's production is, with regard to its private dimension, a matter of indifference. Yet the process also has an objective dimension that is a condition for the realization of its immanent lawfulness."[359]

Perhaps the greatest example of this reciprocity is in the contemplation of the pronoun "I" in a work. Of course, the personal pronoun appears in narrative works such as autobiography, poetry, and first-person fiction narratives. It also appears in paintings and sculptures when they are of the artist himself or herself. Even in music this is possible, as in the use of specific motifs for each other in the compositions of Robert and Clara Schumann, or the allusions to events in childhood in the nostalgic and autobiographical works of Charles Ives.

It is also the I that is most misunderstood in the subject-object dichotomy, leaving a perfect laboratory in the exploration of its implications in a work of art. In the end, says Adorno, it is not possible to insert the I into a work of art without having its subjectivity subverted by the objective "condition for the realization of its immanent lawfulness." Once "I" enters a work, it is subject to certain laws of how a work is envisaged, engaged, and gazed upon (visually or aurally). "Art's linguistic quality gives rise to reflection over what speaks in art; this is its veritable subject, not the individual who makes it or the one who receives it. This is masked by the lyrical 'I,' which in confessing has over the centuries produced the semblance of the self-evidence of poetic subjectivity."[360]

Most astounding, though, is that the universality of art is achieved through the locality in the pure subjectivity of its author. The attempt at a discourse that somehow approximates the subject is erased in the object. As such, art is the chief means for the facilitation of the recursion from Ix to I2 to form homo generator in the Second Negation, for how, after all, is art created except by *homo generator*? "By entrusting itself fully to its material, production results in something universal born out of the utmost individuation. *The force with which the private I is externalized in the work is the I's collective essence; it constitutes the linguistic quality of works* [italics added]."[361]

---

[359] Ibid., p. 166.
[360] Adorno, Theodore W. *Aesthetic Theory.* Minneapolis: U. of Minnesota Press, 1997, p. 166-7.
[361] Ibid., p. 167.

That the ultimate quality of a work is "linguistic," meaning of the mouth and tongue as if in speaking, testifies to the nature of artwork as a *counterdiscourse* – counter to the subjectivity of the prevailing discourse of the Sovereign and the apparatus. That the agents of the sovereign and the apparatus are so eager to support the production, display, and buying and selling of art is a wonder. In the end, the *counterdiscourse* is essential for the discourse itself to remain alive. There must be the blood of creativity flowing in and out of the Star Chamber of the sovereign, and the apparatus needs fresh oil to grease its cogs. *But ultimately, the apparatus needs its negation to Be, for the coming-into-being of both the discourse and the counterdiscourse is mutual and reciprocal, just as the relationship between subject and object and here and there and then and now.* "Only as things do artworks become the antithesis of reified monstrosity. Correspondingly, and this is key to art, even out of so-called individual art work it is a We that speaks and not an I – indeed all the more so the less the artwork adapts externally to a We as its idiom."[362] Herein lies the "problem" with political art, which takes as its *a priori* aesthetic a "We" position, thereby short circuiting its potential as subversive art – the very thing it set out to do.

3.2 The aggregation of the We in plastic arts

Confounding the search for a collective "I," the We of art, as Adorno expresses it above, becomes a *counterdiscourse* and not the collectivized unitary voice or *vox populi*. Adorno points out that even Trotsky did not see the presence or creation of a vox populi: "[A]ccording to Trotsky's thesis, not proletarian art is conceivable, only socialist art."[363] "Socialist art" in this sense is neither the voice of the people of the voice of the state but rather the individual artist expressing the revolutionary in whatever myriad forms it will take. Such art is more concerned with what Adorno calls the "How of apperception," the fabrication and the making (*poesis*), in the plastic arts. "Their We is simply the sensorium according to its historical conditioning pursued to the point that it breaks the relation to the representational objectivity that was modified by virtue of the development of its language of form. So images say: 'Behold!' "[364] The "sic" (thus) of art

---

[362] Adorno, Theodore W. *Aesthetic Theory.* Minneapolis: U. of Minnesota Press, 1997, p. 167.

[363] Ibid., p. 168.

[364] Adorno, Theodore W. *Aesthetic Theory.* Minneapolis: U. of Minnesota Press,

precludes it from discourse just as a terrorist event precludes itself from the attacking or attacked ideology.

What matters is what is abducted and what is not. Socialist art in Trotsky's sense cannot be abducted. If it could, then it would stink of the sovereign and therefore of the aristocracy of exploitation and hierarchical order or what we have called here the "social arch." "That this We is, however, not socially univocal, that it is hardly that of a determinate class or social positions, has its origin perhaps in the fact that to this day art in the emphatic sense has only existed as bourgeois art."[365]

Art "in the emphatic sense" is what we are concerned with as counterdiscourse, which does not mean that it cannot be *engagé* as it is in both political "vox populi" art and bourgeois plastic arts. These distinctions do not so much apply to music, which is not "lingual" in the same sense except when it is paired with words in song. While music does carry discourse, attempts to make music into a nationalistic experience have failed (e.g. the Nazis' use of Wagner). Also, we cannot say "antidiscourse," since one can only oppose *a* discourse and not *all* discourse *as it is the very expression of coming-into-being and Dasein.*

What remains is what Adorno calls "aesthetic truth," a transcendental in the Kantian sense in that it supersedes *a* discourse and *the* Discourse. Moreover, this truth is both subjective and objective, not in equal ratio but as SPO's. They are *coincident.* In as much as art fails to achieve this status – and this is readily observable in all art – the work becomes either too subjective and therefore an excretion of ego and expression of symptomology, or too objective and in thrall to the will of the state or an "other" (such as a wealthy patron's commission of his portrait). "Artists have a hard fate not only because of their always uncertain fate in the world but because through their own efforts they necessarily work against the aesthetic truth to which they devote themselves."[366]

Which also brings us back to the relation of art and personality-disordered pathology. If interruptions in the development of the specular I and the social or real I are carried into the abducted state, there is little hope of a recursion back to the I2 state for reasons we have discussed at length, and therefore little chance for the appearance of homo generator

---

1997, p. 168.
[365] Ibid., p. 168.
[366] Adorno, Theodore W. *Aesthetic Theory.* Minneapolis: U. of Minnesota Press, 1997, p. 169.

and Hegel's Second Negation. However, it seems also that less stable individuals at this critical juncture are more likely to oscillate between the two positions, which is ideal. For an artist to be the full creative being that art demands of "Aesthetic truth," then there must be an easy passing between the two positions – and with a certain rhythm, spasmodic or regular. That is perhaps why the so-called "artistic temperament" (which G.K. Chesterton called "a disease which afflicts amateurs") is the best temperament for art itself as counterdiscourse. "Those who produce important artworks are not demigods but fallible, often neurotic and damaged, individuals."[367]

Another element of the We is in the production of works of so-called genius. The *alterity* of such works belies their genotype. In again transcending the distinction of subject and object we arrive again at the relationship, only now the values are prime because they are of the Second Negation — a transcendence of the transcendence (First Negation):

$$s^1 \rightarrow o^1$$
$$o^1 \leftarrow s^1$$

The work becomes "alien" to the subject who created it because it now expresses a universality that aggregates the We position in safe territory far from the collective We (Us) of the *vox populi* and the commercial We (Us) of the art market and its forms of public display. "The element of self-alienness that occurs under the constraint of the material is indeed the seal of what was meant by 'genius.' If anything is to be salvaged of this concept it must be stripped away from its crude equation with the creative subject, who through vain exuberance bewitches the artwork into a document of its maker and thus diminishes it."[368]

But Adorno is ambivalent about the accusations of genius and authenticity. They are beside the point of the work as counterdiscourse. As such, the combination of the two negations of discourse and counterdiscourse produce a SPO of the contraphasic type, inviting oscillation (as in alternating electrical current, which oscillates at, for instance, 60 cycles per second to produce a non-polarized [indirect] current to power devices), expressed thus: $(I2 \leftrightarrow Ix)n$. Combine with the "neurotic

---

[367] Ibid., p. 171.
[368] Adorno, Theodore W. *Aesthetic Theory.* Minneapolis: U. of Minnesota Press, 1997, p. 170.

and damaged individual" and there is the potential for great flux at the position where art is created and destroyed. Moreover, Adorno also equates it to the *principium individuationis*

Nevertheless, it is not mere individuality or idiosyncrasy that make a work universal in the Second Negation, or what Adorno calls the concept of *Originalgenie:* "originality has turned against the market where it was never permitted to go beyond a certain limit."[369] In its abstraction from the marketplace, there is a return to its prima materia, with an emphasis on the plasticity of the medium, and a plethora of iterations and permutations of original art. At last, we arrive at art's intractability within the realm of the Discourse and the discourses coursing through it. It is in the *Originalgenie* that art becomes the tool of homo generator, the expression of the Second Negation, and the contradiscourse and the difference between ennui and jouissance, boredom and ecstasy. "Not genetically, but in terms of its constitution, art is the most compelling argument against the epistemological division of sensuality and intellect."[370]

4.1 The *'pataphysics* of the Second Negation

Of course, Hegel's Second Negation is a negation of a negation, and as such forms a positive: $[\sim \sim x(y) = x]$, where y is "$\sim$ x" and x is the Second Negation. The first negation never goes away, though, because negation is not a *progression*. As soon as I say $x = \sim y$, then I have said the inverse: $y = \sim x$. I say the two simultaneously when I negate a proposition. Therefore, it is possible to say two things at once which are mutually exclusive but are on the same axis. Baudrillard calls this the "Dead point: the dead center where every system crosses this subtle limit of reversibility, contradiction and doubt and enters into noncontradiction, into its own exalted contemplation, into ecstasy ...."[371] The negation of metaphysics, which itself is a negation of physics, is a negation of a negation and therefore the positive it asserts is the transcendental transcendental.

The ontological implication of the first negation is that the subject has not moved beyond the I2 position (after the negation of the I1

---

[369] Ibid., p. 172.

[370] Adorno, Theodore W. *Aesthetic Theory.* Minneapolis: U. of Minnesota Press, 1997, p. 174.

[371] Baudrillard, Jean. *Fatal Strategies.* Los Angeles: Semiotext(e), 2008, p. 33.

position), and remains in a state, at best, of dialectical conflict between *ennui* and *jouissance*. This is not a happy state, but it is bearable and there are remedies for its irritation and prolonged and ultimate unhappiness. In fact, whole epochs have been characterized by position in the phase shifting from OI to Ix. "To Hegel, spirit in self-estrangement is due to the presence of a first negation without a second negation, resulting in the 'dead form of the spirit's previous state.' [The] Enlightenment stuck to the opposite of faith and superstition, but failed to go on negating itself—the pure consciousness, the culture (superstructure) separated from objective practice."[372]

In the *'pataphysical* world, the rules of both metaphysics and physics are suspended, or they are included but coexist with their negations. In fact, this situation may simply be a confusion of terms in a time of great flux in the set of beliefs associated with the physical universe, akin to the difference between manipulating genes to cure diseases as opposed to other *allopathic* methods – which in turn supplanted in priority the methods of necromancy and divine agency. In quantum mechanics, as Schrodinger hints, the cat can be in two contrary states simultaneously: alive and dead, just as energy can be a particle or wave, or a subatomic particle can be in two places at once or present and decayed at the same instant. So the term " 'pataphysics" may be simply describing the physical world we are beginning to acknowledge exists. Furthermore, the imaginary furniture of the 'pataphysical world can still be observed and measured, fitting Schrodinger's criteria for what is possible epistemologically (if we lop off "awareness," as he does because of its engagement with discourse). "Then all our physical thinking thenceforth has as sole basis and as sole object the results of measurements which can in principle be carried out, for we must not explicitly relate our thinking any longer to any other kind of reality or model."[373]

So we may only say something "is" ontologically if repetition brings about the same result each iteration of the procedure (measurement, observation, analysis, deconstruction). The "awareness" removed from the epistemological parameters is a kind of exorcism of the discursive, which serves as "noise" in our investigation of the 'pataphysical world. "[T]he

---

[372] Anon. "Reflections on Hegel, Marx and Mao." Theory/Practice Newsletters. August-September 2002, p. 2.

[373] Schrodinger, Erwin. John D. Trimmer, trans. "The Present Situation in Quantum Mechanics." *Proceedings of the American Philosophical Society*, 124, 323-38, ND, p. 8.

desired criterion can be merely this: repetition of the measurement must give the same result. By many repetitions I can prove the accuracy of the procedure and show that I am not just playing. All this one must do not twice but very often. Then the predicted statistics are established that is the doctrine."[374]

In a 'pataphysical world there is nothing to know except what can be measured and observed, and that is completed through repetition and without prejudice for what "is and is not" the case. Results are not questioned once obtained, and where they fit into the larger "scheme of things" become irrelevant without awareness. The 'pataphysical orientation of Being in the subject mimics or mirrors that of the 0I stage and serves as the only possible form of recursion to that state. It is a kind of "ad astra" of being, where all is surmounted in the oscillation of $I2 \leftrightarrow Ix$ positions, particularly in homo generator as creator of worlds (art). If the Æpataphysical world is one that homo generator has created as an "artificial world," with the only epistemological value in measurement and observation, then the subject becomes the object in a negation of the real and imaginary. "We arrive at this paradox, at this conjuncture where the position of the subject has become untenable, and where the only possible position is that of the object. The only strategy possible is that of the object."[375]

Trotsky's "socialist art" becomes possible. There is no ontic allegiance to the state or to the *vox populi*. The objectified subject dances nimbly through the gap between the two because it is not encumbered with the need to possess. "It does not believe that anything belongs to it as property," which solves the "genius" problem Adorno describes where the art of the *Originalgenie* becomes merely "individualistic" and ego/market based, rather than the production of the *principium individuationis,* the true genius. "It is not divided with itself — which is the destiny of the subject [at the position I2 as the dialectic of ennui and *jouissance*, specular and real] – and it knows nothing of the mirror phase, where it would come to be caught by its own imaginary."[376] Homo generator does not possess, but is possessed in the only way that precludes abduction: by *jouissance*! "The object is what has disappeared on the horizon of the subject, and it is from the depths of this disappearance that it envelops the subject in its fatal strategy."[377]

---

[374] Ibid., p. 9-10.
[375] Baudrillard, Jean. Fatal Strategies. Los Angeles: Semiotext(e), 2008, p. 143.
[376] Ibid., 144.
[377] Ibid., 144.

BIBLIOGRAPHY

Adorno, Theodore W. *Aesthetic Theory*. Minneapolis: University of Minnesota Press, 1997.

Agamben, Giorgio. *Homo Sacer: Sovereign Power and Bare Life*. Stanford: Stanford University Press, 1998.

Agamben, Giorgio. *What is an Apparatus?* Stanford: Stanford University Press, 2009.

Akera, Atsuchi and Frederik Nebeker. *From 0 to 1: An Authoritative History of Modern Computing*. Oxford: Oxford University Press, 2002.

Ambrose, Alice and Morris Lazerowitz. *Fundamentals of Symbolic Logic*. New York: Rinehart & Co., Inc., Publishers, New York, 1948.

Ayer, Alfred Jules. *Language, Truth and Logic*. New York: Dover Publications, ND.

Badiou, Alain. *Being and Event*. London: Continuum, 2005.

Badiou, Alain. *Theory of the Subject*. London: Continuum, 2009.

Baudrillard, Jean. *Fatal Strategies*. Los Angeles: Semiotext(e), 2008.

Baudrillard, Jean and Sylvere Lotringer. *Forget Foucault*. New York: Semiotext(e), 1987.

Bernays, Edward L. *Propaganda*. Brooklyn: Ig Publishing, 2004.

Camus, Albert. *The Plague*. New York: Vintage Books, 1991.

Chomsky, Noam. *On Language*. New York: The New Press, 1979.

Chomsky, Noam. *Syntactic Structures*. The Hague: Mouton, 1978.

Churchland, Patricia S. and Terrence J. Sejnowski. *The Computational Brain*. Cambridge: MIT Press, 1992.

Deleuze, Gilles and Felix Guattari. *Anti-Oepidpus: Capitalism and Schizophrenia*. Minneapolis: University of Minnesota Press, 1985.

Deleuze, Gilles and Felix Guattari. *Nomadology: The War Machine*. Los Angeles: Semiotext(e), 1986.

de Botton, Alain. *Status Anxiety*. New York: Vintage Books, 2005.

de Saussure, Ferdinand. *Course in General Linguistics*. Chicago: Open Court, 2008.

Descartes, Rene. *Discourse on Method*. Indianapolis: The Bobbs-Merrill Co., Inc., 1975.

Devlin, Keith. *Logic and Information*. Cambridge: Cambridge University Press, 1991.

Doty, William G. *Mythography: The Study of Myths and Rituals*, 2nd ed. Tuscaloosa: University of Alabama Press, 2000.

Fanon, Frantz. *The Wretched of the Earth*. New York: Grove Press, 2004.

Foucault, Michel. *Discipline and Punish: The Birth of the Prison*. New York; Vintage Books, 1979.

Foucault, Michel. *The History of Sexuality: An Introduction*, Vol. 1. New York: Vintage Books, 1990.

Freud, Sigmund. *The Interpretation of Dreams*. New York: Basic Books, 1955.

Godel, Kurt. "On formally undecidable propositions of *Principia Mathematica* and related systems I." 1931.

Goldman, Emma. *Anarchism and Other Essays*. New York: Dover Publications, 1969.

Greenberg, Joseph H., ed. *Universals of Language*, 2nd ed. Cambridge: The M.I.T. Press, 1966.

Hegel, Georg W. F. *Phenomenology of Spirit*. Oxford: Oxford University Press, 1977.

Heidegger, Martin. *Basic Writings*. David Farrel Krell, ed. San Francisco: HarperSanFrancisco, 1992.

Heidegger, Martin. *Being and Time*. New York: HarperPerennial ModernThought, 2008.

Heidegger, Martin. *Discourse on Thinking*. New York: Harper Perennial, 1966.

Innis, Robert E. *Semiotics: An Introductory Anthology*. Bloomington: Indiana University Press, 1985.

Langer, Ellen J. *The Psychology of Control*. London: Sage Publications, 1983.

Kant, Immanuel. *Critique of Pure Reason*. New york: Barnes & Noble, 2004.

Kaufman, Walter, trans. *Basic Writings of Nietzsche*. New York: Modern Library, 2000.

Kern, Stephen. *The Culture of Space and Time: 1880-1918*. London: Weidenfeld and Nicolson, 1983.

Kreisman, Jerold J. and Hal Straus. *I Hate You – Don't Leave Me: Understanding the Borderline Personality*. New York: Perigee, 1989.

Lacan, Jacques. *Ecrits: A Selection*. New York: W.W. Norton & Co., 1977.

Lacan, Jacques. *The Seminar of Jacques Lacan, Book II: The Ego in Freud's theory and in the Technique of Psychoanalysis: 1954-1955*. New York: W.W. Norton, 1978.

Lasswell, Harold D., et al., eds. Propaganda and Communication in World History. Vol. 1: The Symbolic Instrument in Early Times. Honolulu: The University press of Hawaii, 1979.

Lust, Barbara. *Child Language: Acquisition and Growth*. Cambridge: Cambridge University Press, 2006.

Lyons, John. *Introduction to Theoretical Linguistics*. Cambridge: Cambridge University Press, 1968.

Mahler, Margaret S., et al. *The Psychological Birth of the Human Infant: Symbiosis and Individuation*. New York: Basic Books, Inc., Publishers, 1975.

Norberg, Jakob. "Adorno's Advice: *Minima Moralia* and the Critique of Liberalism." PMLA, March 2011, Volume 126, No. 2. pp. 398-411.

Oesterriech, Traugott. *Possession, Demonaical & other Among Primitive Races, in Antiquity, the Middle Ages, and Modern Times*. New Hyde

Park: University Books, 1966.

Plato. *The Apology, Pheado and Crito of Plato*. New York: P.F. Collier & Son Corporation, 1937.

Propp, Vladimir. *Morphology of the Folktale*. Austin: University of Texas Press, 1968.

Quinn, Daniel. *Ishmael: An Adventure of the Mind and Spirit*. New York: Bantam, 1992.

Ronell, Avital. *The Test Drive*. Urbana: University of Illinois Press, 2005.

Rubin, K. and A Silverberg."A Report on Wiles' Cambridge Lectures." *Bulletin of the American Mathematical Society*, Vol. 31, Number 1, July 1994.

Russell, Bertrand. *Introduction to Mathematical Philosophy*. London: George Allen and Unwin Ltd., 1956.

Schirmacher, Wolfgang."After the Last Judgement — Hegel as Philosopher of Artificial Life." New York: Atropos Press. Accessed 27 June 2011.

Schirmacher, Wolfgang, ed. *The Essential Schopenhauer*. New York: HarperPerennial ModernThought, 2010.

Schirmacher, Wolfgang."Ethics and Artificiality" New York: Atropos Press. Accessed 27 June 2011.

Schirmacher, Wolfgang."On the Inability to Recognize the Human Flaw."New York: Atropos Press. Accessed 27 June 2011.

Schirmacher, Wolfgang."Homo Generator: Media and Postmodern Technology." Retrieved on 6 June

Schopenhauer, Arthur. *Essays and Aphorisms*. London: Penguin Books, 2004.

Schopenhauer, Arthur. *The World as Will and Idea*. London: Everyman, J.M. Dent, 1990.

Schrodinger, Erwin."The Present Situation in Quantum Mechanics." *Proceedings of the American Philosophical Society*, 124, pp. 323-38.

Seligman, Martin E.P. *Helplessness: On Depression, Development, and Death*. San Franciso: W.H. Freeman and Co., 1975.

Singh, Simon. *Fermat's Enigma:The Epic Quest to Solve the World's Greatest Mathematical Problem*. New York: Walker and Co, 1997.

Shaumyan, Sebastian. *A Semiotic Theory of Language*. Bloomington: Indiana University Press, 1987.

Spisani, Franco. *The Meaning and Structure of Time*. Bologna: Azzoguidi, 1972.

Toynbee, Arnold J. *Greek Historical Thought: From Homor to the Age of Heraclius*. Boston: The Beacon Press, 1950.

Trevor-Roper, Hugh, ed. *The Goebbels Diaries: The Last Days*. London: Book Club Associates, 1977.

Tuan, Yi-Fu. *Space and Place: The Perspective of Experience*. Minneapolis: University of Minnesota press, 1977.

Tye, Larry. *The Father of Spin: Edward L. Bernays and the Birth of Public*

Relations. New York: Henry Holt and Co., 1998.

von Mises, Ludwig. *Human Action*, 3rd ed. Chicago: Henry Regnery Company, 1963.

Vygotsky, Lev. S. *Mind in Society: The Development of Higher Psychological Processes*. Cambridge: Harvard University Press, 1978.

Watson, James. *Media Communication: An Introduction to Theory and Practice*. New York: St. Martin's Press, 1998.

Whitesitt, J. Eldon. *Boolean Algebra and its Applications*. London: Addison-Wesley Publiching Co., Inc., 1961.

Wittgenstein, Ludwig. *Tractatus Logico-Philosophicus*. New York: Barnes & Noble, 2003

Zielinski, Siegfried. *Deep Time of the Media: Toward and Archaeology of Hearing and Seeing by Technical Means*. Cambridge: The MIT Press, 2006.

Zizek, Slavoj. *The Parallax View*. Cambridge: MIT Press, 2009.

Think Media: EGS Media Philosophy Series

Wolfgang Schirmacher, *editor*

A Postcognitive Negation: The Sadomasochistic Dialectic of American Psychology,
  Matthew Giobbi
A World Without Reason, Jeff McGary
All for Nothing, Rachel K. Ward
Asking, for Telling, by Doing, as if Betraying, Stephen David Ross
Memory and Catastrophe, Joan Grossman
Can Computers Create Art?, James Morris
Community without Identity: The Ontology and Politics of Heidegger, Tony See
Deleuze and the Sign, Christopher M. Drohan
Deleuze: History and Science, Manuel DeLanda
DRUGS Rhetoric of Fantasy, Addiction to Truth, Dennis Schep
Facticity, Poverty and Clones: On Kazuo Ishiguro's 'Never Let Me Go', Brian Willems
Fear and Laughter: A Politics of Not Selves 'For' Self, Jake Reeder
Gratitude for Technology, Baruch Gottlieb
Hospitality in the Age of Media Representation, Christian Hänggi
Itself, Robert Craig Baum
Jack Spicer: The Poet as Crystal Radio Set, Matthew Keenan
Laughter and Mourning: point of rupture, Pamela Noensie
Letters to a Young Therapist: Relational Practices for the Coming Community,
  Vincenzo Di Nicola
Literature as Pure Mediality: Kafka and the Scene of Writing, Paul DeNicola
Media Courage: Impossible Pedagogy in an Artificial Community, Fred Isseks
Metastaesthetics, Nicholas Alexander Hayes
Mirrors triptych technology: Remediation and Translation Figures, Diana Silberman
  Keller
Necessity of Terrorism political evolution and assimilation, Sharif Abdunnur
No Future Now, Denah Johnston
Nomad X, Drew Minh
On Becoming-Music: Between Boredom and Ecstasy, Peter Price
Painting as Metaphor, Sarah Nind
Performing the Archive: The Transformation of the Archive in Contemporary Art from
  Repository of Documents to Art Medium, Simone Osthoff
Philosophy of Media Sounds, Michael Schmidt
Polyrhythmic Ethics, Julia Tell
Propaganda of the Dead: Terrorism and Revolution, Mark Reilly
Repetition, Ambivalence and Inarticulateness: Mourning and Memory in Western
  Heroism, Serena Hashimoto

Other books available from Atropos Press

www.ingramcontent.com/pod-product-compliance
Lightning Source LLC
LaVergne TN
LVHW051509080426
835509LV00017B/2003